A THEORY OF
HUMAN
ACTION

A THEORY OF
HUMAN
ACTION
ALVIN I. GOLDMAN

PRINCETON UNIVERSITY PRESS

Princeton, New Jersey

Published by Princeton University Press,
Princeton, New Jersey

In the United Kingdom: Princeton University Press,
Guildford, Surrey

LCC 76-10021

ISBN 0–691–01974–6 (paperback edn.)

ISBN 0–691–07216–7 (hardcover edn.)

Printed in the United States of America

First PRINCETON PAPERBACK printing, 1976

For Holly

Preface

The prominence of the subject of action on the contemporary philosophical scene can be traced to two sources: first, the extent to which it is intertwined with other areas of philosophy, and second, the intrinsic interest of the subject. Philosophers have come to realize that one cannot go very far in philosophy of mind, philosophy of language, ethics, or many other fields, without confronting crucial problems in the analysis of action. Inquiry into the nature of mind, for example, requires an elucidation of the relation between mental states and actions. Investigation of language reveals the value of distinguishing between various kinds of speech acts and explaining the connections between them. In ethics, most of all, questions about action arise on every front. Responsibility and excuses cannot be adequately discussed without an analysis of ability and inability, and an account of the difference between intentional and unintentional acts. Ethical theories, such as utilitarianism, cannot be properly assessed without an understanding of the relationships between acts, consequences, circumstances and motives.

The frequency with which problems of action are found to underlie problems in other areas is a sufficient explanation for the current prominence of the field. In addition, however, its intrinsic philosophical interest makes it a natural focus of attention. What is an act? What is the relationship between act and agent? Is John's flipping the switch identical with his turning on the light? If not, how *are* they related? How is the concept of a "basic act" to be analyzed, and what role should it play in a general theory of action? What is the nature of the connection between act and desire, logical or causal? These are questions that demand philosophical attention, quite independent of the importance to other fields that their answers might have.

The theory of action presented here is intended to provide answers to these fundamental questions, among others, and in so doing to develop a set of ideas and principles in terms of which various problems of action can be handled. The heart of the theory consists of three main ideas or principles.

v

First, a "fine-grained" approach to the individuation of acts is explained and defended. Secondly, the relationships between acts, so individuated, are studied and exhibited, including the relationships between basic and non-basic acts. Thirdly, the idea that acts are caused by wants and beliefs is not only espoused, but used in the analysis of the concept of an act. The bulk of the book consists in an elaboration and defense of these central ideas and principles, especially the notion of want-and-belief causation. The central role of wants and beliefs is most apparent in the analysis of intentional action and in the discussion of explanations of action.

As in any enterprise of philosophical analysis, one of the purposes here is to explicate certain aspects of our common sense conceptual scheme. Thus, my analysis of action is intended to capture, as closely as possible, our pre-theoretic conception of an "act" or an "action." An analysis of action would be unsatisfactory if it counted salivating or sneezing as cases of "acts." At the same time, it is also my purpose to develop a set of sharp conceptual tools that will be useful for studying action in a systematic way. The achievement of this goal demands that we look beyond the ideas embedded in common sense wisdom. We must look for concepts that will offer the greatest theoretical fruits, and these are not always to be found in everyday thought and language. For example, although it is evident that acts such as turning on the light or signaling for a turn are in some sense "products" of bodily acts and environmental conditions (both physical and social), common sense wisdom does not provide a clear conceptual scheme for analyzing these relationships. At this point the theoretician must introduce novel concepts, the justification for which should ultimately be assessed by their contributions to further investigation and analysis.

As is evident from the problems that occupy most of my attention, the book is aimed primarily at a philosophical audience. But it should also be of interest to behavioral scientists. First, any inquiry into human behavior faces the problem of choosing appropriate units of behavior. The principles of act-individuation and act-interrelation I propose may prove useful for social science as well as for philosophy. Secondly, after elucidating the role of wants and beliefs in our everyday explanations of human action, I spend some time discussing the extent to which our common sense model of action accords with the sorts of models and theories of action found in the behavioral sciences. At first glance, common sense and behavioral science seem to be miles apart. But I contend that there is less incompatibility than initially appears between explanations of behavior appealing to desires, beliefs, goals and intentions, and explanations of the sort sought by behavioral scientists.

The book is based on my doctoral dissertation, which was submitted to Princeton University in 1964. Chapter Six is a slightly revised version of a paper entitled "Actions, Predictions, and Books of Life", which appeared in the *American Philosophical Quarterly*, V (1968), 135-151. A small portion of Chapter Five is adapted from a paper entitled "The Compatibility of Mechanism and Purpose", which was published in *The Philosophical Review*, LXXVIII (1969), pp. 468–82.

Because of the communal nature of the philosophical enterprise, any philosophical work is likely to be the product of many people, and this essay is no exception. I am indebted to numerous people, many more than I can mention, for criticisms and comments of various sorts. My greatest thanks go to William Alston, Jaegwon Kim, and Paul Benacerraf, each of whom, at various stages of my work on the topic of action, helped me enormously. Others to whom thanks are due include Richard Brandt, C.G. Hempel, J.O. Urmson, Arnold Kaufman, Carl Ginet, Bernard Berofsky, Michael Stocker, Charles Stevenson and Elizabeth Beardsley, and former students Lawrence Davis, John G. Bennett, Robert Solomon, Robert Audi, Jerome Segal, and John Immerwahr. I am indebted to the University of Michigan for a Rackham Research Fellowship in the summer of 1968 that enabled me to complete the manuscript. The typing was done by Mrs. Alice Gantt, whose fine work is much appreciated. Finally, I am indebted to my wife, Holly, not only for support and encouragement, but for excellent advice both philosophical and editorial.

Contents

ix

x

A THEORY OF
HUMAN
ACTION

CHAPTER ONE

Acts

1. The Identity Thesis

What is an act? One of the problems concerning the nature of acts is the problem of individuation. Suppose that John does each of the following things (all at the same time): (1) he moves his hand, (2) he frightens away a fly, (3) he moves his queen to king-knight-seven, (4) he checkmates his opponent, (5) he gives his opponent a heart attack, and (6) he wins his first chess game ever. Has John here performed *six* acts? Or has he only performed *one* act, of which six different descriptions have been given? Again, suppose that John (1) moves his finger, (2) pulls the trigger, (3) fires the gun, and (4) kills Smith. Are there four distinct acts that John has performed, or are all of these one and the same act? An answer to such questions will provide a partial answer to the question of the nature of acts.

A straightforward answer to these questions has been proposed by G. E. M. Anscombe and defended in some detail by Donald Davidson. On the Anscombe-Davidson view there is but *one* act that John has performed in each of the two cases. On their view John's moving his hand is *identical* with John's moving his queen to king-knight-seven; John's moving his hand is identical with John's checkmating his opponent; etc. There is but one act here, which has been described in a variety of ways. Miss Anscombe writes:

> ... a single action can have many different descriptions, e.g. "sawing a plank," "sawing oak," "sawing one of Smith's planks," "making a squeaky noise with the saw," "making a great deal of sawdust," and so on and so on. ...
> ... Are we to say that the man who (intentionally) moves his arm, operates the pump, replenishes the water supply, poisons the inhabitants, is performing *four* actions? Or only one? ... In short, the only distinct action of his that is in question is this one, A. For moving his arm up and down with his fingers round the pump handle *is*, in these circumstances, operating the pump; and,

in these circumstances, it *is* replenishing the house water-supply; and, in these circumstances, it *is* poisoning the household.

So there is one action with four descriptions. ...[1]

Similarly, Davidson writes:

> I flip the switch, turn on the light, and illuminate the room. Unbeknownst to me I also alert a prowler to the fact that I am home. Here I do not do four things, but only one, of which four descriptions have been given.[2]

And in another article Davidson writes:

> But what is the relation between my pointing the gun and pulling the trigger, and my shooting the victim? The natural and, I think, correct answer is that the relation is that of identity.[3]

I shall call this thesis the *identity thesis*. It has been espoused not only by Anscombe and Davidson, but also by D. S. Shwayder[4] and Eric D'Arcy.[5]

The identity thesis constitutes one clear and attractive way of individuating acts. But there are several difficulties it encounters. In general, if X and Y are identical, then X must have all and only the properties that Y has. We shall find, however, that some of the pairs of acts which are alleged to be identical do not share all the same properties.

Let us look, for example, at John's pulling the trigger and John's killing Smith, which were mentioned in one of the examples given above. According to the identity thesis, these acts are supposed to be one and the same act. But are they really identical? Consider the act of John's killing Smith and consider the event consisting in the gun's going off. Is it true to say that this act caused this event, that John's killing Smith caused the gun to fire? Surely not. It would be extremely odd to say that John's killing Smith caused the gun to go off. But now consider John's act of pulling the trigger. It is certainly true of *this* act that it caused the event in question, i.e., that it caused the gun to fire. Thus, John's pulling the trigger has the property of causing the gun to fire, whereas John's killing Smith does not have the property of causing the gun to fire. However, since one of these acts has a property which the other lacks, they cannot be one and the same act.

Let us take a slightly different example to illustrate the same point. Suppose that John is playing the piano, and that his playing causes Smith to fall asleep while also causing Brown, who was already asleep, to wake up. John has performed the following acts: (1) he has played the piano, (2) he

---

[1] *Intention* (Ithaca, N. Y.: Cornell University Press, 1958), pp. 11, 45–46.

[2] "Actions, Reasons, and Causes," *The Journal of Philosophy*, LX (1963), p. 686.

[3] "The Logical Form of Action Sentences," in Nicholas Rescher, ed., *The Logic of Decision and Action* (Pittsburgh: University of Pittsburgh Press, 1967), p. 84.

[4] *The Stratification of Behaviour* (New York: Humanities Press, 1965).

[5] *Human Acts* (New York: Oxford University Press, 1963).

has put Smith to sleep, and (3) he has awakened Brown. According to the identity thesis, John's playing the piano = John's putting Smith to sleep = John's awakening Brown. But are these genuine identities? Consider the following two events: (e_1) Smith's falling asleep and (e_2) Brown's waking up. *Ex hypothesi*, both of these events were caused by John's playing the piano. Now let us compare John's playing the piano with John's awakening Brown. Clearly, while John's playing the piano caused (e_1), Smith's falling asleep, John's awakening Brown did *not* cause (e_1). Similarly, compare John's playing the piano with John's putting Smith to sleep. John's playing the piano *did* cause (e_2), Brown's waking up, while John's putting Smith to sleep did *not* cause (e_2). We see, then, that John's act of playing the piano has a property which is lacked by John's act of putting Smith to sleep and has another property which is lacked by John's act of awakening Brown. Hence, John's playing the piano cannot be identical with John's putting Smith to sleep and cannot be identical with John's awakening Brown.

These two objections to the identity thesis make reference to the effects or consequences of two allegedly identical actions. Further objections can be raised to the identity thesis by examining the causes or causal factors of actions. If A and A' are one and the same action, then they are one and the same event. And if they are the same event, one would expect them, if they are caused at all, to be caused by the same set of events or states of affairs. If we find, to the contrary, that A and A' have somewhat different sets of causes or causal factors, that would give us reason to conclude that A and A' are not the same after all.

John answers the phone and says "hello." He says "hello" because he wishes to greet the caller. But John has just been quarreling with his wife and is in a tense emotional state. As a result, he says "hello" very loudly. He doesn't intend to shout over the phone; it just comes out that way. Now consider the following acts: John's saying "hello" and John's saying "hello" loudly. According to the identity thesis, these acts are one and the same. However, they appear to have different sets of causal factors. John's act of saying "hello" loudly is an effect, at least in part, of his being in a tense emotional state. But John's act of saying "hello" (*simpliciter*) is not at all an effect of this emotional state, since John would have said "hello" whether or not he had been angry or tense. Thus, there is a causal factor of John's saying "hello" loudly that is not a causal factor of John's saying "hello."[6]

---

[6] Similar problems arise with respect to physical events generally, not only with respect to human acts. Suppose that a certain piece of wood contains some sodium salts, so that it burns yellow when ignited. The wood's burning *yellow* is partially an effect of the presence of the sodium salts, but the wood's burning *simpliciter* is not an effect of the presence of the sodium salts—at least not an effect in the same way. Thus there is a problem for the contention that the wood's burning (*simpliciter*) is the same event as the wood's burning yellow.

Let us turn next to a slightly different example concerning the causes, or causal conditions, of actions. Suppose there is a light bulb missing from a certain socket and that George fetches a bulb and screws it into the socket. A moment later John comes along, flips the switch and thereby turns on the light. Now consider John's act of flipping the switch and John's act of turning on the light. If we tried to list all the causes or relevant causal factors of John's turning on the light, we would certainly include George's screwing the bulb into the socket. If George had not screwed the bulb into the socket, then John would not have succeeded in turning on the light. He would still have flipped the switch, perhaps, but this would not have resulted in the light's going on. Thus, George's screwing the bulb into the socket is a cause, or causal condition, of John's turning on the light. On the other hand, George's action is not at all a cause, or causal factor, of John's act of flipping the switch. For, as I am imagining the case, John would have performed this act whether or not George had screwed the bulb into the socket.

If the reader finds it a bit odd to say that George's screwing the bulb into the socket is a "cause" of John's turning on the light, we might say instead that John's act of turning on the light was "enabled," or "made possible," by George's screwing the bulb into the socket. We may then add that John's act of flipping the switch was *not* "enabled," or "made possible," by George's activity, since John's success in flipping the switch was quite independent of George's contribution. Thus, John's act of turning on the light has at least one property that is lacked by John's act of flipping the switch.

I turn now to a rather different sort of case in which there is a failure of two putatively identical acts to coexemplify a given property. In this case the property in question is the property of being supererogatory.[7] Suppose that I owe Smith two dollars. Seeing him on the street, I reach into my pocket for some cash, and discover two single dollar bills and one two-dollar bill. I like to collect two-dollar bills myself, but I recall that Smith simply goes wild over them. Bearing this in mind, I pay Smith the money with the two-dollar bill. Now consider my act of giving Smith the two-dollar bill and my act of repaying Smith two dollars. The former is supererogatory, while the latter is not supererogatory in the least. Acccording to the identity thesis, these acts are identical. But since one of them has a property which the other lacks, they cannot be one and the same act.

We have seen that many pairs of acts which are alleged to be identical fail to satisfy the principle of the indiscernibility of identicals: they fail to have all properties in common. A further difficulty confronting the identity thesis stems from a certain relationship that holds between many of these acts which are said to be identical. I wish to turn now to this relationship and to its consequences for the identity thesis.

---

[7] I am indebted here to Michael Stocker.

We often say of a person that he performs one act "by" performing another. We say, for example, that John turns on the light "by" flipping the switch, or that he checkmates his opponent "by" moving his queen to king-knight-seven. As used in these contexts, the term "by" expresses a relationship that holds between acts, between John's act of flipping the switch and his act of turning on the light, and between John's act of moving his queen to king-knight-seven and his act of checkmating his opponent. The relationship in question might be expressed by saying that the one act is a "way" or "method" by which the other act is performed. Typically, when act A is the "way" by which act A' is performed, we can *explain how* act A' has been performed by citing act A. For example, if John checkmates his opponent by moving his queen to king-knight-seven, we can *explain how* he checkmated his opponent by referring to his act of moving his queen to king-knight-seven.

The important point to notice about this relationship is that it is both *asymmetric* and *irreflexive*. Consider first the matter of asymmetry. If agent S does act A' "by" doing act A, then he does not do A "by" doing A'. John turns on the light *by* flipping the switch, but he does not flip the switch *by* turning on the light. He checkmates his opponent *by* moving his queen to king-knight-seven, but he does not move his queen to king-knight-seven *by* checkmating his opponent. We can *explain how* John turned on the light by indicating that he flipped the switch, and we can explain how John checkmated his opponent by saying that he moved his queen to king-knight-seven. But we cannot explain how John flipped the switch by saying that he turned on the light; nor can we explain how John moved his queen to king-knight-seven by saying that he checkmated his opponent.

The irreflexivity of the relationship can be seen in the same examples. We would not say that John turned on the light by turning on the light, nor that John checkmated his opponent by checkmating his opponent. We cannot explain how John flipped the switch by indicating that he flipped the switch; nor can we explain how John moved his queen to king-knight-seven by saying that he moved his queen to king-knight-seven.

The fact that the relationship in question is asymmetric and irreflexive has important consequences for the identity thesis. If A and A' are identical, there can be no asymmetric or irreflexive relation which one bears to the other. If A and A' are genuinely identical, then if a relation R holds of the ordered pair (A, A') it must also hold of the ordered pair (A', A). And if R holds of the ordered pair (A, A'), it must also hold of the ordered pairs (A, A) and (A', A'). But we have seen that there is a relation that holds between the ordered pair (John's moving his queen to king-knight-seven, John's checkmating his opponent) which does not hold of the ordered pair (John's checkmating his opponent, John's moving his queen to king-knight-seven); nor does it hold of the ordered pair (John's moving his queen to king-knight-seven, John's moving his queen to king-knight-seven) or of the ordered pair (John's checkmating his opponent, John's checkmating his opponent).

My final criticism of the identity thesis concerns the contrast between basic actions and non-basic actions. Along with many other philosophers, I am inclined to think that some of our actions are basic actions and that other actions of ours are not basic actions.[8] Moving my hand is a basic action, whereas checkmating my opponent and turning on the light are not basic actions. Rather, they are actions I perform *by* performing some basic actions. Now if the identity thesis is correct, then the distinction between basic actions and non-basic actions must be abandoned. For if John's moving his hand is a basic action, and if it is identical with John's checkmating his opponent, then his checkmating his opponent is also a basic action. This consequence of the identity thesis has been acknowledged by Davidson, who does not find it unacceptable.[9] But I, for one, would regard this as an undesirable consequence.

Having suggested a variety of difficulties for the identity thesis, let us consider how a proponent of the identity thesis might reply to these difficulties. One possible reply would involve an appeal to referential opacity (or intensionality). It is well known that certain phrases, such as "desire," "believe," "necessarily," etc. create contexts in which expected substitutions cannot be made *salva veritate*. The truth of "John believes that Cicero denounced Catiline" does not ensure the truth of "John believes that Tully denounced Catiline," even though Tully *is* Cicero. And the truth of "Necessarily nine is greater than seven" does not ensure the truth of "Necessarily the number of planets is greater than seven," although nine *is* the number of the planets. A proponent of the identity thesis might contend that the phrases used in posing our objections also create referentially opaque contexts, viz. such phrases as "is the cause of," "is an effect of," "is supererogatory," etc. For example, it might be suggested that the context ". . . is the cause of the firing of the gun" is referentially opaque, and because of this the co-referential phrases "John's pulling the trigger" and "John's killing Smith" cannot be substituted *salva veritate*. The non-substitutivity, according to the identity theorist, is not to be accounted for by denying the identity of John's pulling the trigger and John's killing Smith, but rather by observing that ". . . is the cause of the firing of the gun" is an opaque context.

The first point I want to make is that there is a danger here of proliferating opaque contexts. Antecedently, it does not seem very plausible

---

[8] The term "basic action" is due to Arthur Danto. Cf. "What We Can Do," *The Journal of Philosophy*, LX (1963), 435–45, and "Basic Actions," *American Philosophical Quarterly*, II (1965), 141–48. As I shall indicate in Chapter Two, however, I do not agree with Danto's explication of the notion of a basic action.

[9] Davidson has discussed this matter in a paper entitled "Agency," delivered at a 1968 symposium at the University of Western Ontario, *Agent, Action, and Reason*.

that all of the contexts, "... is the cause of X," "... is an effect of Y," "... is supererogatory," and "... is done by - - -," are referentially opaque. Thus, the conclusion that they are all referentially opaque should not be drawn unless this opacity can really be proved.

But can the proponent of the identity thesis *prove* referential opacity in these cases? I think not. The proof of referential opacity could only be accomplished by begging the question. In order to prove the opacity of the belief context in the Cicero-Tully case, it must be granted antecedently that Cicero is identical with Tully. In this case, the identity presents no difficulty, of course. But unless this identity is granted, it cannot be proved that the context in question precludes the substitutivity of identicals. Similarly, in order to prove the opacity of such contexts as "... is the cause of the firing of the gun," we must have antecedent agreement on the question of whether John's pulling the trigger is identical with John's killing Smith. But here there is a difficulty, for whether or not these are identical is the very point at issue. To presuppose that they are identical is to beg the question.

Another possible reply of the identity theorist is to claim that the properties we have considered do not apply, strictly, to actions *per se*, but rather to actions *"under certain descriptions."* We cannot say, for example, that actions *per se* are supererogatory, but only that actions, *under certain descriptions*, are supererogatory. Talk of actions "under descriptions" appears in Davidson's article, "Actions, Reasons, and Causes." He writes: "*R* is a primary reason why an agent performed the action *A* under the description *d* only if *R* consists of a pro attitude of the agent toward actions with a certain property, and a belief of the agent that *A*, under the description *d*, has that property."

This reply of the identity theorist seems to me to have unfortunate consequences. In particular, it requires us to do violence to some of the things that it seems most natural to say about human actions. It seems perfectly natural, for instance, to say that actions cause certain events. But if we accept this reply of the identity theorist, we shall be forced to deny that actions cause events, and to say instead that only actions under descriptions cause events. This has the unattractive consequence of committing us to the view that causation is somehow *language-dependent*. Again, it seems perfectly natural to think that acts are often caused by antecedent events, or at least made possible by antecedent events. But if the identity theorist is right, we shall have to revise this view, and say instead that only actions under certain descriptions are caused or made possible by prior events. Similarly, if we adopt the identity thesis, we shall be forced to deny that agents often perform one act by performing another act. We shall be forced to say that only acts under certain descriptions are performed by performing acts under other descriptions.

All this talk of acts "under descriptions" strikes me as unnecessarily cumbersome as well as questionable. A more natural and straightforward way of talking about action would allow us to speak of acts *per se* as causes, as effects, as supererogatory, etc. In order to achieve this more natural way of speaking about action, however, we must abandon the identity thesis. Instead of saying that John's pulling the trigger = John's killing Smith, we must say that John's pulling the trigger is a different act from John's killing Smith. Instead of saying that John's moving his queen to king-knight-seven is the same as John's checkmating his opponent, we must say that these are distinct acts. And instead of saying that John's turning on the light is identical with John's flipping the switch, we must contend that these are not identical.

Such an approach to the individuation of acts has at least some precedence. In J. L. Austin's William James Lectures, *How to Do Things with Words*,[10] he distinguishes between a variety of different acts, all of which would be considered the same act according to the identity thesis. In a given bit of speech, Austin distinguishes a phonetic act, a phatic act, a rhetic act, a locutionary act, an illocutionary act, and a perlocutionary act. It is not my purpose here to discuss or evaluate the nature and justification of the particular distinctions which Austin draws. I mention Austin's work only in order to draw the reader's attention to one example of an attempt to individuate acts in a way quite different from the Anscombe-Davidson approach. I shall try to develop a similar project of individuating acts, but I shall make no further reference to Austin's work.

There are two immediate objections that might be raised to a more "fine-grained" manner of individuating acts. The first objection is that such a fine-grained manner of individuating acts would generate a proliferation of entities. If we individuate acts in such a manner that in the chess case, for instance, John performs (at least) six different acts, we would commit ourselves to a prodigal ontology; we would increase the furniture of the world in an unconscionable manner. There is a danger, in fact, that at any given moment an agent will be performing indefinitely many acts. And such a view would surely be ontologically unacceptable.

This objection is misguided. A fine-grained method of act-individuation cannot justly be accused of "increasing the furniture of the world," for such an approach would not countenance any entities that would not be admitted by a rival method of act-individuation. What, after all, are the acts it would allow in its ontology? They are acts such as John's moving his hand, John's frightening away a fly, John's moving his queen to king-knight-seven, John's checkmating his opponent, etc. But surely these are all acts that would be countenanced by any theory whatever, including the identity thesis.

---

[10] (Cambridge: Harvard University Press, 1962).

The bone of contention, then, is not whether these acts exist, but whether they are identical with one another. Though the fine-grained method of act-individuation diverges from the identity thesis on the question of identity or diversity, it would not postulate any acts the existence of which would be denied by the identity thesis. The difference between the two approaches, therefore, is not to be settled by the use or disuse of Ockham's razor.

While conceding that a fine-grained approach to act-individuation would not postulate any "new" acts, the critic might maintain that this approach would slice behavior up into too many units, "too many" as compared with our *ordinary* procedure for individuating acts. But what is our ordinary procedure for act-individuation? In fact, ordinary language is very vague on this matter. In everyday speech we seldom explicitly address ourselves to the question of whether the acts in the chess case, for example, are identical or distinct. And when asked such a question, people are frequently uncertain about the issue. This is not to say that ordinary language provides no clues for the best resolution of the matter. As we have seen, appeals to ordinary language, e.g., appeal to the use of the "by" locution, combined with appeals to relevant logical or ontological principles, provide strong reasons for abandoning the identity thesis in favor of a fine-grained method of act-individuation. Nevertheless, the adoption of a fine-grained approach does carry us beyond ordinary language, in the sense that it does not merely restate a standard procedure for act-individuation already explicit in ordinary language. But this is to be expected. It is characteristic of philosophical explications that they introduce refinements where ordinary language is unclear or indeterminate. Hence, although we do not say things in ordinary speech that explicitly commit us to the view that agents typically perform many acts at a given moment, an analysis of the notion of an act which has this consequence is not on this account defective.

The second objection to a "fine-grained" procedure of act-individuation is that it leaves as a puzzle the nature of the relationships between the various acts. It is evident that John's act of moving his hand is intimately related with his act of moving his queen to king-knight-seven, with his act of checkmating his opponent, etc. If the relationship is not that of identity, what is it? This question is clearly formulated by Davidson in "The Logical Form of Action Sentences." He writes:

> Excuses provide endless examples of cases where we seem compelled to take talk of "alternative descriptions of the same action" seriously, i. e., literally. But there are plenty of other contexts in which the same need presses. *Explaining* an action by giving an intention with which it was done provides new descriptions of the action: I am writing my name on a piece of paper with the intention of writing a check with the intention of paying a gambling debt. List all the different descriptions of my action. Here are a few for a start: I am writing my name. I am writing my name on a piece of paper. I am writing my

name on a piece of paper with the intention of writing a check. I am writing a check. I am paying my gambling debt. It is hard to imagine how we can have a coherent theory of action unless we are allowed to say here: each of these sentences describes the same action.[11]

This passage can be taken as a challenge. Unless we can find a way of relating acts other than by the relation of identity, the "fine-grained" procedure of act-individuation will not prove satisfactory. I think, however, that such relationships can be found. This matter will constitute the heart of Chapter Two in this volume.

2.   Act-Types and Act-Tokens

In the foregoing section I expressed my intention of adopting a "fine-grained" procedure for the individuation of acts. But the precise nature of this procedure is yet to be spelled out. To this matter I now turn.

I begin by distinguishing between *act-types* and *act-tokens*. An act-type is simply an act-property, a property such as mowing one's lawn, running, writing a letter, or giving a lecture. When we ascribe an act to an agent, we say that the agent exemplified an act-property (at a certain time). When we say, for example, "John mowed his lawn," we assert that John exemplified the property of mowing his lawn. Mowing one's lawn is a property because it can be *true of*, or *exemplified by*, a particular object at a particular time. Normally philosophers tend to apply the term "property" to such things as being six feet tall, being a bachelor, or having red hair. But we need not restrict the term "property" to *static* properties. Just as *owning* a Jaguar is a property that can be exemplified by John at time *t*, so *buying* a Jaguar is a property that can be exemplified by John at time *t*.

To perform an act, then, is to exemplify a property. To perform the act of giving a lecture is to exemplify the property of giving a lecture. A particular act, then, consists in the exemplifying of an act-property by an agent at a particular time. I shall call such particular acts: "*act-tokens*." An act-token is not itself a property. It is the exemplifying of a property by an agent. Act-tokens include John's mowing his lawn (at *t*), John's flipping the switch (at *t*), John's giving a lecture (at *t*), etc.

Since an act-token is the exemplifying of a property by an agent at a time, it is natural so to individuate act-tokens that *two act-tokens are identical if and only if they involve the same agent, the same property, and the same time.*[12]

---

[11] Rescher, ed., *The Logic of Decision and Action*, p. 85.

[12] This analysis of an act-token is very similar to Nicholas Rescher's characterization of a "concrete act" or a "specific action" given in *Introduction to Value Theory*, (Englewood Cliffs, N. J.: Prentice-Hall, Inc., 1969), p. 30. It also closely resembles the account of events given by Jaegwon Kim in "On the Psycho-Physical Identity Theory," *American*

First, if George and Oscar are distinct persons, then no act performed by one of them is identical with any act performed by the other. Secondly, if ϕ and ϕ' are distinct act-properties, no exemplifying of ϕ is identical with any exemplifying of ϕ'. Thirdly, if John exemplifies property ϕ at t and exemplifies ϕ at a different time t', then his exemplifying ϕ at t is a different act-token from his exemplifying ϕ at t'. Finally, if a given person S exemplifies act-property ϕ at time t, then any exemplifying of ϕ by S at t is identical with the first exemplifying of ϕ by S at t.[13]

If we adopt this analysis of act-tokens, we shall obtain the result sought in the previous section; that is, it will follow that John's moving his hand (at t), John's moving his queen to king-knight-seven (at t), John's checkmating his opponent (at t), John's giving his opponent a heart attack (at t), etc., are all different act-tokens. This is because the properties exemplified in these cases are different properties. The property of moving one's hand $\neq$ the property of moving one's queen to king-knight-seven $\neq$ the property of checkmating one's opponent $\neq$ the property of giving one's opponent a heart attack, etc.

I shall say that John's moving his hand (at t) is a *token of* the type (or property), moving one's hand. Each act-token is a token of one and only one type (property). Thus, John's moving his hand (at t) is a token of the type "moving one's hand," but not a token of the type "moving one's queen to king-knight-seven," or of the type "checkmating one's opponent." *Being a token of a property* should not be confused with *exemplifying a property*. John's moving his hand (at t) is a token of the property "moving one's hand," but it does not exemplify that property. (*John* exemplifies that property.) John's moving his hand (at t) does exemplify a variety of properties, however. It exemplifies the property of causing the fright of a fly; it exemplifies the property of causing the movement of the queen; etc. Act-tokens, like anything else, may *exemplify* indefinitely many properties, although they are *tokens of* only one property each.

Since John's moving his finger, John's pulling the trigger, John's firing the gun, and John's killing Smith are all distinct acts, one might be inclined to think that every act can be described, or referred to, by only one expression, or by synonymous expressions only. But this does not follow from my position. Any act-token can be referred to by different, nonsynonymous expressions that pick out the same agent, the same property, and the same time. For

---

Philosophical Quarterly, III (1966), 231, and by Richard Brandt and Jaegwon Kim in "The Logic of the Identity Theory," *The Journal of Philosophy*, LXIV (1967), 516–18.

[13] Perhaps a fourth determinant of act-tokens is needed beyond agent, property, and time. Suppose that John makes a certain signal twice at the same time, once with his right hand and once with his left. The agent, time, and property are identical here—the property being that of making a certain signal—yet there seem to be two distinct act-tokens. This sort of case could be handled by introducing a fourth determinant,—viz., the *way* in which the property is exemplified, e.g., by moving the right hand, or alternatively, by moving the left hand. This complication can safely be ignored in the future, however.

example, two expressions may refer to the same act-token even though they contain different, nonsynonymous phrases for the same agent. If "John" and "the mayor" designate the same agent, then "John's killing Smith (at *t*)" and "the mayor's killing Smith (at *t*)" designate the same act-token. Moreover, we can refer to a given act-token by definite descriptions of the form "the act-token mentioned by Brown" or "the act-token which shocked Jones." Thus, the nonsynonymous expressions "John's killing Smith (at *t*)" and "the act-token mentioned by Brown" might refer to the same act-token.

It does follow from my position, however, that "John's killing Smith (at *t*)" and "John's moving his finger (at *t*)" do not refer to the same act-token. This is because the *properties* picked out by these phrases—viz., killing Smith and moving one's finger—are distinct properties. The heart of my position is that act-token *A* and act-token *A'* are identical only if they are tokens of the same type (property). But since killing Smith and moving one's finger are distinct types, John's killing Smith (at *t*) and John's moving his finger (at *t*) are distinct act-tokens.

We may note parenthetically that the reason why Davidson would say that these acts *are* identical is because he treats the phrase "John's killing Smith" as a definite description. He would analyze "John's killing Smith" as "the act of John's which caused the death of Smith," and would contend that this act *is* John's moving his finger. But, as we have seen, such an analysis has counter-intuitive consequences—e.g., the fact that John's killing Smith would be the cause of the gun's firing. On my view, "John's killing Smith" is not to be analyzed as "the act of John's which caused the death of Smith," but rather as "John's exemplifying the property of killing (causing the death of) Smith."

Since my account of act-tokens depends crucially on the notion of a property, the individuation of properties becomes a critical problem. Unfortunately, it is also a very difficult problem. As a first stab we might say that properties ϕ and ϕ' are identical just in those cases when they are expressible by synonymous expressions. Being a bachelor is thus the same property as being an unmarried man, since the former can be expressed by the phrase "being a bachelor" and the latter by the synonymous phrase "being an unmarried man." Of course, we do not want to require that there actually be some suitable expression in some actual language. The most we want to say is that, *if* there are phrases in a language which express ϕ and ϕ', then their being synonymous is a necessary and sufficient condition for their expressing the same property. This allows for the possibility of identical properties ϕ and ϕ' which are not expressed by phrases in any actual language.

We must note at once, however, that properties can be identified or designated in a variety of ways. The phrase "being blue" identifies or picks out the property of being blue. But this same property can be referred to by a definite description, such as "the color property of the sky," which is clearly not synonymous with "being blue." However, although we can *refer* to this property with the expression "the color property of the sky," this phrase does not *express* this property in the way that "being blue" *expresses* it. The proposed synonymy criterion must be restricted to phrases that *express* properties, and must not be applied to definite descriptions that merely refer indirectly to properties.

Problems still arise, however, for the synonymy test. Consider, for example, the property of having temperature T and the property of having mean molecular kinetic energy M. Might these be the same property? On the one hand, the phrases "temperature T" and "mean molecular kinetic energy M" do not appear to be synonymous, and yet, it might be argued, physics has shown that these properties are identical. This is indeed a problem for the synonymy test. But since it is not the sort of problem that will concern us much in this work, we might well sidestep it and accept the synonymy test at least as a working principle.[14]

Another objection that might be raised against the synonymy test is that it yields the result that *running* and *running at ten miles per hour* are different properties. Perhaps this in itself is not a problem. But when this is combined with the principle for individuating act-tokens, it will turn out that John's running (at t) is a different act-token from John's running at ten miles per hour (at t).

Although the latter consequence may seem counter-intuitive at first, I think it is one with which we can live. Indeed, in Section 1 we found positive reasons for distinguishing between John's saying "hello" and John's saying "hello" loudly. Similar reasons might be adduced for distinguishing between John's act of extending his arm and John's act of extending his arm out the window, and for distinguishing between John's act of running and John's act of running at ten miles per hour. To be sure, if we say these pairs of acts are distinct, we must also indicate that they are closely related. This will be provided for in Chapter Two.

The most serious problem facing the synonymy test concerns relational properties. Consider the property of hitting the tallest man in the room and the property of hitting the wealthiest man in the room. Suppose that the tallest man in the room *is* the wealthiest man in the room. Are these properties the same or different? If we employ the synonymy test in this case, we shall obtain the result that the properties are different. And then we shall obtain the further result that John's act of hitting the tallest man in the room (at t) is different from John's act of hitting the wealthiest man in the room (at t). Such a result surely appears unwelcome.

At this point one might decide to modify the synonymy test. One might decide to say that two properties are identical even if they contain different

---

[14] It does become important, however, when the mind-body issue is broached in Chapter Five, Section 5. For a discussion of this issue, cf. Brandt and Kim, "The Logic of the Identity Theory," *op. cit.*

individual concepts of the same individual. I am prepared, however, to use the synonymy test even for relational properties, and to accept the consequences of this for the individuation of acts. Having already committed myself to a "fine-grained" procedure for individuating acts, I do not think I will have difficulty in accommodating the further distinctions that flow from this decision. Specifically, given the techniques that will be developed for relating such acts as John's flipping the switch and John's turning on the light, I do not think it will be difficult to introduce further techniques for relating such acts as John's hitting the tallest man in the room and John's hitting the wealthiest man in the room, even if these acts are considered to be distinct. It should be remembered, however, that this decision regarding relational properties is by no means an essential ingredient of my theory. The rest of the theory does not depend on this decision. Hence, if the reader finds this particular element of the account unattractive, it can easily be detached from the remainder and discarded.

The individuation of properties is a difficult problem which I have not tried to settle completely here. But I turn now to a different point, concerning the relationship between acts and act-ascribing sentences. Consider the two sentences, "John killed Smith (at t)" and "The mayor killed Smith (at t)." Although these sentences are not logically equivalent, both of them (if true) identify the very same act-token. Thus, two act-ascribing sentences need not be logically equivalent in order to identify the same act-token. But although logical equivalence is not a necessary condition of act-identity, one might think it is a sufficient condition. Yet this too, I think, is incorrect. There are some logically equivalent pairs of act-ascribing sentences, I believe, such that one member of a given pair ascribes a certain act to a certain person though the other member of the pair ascribes a different act to a different person. Secondly, there are some logically equivalent pairs of sentences such that one member of a given pair is an act-ascribing sentence though the other member does not ascribe an act at all.[15]

First, consider sentences P and Q.

P: "John married Mary (at t)."

Q: "Mary married John (at t)."

Now it might be claimed, though this perhaps is not obvious, that P and Q are logically equivalent, that necessarily they have the same truth-value. Mary's marrying John may be a (logically) necessary condition of John's marrying Mary, and conversely. Nevertheless, I deny that P and Q, if true, pick out the same act-token. For P, if true, picks out the act-token "John's marrying Mary (at t)," an act-token that consists of John as agent and marrying Mary as act-type. Q on the other hand, if true, picks out the act-token

---

[15] On both points I am indebted to Jaegwon Kim.

"Mary's marrying John (at *t*)," which consists of Mary as agent and marrying John as act-type.

Next consider sentences R and S.

R: "John ate lunch (at *t*)."

S: "The class of objects x such that x is self-identical and such that John ate lunch (at *t*) is identical with the class of objects x such that x is self-identical."[16]

R and S are logically equivalent, yet only one of them, I think, ascribes an act to anyone. R ascribes to John the act of eating lunch, but S, far from ascribing an act to John, is not about John at all. S is about a certain class or pair of classes, and what it asserts of these classes is not that they performed any acts, but that they are identical. Thus, although necessarily R is true if and only if S is true, R might (if true) pick out an act-token, but S could not under any circumstance pick out an act-token. Therefore, though R may pick out an act-token and though S is logically equivalent to R, S could not pick out the same act-token as R.[17]

3. Act-Tokens and Other Property-Exemplifications

I have said that an act-token consists in the exemplifying of an act-property by a person at a time (or during a time interval). The next problem that faces us, then, is to explain which properties are act-properties. Clearly, being a bachelor, being six feet tall, and having brown eyes are not *act*-properties; nor are John's being a bachelor (at *t*) or John's being six feet tall (at *t*) *act*-tokens. How, then, can act-properties be distinguished from other properties?

Before worrying about this problem, we must note a further and perhaps more serious problem. My analysis of act-tokens suggests that there is a class of properties—viz. act-properties, such that *any* exemplification by a person of one of these properties is an act-token. For each act-property P, it suggests, any instance of P is an act-instance. Unfortunately, matters are not this neat.

---

[16] This example is patterned after one by Davidson, "Truth and Meaning," *Synthese*, XVII (1967), 304–23, and "The Logical Form of Action Sentences," *loc. cit.* A similar example is from W.V.O. Quine, *Word and Object* (Cambridge, Mass.: The M.I.T. Press, 1960), pp. 148–49, and ultimately derives from Frege.

[17] The rejection of the view that R and S pick out the same act-token helps us forestall an argument which threatens to prove that *all* true act-ascribing (or event-ascribing) sentences ascribe, or refer to, the *same* act (or event). Such a conclusion, of course, would be disastrous. For a discussion of these issues, see Jaegwon Kim, "Events and Their Descriptions: Some Considerations," in *Essays in Honor of Carl G. Hempel*, eds., Nicholas Rescher et al (Dordrecht: D. Reidel Publishing Company, 1969).

Consider the property *coughing*, for example. Some, but not all, of the instances of this property are act-instances. If John coughs artificially, as a signal to his henchmen, then his coughing is an act-token. But coughing *naturally*, because of a certain familiar bronchial state, is not an act-token. The latter sort of coughing is not something you *do*, but rather something that *happens* to you, that you *undergo*.

This shows that we cannot complete our analysis of act-tokens even with an adequate characterization of act-properties at our disposal. A necessary condition of x's being an act-token is that x be the exemplification by a person of an act-property at a time; but this is not a sufficient condition of x's being an act-token. Despite this problem, it would be helpful to have a definition of an act-property—i.e., of a property such that *at least one* of its instances is an act-token. But even this is extremely difficult.

In his book *Action, Emotion and Will* Anthony Kenny distinguishes between three kinds of verbs: static verbs, performance verbs, and activity verbs.[18] Static verbs are ones which do not have continuous tenses, whereas both performance verbs and activity verbs do have continuous tenses. Performance verbs are distinguished from activity verbs by the following criterion: where "S is ϕing" implies "S has not ϕed" the verb is a performance verb; where "S is ϕing" implies "S has ϕed" the verb is an activity verb. Performance verbs are said to stand for performances and activity verbs for activities; the term "action" stands indifferently for a performance or an activity. Thus, we might say that any activity verb or verb phrase and any performance verb or verb phrase expresses an act-property.

Kenny's account works fairly well up to a point. Predicates like "is tall" "is a bachelor," "has brown eyes," or " owns an Alfa Romeo" should not express act-properties; and on Kenny's criterion they would not express act-properties since they do not have continuous tenses. But the account fails when examined more closely. Consider the verb "dying," for example. This turns out to be a performance verb on Kenny's criterion, and hence it should express an act-property. But I do not think that *dying* is an act-property. Although committing suicide is certainly an act, dying—i.e. actually expiring —is never something one does. Or consider the verb phrases "growing taller" and "getting bald." These phrases stand for activities, on Kenny's criterion, and hence should express act-properties. But growing taller or getting bald are never *done* by people. Similarly, "catching a cold" and "fainting" have continuous tenses and should express act-properties, but in fact catching a cold or fainting are never things that we *do*.

Another possible approach to the elucidation of act-properties might use the notions of purpose, intention, or reason. It has often been remarked that the distinguishing feature of human action is the element of purpose. Doing something in order to achieve a certain end, or for a certain reason, or with a

---

[18] (London: Routledge and Kegan Paul, 1963), pp. 172–73 ff.

certain intention is central to the concept of a human doing. We could not define an act-property, however, as a property all of whose instances are intentional or purposeful. (For one thing, this would make the notion of an act-instance logically prior to that of an act-property, instead of vice versa.) *Insulting John* is clearly an act-property, but not *all* of its instances are intentional, since there may have been an act-token of insulting John that was unintentional. Similarly, not all of the tokens of *turning on the light* are intentional, yet this is an act-property.

A weaker proposal would say that an act-property is a property that *can* be exemplified intentionally, or such that *some* of its instances are intentional. The second version will not work, since there are many act-properties that are never exemplified at all, hence not exemplified intentionally. Thus, we must concentrate on its *possible* instances, which returns us to the first version. Even this weak proposal may be too strong, however; there are properties like *misspeaking*, *miscalculating* or *miscounting* that are act-properties though they seem to *preclude* intentionality. A second problem for this proposal concerns the nature of the modality. How shall we decide if it is *possible* for a property to be exemplified intentionally? Is it possible for the property *dying* to be exemplified intentionally? Or the property *growing taller*? Perhaps some yoga could die intentionally or grow taller intentionally, just as some of us can wiggle our ears intentionally.

The problems here are serious. But, since a definition of act-properties will not complete our analysis of act-tokens anyway, perhaps we should abandon the idea of analyzing act-properties prior to act-tokens. Perhaps, after all, there is no need to provide criteria for distinguishing act-properties from all other properties prior to providing a definition of act-tokens. If we can give a definition of act-*tokens* without first defining act-*properties*, this will be adequate for our purposes. Of course, the newly envisaged definition of act-tokens would not override the old characterization of them. We shall still say that an act-token is an exemplification of an act-property by a person at (during) a time. But while retaining this characterization, we shall not *use* it to distinguish act-tokens from other property-exemplifications. Instead, we shall employ the envisaged definition to ascertain which property-exemplifications are *act*-tokens; then we shall say that any property which has an *act*-token as one of its instances is an *act*-property. In giving the new definition of act-tokens we shall have to define a certain narrow class of act-properties first; but we shall not be forced to define act-properties in general.

The preceding paragraph hints at the procedure I shall follow, but let me spell it out more fully. I shall try to give a "recursive" or "inductive" definition of an act-token. I shall demarcate a certain class of act-tokens and a certain set of relations, and then I shall say that anything which bears an appropriate combination of these relations to a member of the originally demarcated class of act-tokens is itself an act-token. This, actually, is a logical reconstruction of the procedure I shall follow, not an indication of the order of exposition. In fact, I shall be forced first to discuss the nature of the relations involved (Chapter Two) and only later (in the middle of Chapter Three) shall I fully define the originating class of act-tokens. There is a danger that the structure of the inductive definition may get lost because of the order of exposition. But I hope that by giving a sketch of that structure now, I shall give the reader enough guidelines to reconstruct it from the various sections of chapters in which it occurs. It would be nice to give the complete definition and its justification in Chapter One, but unfortunately this is impossible.

The originating class of act-tokens on which the inductive definition will be based is the class of *basic* act-tokens. A person's action often has far-reaching effects in the world, but whatever one does in the world at large must come, in one way or another, from one's body, especially from the movements of one's body. Thus, there is a central role that bodily acts play *vis-à-vis* our acts in general, and this special role is intended to be captured by the phrase "basic acts." This concept will be left undefined until the middle of Chapter Three, but the idea can be easily grasped with the aid of some examples. Here, then, is a sample list of basic act-types (basic act-properties).

    Extending one's arm
    Moving one's finger
    Bending one's knee
    Shrugging one's shoulder
    Opening one's eyes
    Turning one's head
    Puckering one's lips
    Wrinkling one's nose

The negations of these properties are also basic act-properties—viz., *not extending one's arm*, *not moving one's finger*, etc. Actually, to call all of these properties basic act-properties is something of an oversimplification. More precisely, basic act-types should be relativized to persons and times. Instead of saying that A is a basic act-type, we should say that A is a basic act-type *for* person S *at* time t. *Wiggling one's ears* may be a basic act-type for one person but not for another, and *extending one's arm* may be a basic act-type for S at t but may cease to be a basic act-type for S at t' when the arm becomes paralyzed.

Not all tokens of basic act-types are basic act-tokens; some are not acts at all. The property *coughing*, for example, is a basic act-type, but not all of its tokens are acts. Although an intentional cough is a basic act-token, when one coughs naturally, rather than by intent, one has not performed an act. With this in mind, I shall say that a token of a basic act-type is a basic act-token only if it is intentional. (Details on the concept of intentionality must await Chapter Three) This does not imply, of course, that *all* act-tokens are intentional, only *basic* act-tokens. But since all act-tokens must be somehow related to basic act-tokens, this imports the concept of purpose or intention into the heart of the concept of human action.

Act-tokens in general are either basic act-tokens or things related in specific ways to basic act-tokens. The most important of these relations can be illustrated by our chess example. John's moving his hand is a basic act-token, and each of the other acts—John's frightening away a fly, John's moving his queen to king-knight-seven, John's checkmating his opponent, etc.—is *generated* or *produced* by this basic act-token. In a different context, John's extending his arm might generate or produce the act-token John's signaling for a turn. The nature of the relations that obtain when one act generates or produces another will be studied in Chapter Two. Once these and other relations are explicated, we shall be in a position to define act-tokens in general. Throughout Chapter Two and much of Chapter Three, however, I shall take for granted the notion of a basic act-token and the notion of an act-token in general. I shall not operate on the assumption that use of these notions is illegitimate until a complete definition has been given. On the contrary, these notions must be used in the process of explaining precisely those tools that will be used to define them. If this involves some lifting by the bootstraps, I can only say that I find this an inevitable, and hence not very objectionable, feature of most philosophical theorizing.

One final note on the analysis of acts to be presented. In discussing a topic like action it is well to bear in mind the large degree of vagueness in our ordinary concept. The words "act" and "action" are susceptible of various stricter and looser uses in ordinary speech, and in consequence, there is room for analyses both of a broader range and of a narrower range of cases. One analysis might center on purposeful and intentional behavior, while another analysis might seek to accommodate more thoroughly the cases of automatic, habitual, and mindless behavior. My analysis will tend to focus on purposeful behavior. This does not mean that unintentional acts will be neglected, but it does mean that relatively slight attention will be paid to behavior of a mechanical or habitual sort. I do not contend that mine is the *only* defensible range of cases to concentrate on, but I do claim that it is *a* defensible range of cases.

CHAPTER TWO

The Structure
of Action

1. Level-Generation

We saw in Chapter One that a delineation of the class of act-tokens requires an explanation of the way in which nonbasic act-tokens are related to basic act-tokens. Such an explanation will be provided in this chapter. In the process of giving this explanation, however, I shall have to presuppose an intuitive idea of an act-token. Thus, I shall make use of the notion of an act-token even though I have yet to give a full definition of it.

The importance of the present study is not confined to its usefulness in defining the concept of an act (-token). It is also essential to my defense of the "property" criterion of act-individuation. According to this criterion, pairs of acts such as John's moving his hand and John's moving his queen to king-knight-seven are not identical. But, if not identical, such acts are surely connected in some intimate way. If we are to develop a coherent theory of action using the "property" criterion, it is imperative that we explicate the nature of such connections. Much of the present chapter, therefore, will be devoted to the study of the relation holding between pairs of acts such as (a) John's moving his hand and John's moving his queen to king-knight-seven, (b) John's extending his arm out the car window and John's signaling for a turn, and (c) John's turning the key and John's unlocking the door.

We have already seen that the preposition "by" is often used where pairs of acts are related in the indicated way. In each of the three examples which follow, it is appropriate to say that act A' was done "by" act A, or that the agent did A' "by" doing A. We can say that John moved his queen to king-knight-seven "by" moving his hand; that he checkmated his opponent "by" moving his queen to king-knight-seven; and that he gave his opponent a heart attack "by" checkmating his opponent. (In some of these cases, the preposition "in" can be substituted for "by." We may say that "in" moving

Act A	Act A'
John's moving his hand ————→	John's moving his queen to king-knight-seven
John's moving his queen to king-knight-seven ————→	John's checkmating his opponent
John's checkmating his opponent ————→	John's giving his opponent a heart attack

his queen to king-knight-seven, John checkmated his opponent.) The relationship which obtains between pairs of act-tokens such as these will be called "*level-generation*," or more simply, "*generation*." Thus, level-generation is a relation holding between ordered pairs of act-tokens of the same agent. In general, level-generation will obtain when the "by" locution is appropriate; but the notion of level-generation will not be completely tied to this locution.

The term "*level*-generation" has been chosen because I shall draw diagrams of act relationships in which generated acts are drawn above their corresponding generating acts. This will produce diagrams in which basic act-tokens are at the bottom of act-trees and nonbasic act-tokens at higher levels on the act-trees. As is suggested by these diagrams, level-generation is intended to be an *asymmetric, irreflexive,* and *transitive* relation.

Let us begin the study of level-generation by noting some temporal properties of pairs of acts related by generation. The first thing to notice is that neither one of a pair of generational acts is *subsequent* to the other. Let us say that S's doing A' is *subsequent* to S's doing A if and only if it is correct to say that S did A "*and then*" (or "*and later*") did A'. If S shaves at 8:00 o'clock and eats breakfast at 8:15, then his eating breakfast is subsequent to his shaving. For it is correct to say that he shaved "and then" (or "and later") ate breakfast. On the other hand, if S checkmates his opponent by moving his queen to king-knight-seven, his checkmating his opponent is not subsequent to his moving his queen to king-knight-seven. It would be incorrect to say that S moved his queen to king-knight-seven "and then" checkmated his opponent, for that would wrongly suggest that it took an additional move to perform the checkmate. Similarly, if S turns on the light by flipping the switch, his turning on the light is not subsequent to his flipping the switch. His turning on the light is not subsequent to his flipping the switch even if the light does not go on until a few seconds after the switch is flipped. (Imagine a delaying mechanism in the switch.) Although the light does not go on until a few seconds later, it would still be incorrect to say that he flipped the switch "and then" turned on the light. Likewise, although the opponent's heart attack begins several moments after the checkmate, it would be inappropriate to say that S checkmated his opponent "and then" gave him a heart attack.

There is a sense, then, in which pairs of generational acts are always done *at the same time;* i.e., neither of a pair of generational acts is subsequent to the other. Nevertheless, nonsubsequence is not a sufficient condition for two acts to be related by generation. Many pairs of acts done by a single agent at the same time are completely *independent* acts, neither of which is done "by" doing the other. Suppose, for example, that S wiggles his toes while, at the same time, strumming a guitar. Neither of these acts is subsequent to the other, but they are not related by level-generation. I shall call pairs of acts of this sort "*co-temporal*" acts. The criterion of co-temporality is the correctness of saying that one of the acts is done "*while also*" doing the other. It is correct to say that S wiggled his toes "while also" strumming a guitar; hence these two acts are co-temporal. But it is incorrect to say that S checkmated his opponent "while also" moving his queen to king-knight-seven (or vice versa), and it is incorrect to say that S turned on the light "while also" flipping the switch (or vice versa). Hence, neither of these pairs of acts is co-temporal. Pairs of acts are related by level-generation only if they *fail* to be co-temporal.

Although level-generational acts must not be co-temporal, we do want them to be performed at the same time—more precisely, during the same *interval* of time. The nonsubsequence requirement helps to ensure that they occupy the same interval of time. We must add to this, however, the requirement that no member of a level-generational pair be a *temporal part*, i.e. proper part, of its level-generational mate. Consider, for example, S's act of playing the C-scale. This act is composed of a series of smaller acts ordered by the relation of subsequence—viz., S's playing note C, followed by S's playing note D, followed by S's playing note E, etc. Each of these shorter acts is a temporal part of S's playing the C-scale. Because of this, none of these shorter acts is level-generationally related to the longer act of playing the C-scale. Furthermore, no act which is generationally related to a temporal part of playing the C-scale is generationally related to playing the C-scale. For example, since S's moving his thumb generates S's playing note C, and since S's playing note C is a temporal part of S's playing the C-scale, S's moving his thumb is not level-generationally related to S's playing the C-scale.

Our three temporal requirements provide necessary conditions to be satisfied by any pair of level-generational acts. These necessary conditions, however, do not give us much insight into the nature of level-generation. Nor do they give us any indication of the direction of level-generation: *which* of a pair of generational acts level-generates the other. A detailed study of level-generation is therefore in order. I shall proceed by dividing cases of level-generation into four categories, each of which will be examined at some length. The four categories are: (1) *Causal generation*, (2) *Conventional generation*, (3) *Simple generation*, and (4) *Augmentation generation*.

The most common species of level-generation is *causal* generation. Four examples are given below. In each of these examples, S's act-token A has a certain effect, E, and because it has this effect, S may be credited with performing act A'. For example, S's flipping the switch has the effect of the

Act A	Act A'
S's flipping the switch ⟶	S's turning on the light
S's shooting the gun ⟶	S's killing George
S's moving his arm ⟶	S's closing the door
S's closing the door ⟶	S's preventing a fly from entering the house

light's going on. And in virtue of this, S may be credited with the act of turning on the light. That is, we may say that S exemplified the property of turning on the light. Similarly, S's closing the door has the effect that a fly is unable to enter the house. Because of this, we may say that S exemplified the property of preventing a fly from entering the house. To generalize: *Act-token* A *of agent* S *causally generates act-token* A' *of agent* S *only if* (a) A *causes* E, and (b) A' *consists in* S's *causing* E.

In cases of causal generation the generated act-token A' is always a token of an act-type of the form *causing* E (or *bringing about* E), where E is either an event or a state of affairs. For example, S's turning on the light is a token of the type *turning on the light*, which can be analyzed (roughly) as *causing the light to go on*. S's closing the door is a token of the type *closing the door*, which can be analyzed (roughly) as *causing the door to close*. And S's preventing a fly from entering the house is a token of the type, *preventing a fly from entering the house*, which can be analyzed (roughly) as *causing a fly to be unable to enter the house*. Admittedly, there are sometimes restrictions implicit in these act-types. S might *cause* the door to be closed by asking another person to close it, and here S would not be credited with "closing the door." For the sake of simplicity, however, I shall ignore such complications.

It is extremely important to distinguish between *causal generation* and *causation*. Although the notion of causation is presupposed in the notion of causal generation, the two must not be identified. Indeed, they are mutually exclusive. Two acts can never be related both by causal generation and by causation. Suppose that S locks himself out of his car, and this deed of his forces him to break the window in order to get back in. S's act of locking himself out of the car *causes* his act of breaking the window; but it does not causally generate the latter act. Level-generation is precluded between these acts because one of them is subsequent to the other. In cases of causal generation, a causal relation obtains between act-token A and event E, not between act-token A and act-token A'. S's act of flipping the switch *causes* the event of *the light's going on*. And since S's turning on the light consists in S's causing the light's going on, we may say that S's flipping the switch *causally generates* S's turning on the light.

One final example may help clarify the difference between causation and causal generation. John takes a sleeping pill at 1:00 o'clock and he falls asleep fifteen minutes later. By taking the sleeping pill, John causes himself to fall asleep. There are, then, three distinct things to be considered: (a) John's act of taking the sleeping pill, (b) John's falling asleep (not an act), and (c)

John's act of causing himself to fall asleep. They are related as follows. Act (a) causes event (b), but does not causally generate it. Act (c) is causally generated by act (a), but is not caused by it.

In Arthur Danto's article "What We Can Do"[1] there is a confusion between causation and causal generation that results in an inadequate definition of the notion of a basic action. According to Danto's definition, A is a basic action if and only if (1) A is an action, and (2) whenever S performs A, there is no other action A' performed by S such that A is caused by A'. To see that this definition is incorrect, consider S's act of killing George. Suppose that this act is not caused by any other act of S (although, of course, it is causally *generated* by other acts of S—e.g., S's shooting the gun). Then according to Danto's definition, S's killing George is a basic action. But this sort of action is not the sort we want to classify as a basic action. Danto's definition is also inadequate because it *rules out* actions which we *want* to class as basic. Suppose, for example, that S performs the act of (accidentally) locking himself out of the house, and this causes him to climb back in through a window. In climbing through the window, he moves his legs in a certain way, and this act of moving his legs is the sort we want to consider a basic action. But since his moving his legs in this way is caused by his (earlier) act of locking himself out of the house, Danto's definition would not allow the moving of his legs to be counted as a basic action.[2]

Danto would come closer to an adequate definition of a basic act (-token) if he substituted the notion of causal generation for that of causation. Whereas an act *caused* by another act of the same agent may still be a basic act, no act *causally generated* by another act is a basic act. Nevertheless, even the substitution of "causal generation" for "causation" will not effect a fully adequate definition of a basic act. The requirement that A not be causally generated by any other act is a *necessary* condition of its being a basic act, but it is not a *sufficient* condition. As we shall see later, S's act of signaling for a turn is not a basic act, even though it is not *causally* generated by any other act. (It is *conventionally* generated by other acts.)

Although the notion of causal generation depends on the notion of causation, I shall not offer any account of causation. I shall simply presuppose our ability to make the necessary judgment that a given act has caused a given effect. One point worth making, however, is that acts can have varying degrees of causal relevance *vis-à-vis* a given effect. Sometimes we say without qualification that a certain act caused a certain event, while at other times we would only say that a given act was a "partial" or "contributing" cause of a given event. The notion of causal generation is intended to be quite inclusive, however, so as to cover all such cases.

[1] *The Journal of Philosophy*, LX (1963), 435–45.

[2] Similar criticisms of Danto are made by Myles Brand, "Danto on Basic Actions," *Nous*, II (1968), 187–90, and by Frederick Stoutland, "Basic Actions and Causality," *The Journal of Philosophy*, LXV (1968), 467–75.

When S's act A causes event E, we say that S exemplified the property of causing E. In other words, we say that the event E was caused, or brought about, by the *agent* S. To say that S caused E, however, is not to imply that S caused E *intentionally* or *on purpose;* nor does it imply that S is *responsible* or *liable* for the occurrence of E. At any rate, as I am using the expression "S caused E," such a statement has no implications concerning intentionality or responsibility. Admittedly, the phrase "S was the cause of E" or "S caused E" is sometimes used to impute responsibility, fault, or blame. But the phrase need not be used in this way.[3]

I turn from causal generation to the second species of level-generation: *conventional* generation. Conventional generation is characterized by the existence of rules, conventions, or social practices in virtue of which an act A' can be ascribed to an agent S, given his performance of another act, A. Here are some examples.

Act A	*Act A'*
S's extending his arm out the car window	⟶ S's signaling for a turn
S's moving his queen to king-knight-seven	⟶ S's checkmating his opponent
S's trying to save Jones' life	⟶ S's doing his duty
S's breaking his promise	⟶ S's doing what he ought not to do

In each of these cases there is a rule, R, according to which S's performance of A justifies the further ascription of A' to S. In the first example there is the rule, "extending one's arm out the car window while driving counts as signaling for a turn." In the second example, the relevant rules are rules of chess: the rules stipulating what counts as checkmate and rules saying how the pieces can move. In the third example the rule is: "Lifeguards, while on duty, are obliged to try to save the life of anyone in the water who calls for help." (It is imagined, in this example, that S is a lifeguard currently on duty, and that Jones has just called for help.) In the fourth example the rule is: "One should not break one's promises."

For our purposes, rules can be divided into two classes: normative rules and non-normative rules. Normative rules specifiy acts that are obligatory, forbidden, etc. They include the rules of the third and fourth examples. Non-normative rules typically indicate the sort of significance a certain act has within a game or institutional framework. A good example of this is the rule in our first example: "Extending one's arm out the car window while

---

[3] For a discussion of these issues, see Joel Feinberg, "Action and Responsibility," in Max Black, ed., *Philosophy in America* (London: George Allen and Unwin, 1965), pp. 134–60.

driving counts as signaling for a turn." This rule indicates that the significance or force of extending one's arm out the car window is that of signaling for a turn.

In most instances of conventional generation there are *circumstances* accompanying act *A* which are essential for the performance of act *A'*. In the first example, such a circumstance is the fact that *S* was driving his car at the time that he extended his arm out the window. If this circumstance had not obtained—if, say, the car had been sitting in the garage at the time—then *S*'s extending his arm out the window would not have generated his signaling for a turn. In the second example the relevant circumstances include the positions of the various pieces on the chessboard. Had their positions been relevantly different, *S*'s moving his queen to king-knight-seven would not have generated *S*'s checkmating the opponent. In the third example the relevant circumstances include (a) the fact that *S* is a lifeguard, (b) the fact that *S* is on duty, and (c) the fact that Jones has just called for help. If no such circumstances had obtained, *S*'s trying to save Jones' life would not have generated the act of performing (or fulfilling) his *duty*.

In some cases, however, conventional generation occurs without any particular "circumstances" being involved. The performance of act *A* and the existence of rule *R* together suffice for the ascription of act *A'*. In the fourth case, for example, the rule forbidding promise-breaking and the fact that *S* broke his promise warrant us in ascribing to *S* the act of doing what he ought not to do. No special circumstances are required to warrant this ascription.

With these examples in mind, we can state the following condition for conventional generation. *Act-token* A *of agent* S *conventionally generates act-token* A' *of agent* S *only if the performance of* A *in circumstances* C (*possibly null*), *together with a rule* R *saying that* A *done in* C *counts as* A', *guarantees the performance of* A'.

The third species of level-generation, *simple* generation, is best characterized by contrast with causal generation and conventional generation. In contrast with causal generation, simple generation involves no causal connection between the generating act, *A*, and an effect, *E*. And unlike conventional generation, there are no rules involved in the relationship between *A* and *A'*. In simple generation the existence of certain circumstances, conjoined with the performance of *A*, ensures that the agent has performed *A'*. In other words, simple generation is like conventional generation minus the rules. (Except, of course, that in conventional generation the "circumstances" may be null; whereas they cannot be null in the case of simple generation.) While conventional generation might be schematized as "*A* and *R* and *C* jointly imply *A'*," simple generation could be schematized as "*A* and *C* jointly imply *A'*." Below are some examples of simple generation.

In the first example the relevant circumstance is that George has just jumped six feet. Together with the fact that *S* jumps 6 feet 3 inches (act *A*), it

Act A	*Act A'*
S's jumping 6 feet 3 inches	⟶S's outjumping George
S's asserting that p	⟶S's contradicting his earlier statement
S's coming home after 12:00	⟶S's breaking his promise
S's asserting that p	⟶S's lying
S's dangling a line in the water	⟶S's fishing

follows that S outjumps George (act A'). The circumstance of the second example consists in S's having asserted that not-p at an earlier time. The circumstance of the third example consists in S's having promised not to come home after 12:00.

Notice the difference between this third example and the case of conventional generation in which S's breaking his promise generates S's doing what he ought not to do. It does not follow from the definition of "doing what one ought not to do" or from the definition of "break one's promise" that breaking promises is something one ought not to do. Thus, the fact that S breaks his promise does not by itself imply that he does what he ought not to do. To get the required implication, we must add a *rule* to the effect that one ought not to break one's promises. In the example of simple generation, however, no rule is presupposed. From the definition of "break one's promise" it follows that if S promised to do x and failed to do x, then he has broken his promise. Thus, given the "circumstance" that S promised not to come home after 12:00 and given his act of coming home after 12:00, it follows that he has performed the further act of breaking his promise.

The fourth and fifth examples of simple generation are interesting because the relevant circumstances consist in the agent's being in certain mental states. In the fourth example it is assumed that lying is asserting something that one *believes* to be false. Since S believes that p is false, his asserting that p generates his performing the act of lying.

The circumstance of the fifth example is the presence of a certain *desire* or *hope* of the agent—viz., to catch fish. Since S is dangling a line in the water with (or *out of*) a desire to catch fish, he is performing the act of fishing. An agent's desires, intentions, or motives often occur as circumstances for simple generation. The act of crouching behind a car, if done with the intention of preventing oneself from being seen, generates the act of *hiding*. And playing the piano, if done out of the desire to improve one's playing, generates the act of *practicing* the piano.

It might be claimed that an agent's intentions, motives, beliefs, etc. are a sufficiently distinctive class of circumstances to warrant a separate species of level-generation entirely, on a par with the four others I have mentioned. This may be so; but since the categorization of species of level-generation is largely arbitrary, I shall leave these cases under the heading of simple generation.

I turn now to the fourth and final species of generation, *augmentation* generation. The following examples illustrate this species of level generation.

Act A	*Act A'*
S's extending his arm	————→*S*'s extending his arm out the car window
S's saying "hello"	————→*S*'s saying "hello" loudly
S's running	————→*S*'s running at 8 m.p.h.
S's shooting (a basketball)	————→*S*'s jump-shooting

What is distinctive in these cases is the fact that the performance of the generated act, *A'*, entails the performance of the generating act, *A*. On the other hand, the performance of the generating act does not entail the performance of the generated act. The generated act is formed by "augmenting" the generating act with some relevant fact or circumstance. The fact that the generating act is not merely performed, but performed *in a certain manner*, or *in certain circumstances*, entails that the generated act is also performed.

The sorts of facts or circumstances with which an act may be augmented are quite varied. In the first example given above *S*'s act of extending his arm is augmented by the fact that, when extended, his arm goes out the window. From this it follows that he performs the act of extending his arm out the car window. In the second example the augmenting circumstance is the manner in which *S* says "hello," viz. loudly. And in the third example *S*'s act of running is augmented by the specific speed at which he runs.

A special case of augmentation generation occurs when the augmenting circumstance is a co-temporal act of the agent. Suppose, as in the fourth case shown above, that *S* shoots the basketball at the basket. While shooting, he is also jumping in the air. Now if we regard his jumping as a "circumstance" *vis-à-vis* his act of shooting, we can add this circumstance to the act of shooting and form the act of jump-shooting. Thus, we may say that *S*'s shooting generates his jump-shooting. Of course, we could equally start with *S*'s jumping and regard his co-temporal act of shooting as a "circumstance" *vis-à-vis* his act of jumping. The act of jump-shooting, therefore, is also generated by the act of jumping. Needless to say, since *S*'s jumping and *S*'s shooting are co-temporal acts, neither of them generates the other. But *S*'s jump-shooting is not co-temporal with *S*'s shooting nor co-temporal with *S*'s jumping. (It would be incorrect to say that *S* took a jump-shot "while also" jumping, and incorrect to say that he took a jump-shot "while also" shooting.) Hence, *S*'s jump-shooting can be generated by *each* of the co-temporal acts. I shall call such special cases of augmentation generation "*compound generation*."

The concept of augmentation generation, as I have characterized it, does not mesh completely with the other three forms of generation. And I think that, in general, it is not intuitively as attractive as these other species of generation. The feeling that it is rather different from the other three species is supported by the fact that the preposition "by" is inapplicable in connection with it. In all cases of causal, conventional, or simple generation it is appropriate to say that S did act A' "by" doing A. But we would not ordinarily say that S ran at 8 m.p.h. "by" running or that S extended his arm out the window "by" extending his arm. Nor would we say that S jump-shot (or "took a jump-shot") "by" shooting.

Despite the failure of the prepositional test, I think that augmentation generation is a defensible notion. The main defense lies in its superiority to the other alternatives. How *should* one deal with pairs of acts like S's running and S's running at 8 m.p.h., or S's extending his arm and S's extending his arm out the car window? One possibility, of course, is to say that they are identical. We saw in Chapter One, however, that there are reasons for rejecting this approach. For it appeared that one of the acts of such a pair—e.g., S's saying "hello" loudly—may have a different set of causal factors from its partner—S's saying "hello." S's tense emotional state may be a causal factor of his saying "hello" *loudly*, though not a causal factor of his saying "hello."

Another example of the same sort is the following. Suppose that S runs a mile in 3 minutes 40 seconds, and that this is accomplished with the help of a new breathing technique. Then S's running the mile in 3:40 is partially caused by his use of this breathing technique. But S's running the mile (*simpliciter*) is not caused even in part by the breathing technique, for S would have run the mile with or without that technique. Thus, we cannot say that *S's running the mile in 3:40* is identical with *his running the mile*. Still another objection to the identification of pairs of acts involving augmentation is this. Suppose that S is driving to his mother-in-law's house, and, in a certain 60 m.p.h. zone, drives 70 m.p.h. Consider these three acts: (1) S's driving at 70 m.p.h., (2) S's driving, and (3) S's driving to his mother-in-law's house. If we say that pairs of acts involving augmentation are identical, then (1)=(2), (2)=(3), and by the transitivity of identity, (1)=(3). But act (1) is clearly a violation of the law, whereas act (3) *clearly* is *not* a violation of the law.

Another possible way of dealing with pairs of acts involving augmentation is to say that the more inclusive act generates the less inclusive act (rather than vice versa). On this alternative, S's running at 8 m.p.h. would generate S's running. This alternative, however, is not in conformity with the other species of generation. In all of the other species of generation, a generated act is formed by making use of some *additional* fact not implicit in the generating act. This feature of generation is preserved by saying that S's running generates S's running at 8 m.p.h.; it would run contrary to this feature to say that S's running at 8 m.p.h. generates S's running.

Of course, we do not exhaust all the possible act relationships by considering identity and generation (in either direction). Perhaps the relationship between S's running and S's running at 8 m.p.h., or between S's driving and

S's driving to his mother-in-law's house is some further relationship yet to be considered. Upon reflection, however, it does seem that the generation relation, in the direction I have chosen, fits these cases rather well. Augmentation generation as I have defined it comes very close to simple generation in a variety of cases. The relationship between *S*'s driving and *S*'s driving to his mother-in-law's house depends on *S*'s intention in driving, just as the relationship between *S*'s crouching behind a car and *S*'s hiding from George depends on *S*'s intention in crouching behind a car. Similarly, the relationship between *S*'s extending his arm and *S*'s extending his arm out the car window depends on the "circumstance" that the car window is present, just as many cases of simple generation depend on similar circumstances. Indeed, the only reason why these are cases of augmentation generation rather than simple generation is that the performance of the generating act is entailed by the performance of the generated act. In view of these similarities, it seems appropriate to define augmentation generation as I have done.

This completes my elucidation of the four species of level-generation. It should be noted that these categories, while intended to be exhaustive, are not intended to be mutually exclusive. There need not be one and only one species of generation involved whenever one act generates another. First, since generation is transitive, act *A* and act *A'* may be related by a series of steps of different kinds of generation. John's moving his hand generates John's giving his opponent a heart attack, but this involves causal generation, conventional generation, and even augmentation generation. Secondly, many cases of generation fall on a borderline between two (or more) of the different categories. In general, the significance of my categorization should not be overemphasized. The classification I have presented is intended as a guide to level-generation, and not more than that. Alternative classifications might prove equally useful.

2.   Act Diagrams

Structural relationships can frequently be elucidated with the aid of diagrams, and I think that diagrams can be useful in exhibiting and clarifying the various relationships that hold among the act-tokens of a single agent. Let us start with a simple procedure for diagraming level-generation. Each act-token is to be represented by a circle. To indicate that act *A* generates act *A'*, we draw a circle for act *A* and then another circle *above* the first to represent act *A'*. A vertical line connecting these circles is drawn, and a number representing the species of generation—"1" for causal generation, "2" for conventional generation, etc.—is written adjacent to this vertical line. In some cases we may want to draw the circle representing act *A'* above but *at an angle* to the circle representing act *A*. In these cases we will have a diagonal line connecting the two circles, but it too, like a vertical line, symbolizes level-generation. Since generation is transitive, any two circles connected by a *sequence* of vertical (or diagonal) lines represent a generationally related pair of acts.

Our simple technique for picturing level-generation is illustrated by the two diagrams in Fig. 1. In all such diagrams, of course, the agent is the same for every act. Hence, to avoid repetition, I simply omit the name of the agent from each act description.

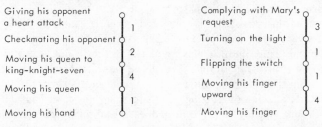

FIGURE 1

Now level-generation is not the only act-relationship worth exploring. In fact, the attempt to diagram act-relationships suggests various kinds of relationships which might not otherwise be apparent. The first such relationship is not especially important, but it does enable us to deal effectively with one of the (smaller) problems that arose in Chapter One. The possibility of diagraming acts suggests the question of whether there are any same-level acts, that is, distinct acts which should nevertheless be drawn on the same level rather than one above the other. A natural candidate for such a position is a pair of relational acts which differ only in having different individual concepts of the same object. It will be recalled that in Chapter One I allowed that *hitting the tallest man in the room* and *hitting the wealthiest man in the room* are distinct properties, even though the tallest man in the room is identical with the wealthiest man in the room. It follows from this that S's hitting the tallest man in the room (at t) and S's hitting the wealthiest man in the room (at t) are distinct act-tokens. But how are these act-tokens related? They certainly are not related by level-generation; for level-generation is an asymmetric relation, whereas any relation holding between these acts would seem to be symmetric. Given our diagrammatic conception of acts, it is natural to regard these two acts as being *on the same level*, and to represent them by circles connected with a horizontal line. Moreover, we can stipulate that if A and A' are same-level act-tokens, then any act which generates A also generates A'; and any act which is generated by A is also generated by A'. Thus, any act which generates S's hitting the tallest man in the room also generates S's hitting the wealthiest man in the room; and any act generated by S's hitting the tallest man in the room is also generated by S's hitting the wealthiest man in the room.

Another relationship suggested by diagraming acts is that of *"branching."* In each of the two preceding diagrams there was a vertical column of acts, each generated by every act below it. This raises the question, however, of whether there might be cases in which act A_1 generates *both* act A_2 and act A_3, but where *neither* act A_2 nor act A_3 generates the other. If there are such cases, they could be diagramed by drawing A_2 and A_3 above but at an angle from A_1. Each would be connected with A_1 by a diagonal line, but A_2 and A_3 would not be connected with each other by a vertical or diagonal line. This would form a pair of "branches" from act A_1.

As soon as this possibility is suggested, suitable examples come to mind immediately. Consider our piano-playing example from Chapter One. John is playing the piano, and his playing causes Smith to fall asleep but causes Brown to wake up. Thus, John's playing the piano causally generates the act of putting Smith to sleep, and it also causally generates the act of awakening Brown. But since John's putting Smith to sleep does not cause Brown to wake up, John's putting Smith to sleep does not causally generate his awakening Brown. And since John's awakening Brown does not cause Smith to fall asleep, John's awakening Brown does not causally generate his putting Smith to sleep. It would be inappropriate to say that John put Smith to sleep *by* awakening Brown, and equally incorrect to say that he awakened Brown *by* putting Smith to sleep.

The way in which this sort of case should be diagramed is shown in Fig. 2. John's putting Smith to sleep and John's awakening Brown are drawn above, but at different angles to, John's playing the piano. The diagonal lines from John's playing the piano indicate that this act generates each of the others. The absence of a vertical or diagonal line connecting John's putting Smith to sleep and John's awakening Brown indicates that these acts are not related by level-generation. As I have drawn the diagram, these two acts are drawn at the same height. But they are not same-level acts, a fact symbolized by the absence of a horizontal line between them. Actually, there is no need to draw these acts at the same height; they could be drawn at different distances above the act of playing the piano. The important thing in drawing branching acts is that they not be connected by a diagonal or vertical line or by a horizontal line. This shows that they are, strictly speaking, *level-indeterminate* with respect to each other. Each is *higher* than, i.e., *generated by*, some common act; but neither is higher than the other nor on the same level as the other.

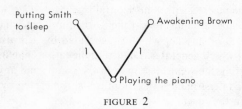

FIGURE 2

Suppose we have three acts, A_1, A_2, and A_3, and that we know that A_2 and A_3 is each generated by A_1. How shall we decide between the following three alternatives? (1) A_2 and A_3 are branching acts (level-indeterminate acts); (2) A_2 generates A_3; or (3) A_3 generates A_2. The important question in deciding whether a given act, say A_2, generates another act, say A_3, is whether the performance of A_3 depends on the performance of A_2. For example, to decide whether John's putting Smith to sleep generates John's awakening Brown, we must decide whether John's awakening Brown depended on his putting Smith to sleep. Given that John was playing the piano, would he have a-wakened Brown even if he had not put Smith to sleep? The answer to this counterfactual question is "Yes." He would have awakened Brown whether or not he put Smith to sleep. Thus, it is false to say that his putting Smith to sleep generated his awakening Brown. Since it is equally false that his awakening Brown generated his putting Smith to sleep, the two acts are clearly branching acts. Similarly, suppose an agent has extended his arm, and thereby performed two further acts: extending his arm out the car window and frightening away a fly. What is the relationship between his extending his arm out the car window and his frightening away the fly? Obviously his frightening away the fly did not generate his extending his arm out the car window, but did his extending his arm out the car window generate his frightening away the fly? This depends on why the fly was frightened. If we assume that the fly was simply frightened by the movement of the arm, and that the arm's going out the car window was not a matter of concern to the fly, then his extending his arm out the car window did not generate his frightening the fly. Contrast this with the relationship between his extending his arm out the car window and his signaling for a turn. Here it is clear that his signaling for a turn was dependent on his extending his arm out the car window. If he had merely extended his arm, but not *out the car window*, then he would not have signaled for a turn. For this reason, we must say that his signaling for a turn was generated by his extending his arm out the car window, and not just by his extending his arm.

It is apparent that the drawing of correct act diagrams generally requires answers to certain counterfactual questions. And answers to these counter-factual questions require information concerning the details of the situation in which the act-tokens occurred. A list of act-types which an agent exemplified at a given time does not (normally) provide enough information to draw a diagram of his act-tokens. Information concerning the entire context of his action is usually necessary.

Figures 3 and 4—which I shall call "act-trees"—make use of all the tech-niques introduced thus far. Needless to say, neither of these diagrams depicts *all* the acts performed by the agent at the time in question, even setting aside his performance of co-temporal acts. No actual act-tree diagram is a *complete* diagram of an agent's behavior. This follows from the fact that, on my analysis of acts, a person performs indefinitely many acts at any time (at least whenever he is performing any acts at all). Any act-tree diagram containing finitely many acts, therefore, could be supplemented by further acts—e.g., acts on the same level as pictured acts or acts causally generated by the highest of the pictured acts.

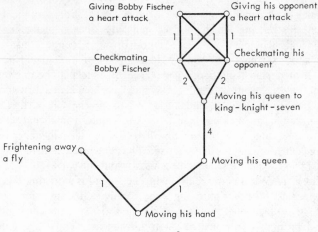

FIGURE 3

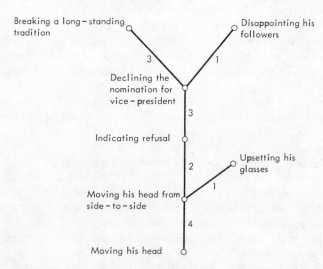

FIGURE 4

Let us next consider the problem of diagraming co-temporal acts, such as *S*'s shooting and *S*'s jumping, and the related problem of diagraming compound generation. One might think that any pair of independent, co-temporal acts should be drawn on completely distinct act diagrams. We have seen, however, that compound acts are generated by *each* of two independent acts. *S*'s act of jump-shooting is generated both by his act of jumping and by his act of shooting. We must, therefore, have some means of placing all of these acts on a single diagram.

The sort of solution I suggest is illustrated in Fig. 5. This diagram depicts the behavior of a flagman on an aircraft carrier, who gives directions to incoming pilots by waving two flags, one in each hand. When he holds the left flag extended outward while at the same time moving the right flag in a rotating fashion, this compound act counts as a signal to land. On the particular occasion imagined, his signaling the plane to land results in an accident.

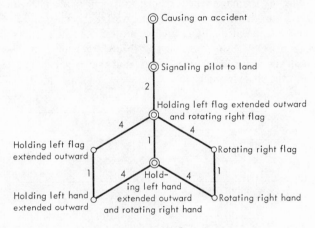

FIGURE 5

The diagram shows two independent, basic act-tokens which together generate (either singly or jointly) the rest of the acts in the diagram. These two basic act-tokens are (A_1) *S*'s holding his left hand extended outward and (A_2) *S*'s rotating his right hand. Despite the fact that they are opposite each other in the diagram, the absence of a horizontal line between them indicates that they are not same-level acts. They are also unlike branching acts, inasmuch as there is no *common* act which generates them. Thus, they are completely level-indeterminate. These two basic acts, however, generate by compound generation *S*'s act of *holding his left hand outward and (while) rotating his right hand*. The latter act, being a compound act, is represented by a pair of concentric circles. The two concentric circles symbolize the fact that this act has its source in two co-temporal basic acts.

A final problem for diagraming acts is that of diagraming the relationships between acts and their temporal parts. Consider, for example, *S*'s act of driving a nail into the wall. Suppose this was accomplished by striking the nail four times with a hammer. The behavior in question is pictured in Fig. 6. In contrast with our previous diagrams, the horizontal axis in this diagram represents the temporal dimension. There are four relevant basic acts performed during the period in question, at times t_1, t_2, t_3, and t_4 respectively. (Actually, each of these acts occurs over an interval of time, but for simplicity I shall speak as if each occurs at a moment of time.) Each of these basic acts is an act of S's swinging his hand, each of which generates an act of S's swinging the hammer, which in turn generates an act of driving the nail a little way into the wall. Thus, S's swinging his hand at t_1 generates S's swinging the hammer at t_1 which generates S's driving the nail a little way into the wall at t_1. The sequence of these four basic acts constitutes a larger act, viz., S's swinging his hand four times (between t_1 and t_4). This larger act generates S's act of swinging the hammer four times (between t_1 and t_4), which in turn generates S's act of driving the nail into the wall (between t_1 and t_4). None of the larger acts is generationally related to any of the smaller acts, but there are generational relationships among the three larger acts. In the diagram, the larger acts are depicted by oval figures; and these ovals are connected by vertical lines at their extreme right.

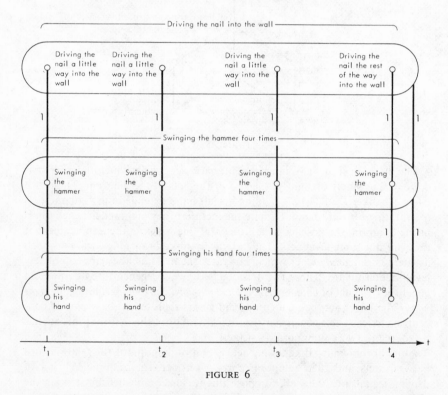

FIGURE 6

The diagram may be taken to suggest that the shortest unit of action in the imagined case is an act of swinging one's hand. But this is not an intended implication of the diagram. There is no minimal (or maximal) temporal length for a unit of action. Although the shortest unit depicted in the diagram has the length of an entire swing, this is quite arbitrary. Acts of this length could be subdivided into their temporal parts—e.g., S's moving his hand one inch—which would also be act-tokens.

Having developed techniques for individuating and interrelating acts of various kinds, we might pause to notice that our scheme provides a fairly natural way of interpreting the sort of thing which Anscombe and Davidson would regard as a "single" action. Setting aside the complications introduced by co-temporal acts or temporal sequences of acts, let us consider a single act-tree at the bottom of which is some basic act. Two acts are on the same act-tree if and only if they satisfy one of the following conditions: (A) they are identical; (B) they are same-level acts; (C) one of them generates the other; (D) both are generated by some common act. All the acts in our chess case, for example, are on the same act-tree. Now Anscombe's or Davidson's notion of a single action, I think, corresponds to our notion of a single act-tree. Their single *action* corresponds to the set of all acts on a single *act-tree*, or perhaps to whatever "underlies" the acts on a single act-tree. Of course Anscombe and Davidson have not spelled out their notion of a single action in great detail, so it is difficult to be sure just what they would say. Their notion of a single action is an intuitively attractive one, however, and it is important to see that some such notion can be captured and expressed within our framework.

While our framework enables us to capture the intuitive force of the Anscombe-Davidson notion of an action, our scheme also enables us to refine that intuitive idea. These refinements make it possible to avoid the difficulties posed in Chapter One against the Anscombe-Davidson account. On their account, for example, one would be forced to say that John's killing Smith is a cause of the firing of the gun. This follows from the fact that John's killing Smith is supposedly identical with John's pulling the trigger, and John's pulling the trigger is a cause of the firing of the gun. Our theory spares us this counter-intuitive result. We are free to say, what is surely the intuitive thing to say, that John's pulling the trigger, but *not* John's killing Smith, is a cause of the gun's firing. We are free to say that John's pulling the trigger causally generates John's firing the gun, whereas John's killing George does not causally generate John's firing the gun.

The other puzzles confronting the Anscombe-Davidson approach can also be easily handled within our scheme. Their approach would force one to say, for example, that John's playing the piano = John's putting Smith to sleep = John's waking up Brown. And this has the undesirable consequence that John's putting Smith to sleep causes Brown's waking up. On our approach these three acts can be distinguished, and we can say that John's playing the piano, but not John's putting Smith to sleep, causes Brown's waking up. We can say that John's playing the piano, but not John's putting Smith to sleep, causally generates John's waking up Brown. Again, on the Anscombe-Davidson approach, one is forced to say that John's putting Smith to sleep and John's waking up Brown have all the same causal conditions, or "enabling" conditions. On our approach we are allowed to say that Smith's being tired is a causal condition, or an "enabling" condition, of John's putting Smith to sleep, but *not* a causal condition of John's waking up Brown. Finally, the theory I have presented makes it possible for us to appreciate the *asymmetry* implicit in our willingness to say that John turned on the light *by* flipping the switch but our unwillingness to say that John flipped the switch *by* turning on the light. This asymmetry is precisely what is expressed by saying that John's flipping the switch *level-generated* John's turning on the light while *denying* that John's turning on the light *level-generated* John's flipping the switch. We see, then, that the theory presented here enables us to deal comfortably with the cases that prove difficult for the identity thesis, yet at the same time providing the tools for capturing the intuitive idea that lies at the heart of the identity thesis.

3.   The Definition of Level-Generation

The notion of level-generation is obviously the central notion in the scheme of action I have been constructing. Although various restrictions have been placed on it, and although a variety of illustrations of it have been given, a formal definition remains to be presented. Now the idea of level-generation, I think, is an intuitive or pre-analytic idea, implicit within our commonsense framework. To be sure, I have tried to streamline our commonsense notion by making certain technical stipulations; and I have introduced a technical vocabulary for dealing with the concept. Nevertheless, the idea of level-generation is implicit in our use of the phrase, "S did . . . *by* doing - - - ," and in our use of the phrase, "S did . . . *in* doing - - - ." That it is an intuitive notion is reflected in the fact that once a few examples of it are given, any ordinary speaker can readily identify numerous other cases that fall under the same concept. Moreover, ordinary people will normally agree, with respect to any pair of acts A and A', whether or not A' was performed "by" performing A. Since there is a prior notion to be analyzed, we do not want to provide merely a *stipulative* definition. We want to provide a definition that captures our antecedent notion (while also capturing the amplifications of the notion—e.g., augmentation generation—which I have introduced). But providing analyses of interesting concepts is always a difficult enterprise. What must be remembered, therefore, is that the tenability of the intuitive concept should not depend on the success of any particular analysis.

Before proposing an analysis of level-generation, let me examine some possible definitions that are clearly inadequate.

At first glance, it seems possible to define the notion of level-generation in terms of means and ends, or some other teleological notion. There are many cases in which a lower act is done *in order to* do a higher act, or as a *means* to performing a higher act. John moves his queen to king-knight-seven in order to checkmate his opponent. *S* flips the switch in order to turn on the light. Unfortunately, teleological notions will not provide us with an adequate definition of generation. For while many instances of level-generation are accompanied by an appropriate purpose, intent, or goal of the agent, many are not. Act *A* often generates act *A'* though the agent does not do *A in order to* do *A'*. John's checkmating his opponent causally generates his giving his opponent a heart attack, but John does not checkmate his opponent *in order to* give his opponent a heart attack. John's moving his hand causally generates his frightening away a fly, but John does not move his hand with the *intent* of frightening away a fly.

Another apparently promising line of approach makes use of the concept of *reduction*. It appears that generated acts are in some sense more *complex* than the acts which generate them; perhaps they are even in some sense "constructed" out of the acts which generate them. Hence, it might appear that generation implies that a generated act can be *reduced to* its generating acts, and ultimately to some basic act or acts.

In what sense of the term "reduction" might it be said the generated acts are reducible to generating ones? One familiar sense of "reduction" is micro-reduction: the analysis of entities or classes of entities into their constituent parts. But this sense of "reduction" clearly does not apply to the relation between generated and generating acts. For in general the relation between a generated act and a generating act is not that of whole to part. Admittedly, in the special case of augmentation generation, and in particular compound generation, there is a whole-part relation. *S*'s shooting (at *t*) is certainly *part of S*'s jump-shooting (at *t*). But the part-whole relation does not obtain in the other species of generation. *S*'s flipping the switch is not *part of S*'s turning on the light; and *S*'s extending his arm out the window is not *part of S*'s signaling for a turn. It would be a mistake to think that *S*'s signaling for a turn is made up of parts including (a) his extending his arm out the car window, (b) the circumstance that he was driving at that time, and (c) the rule that extending one's arm out the car window while driving counts as signaling for a turn. It makes no sense to say that the *rule*, for example, is *part of* the act of signaling. Acts are not *composed* of rules, though the performance of them may *presuppose* rules. Similarly, many acts *presuppose* certain circumstances without being composed of those circumstances. *S*'s outjumping George *presupposes* the fact that George jumped only six feet, but *S*'s act of outjumping George is not *composed*, in part, of *George's* jumping six feet. George's act is not *part of S*'s act.

A second use of the term "reduction" might be more pertinent to the notion of level-generation. Philosophers in the past have claimed that material objects are "reducible" to sense data, or that unobservable entities are "reducible" to macroscopic, observable entities. And what they have meant (at least some of them) is not that material objects are "composed" of sense data, or that microscopic, unobservable particles are "composed" of macroscopic entities, but rather that *statements* about material objects are *translatable* into *statements* about sense data, and that statements about unobservable particles are *translatable* into statements about macroscopic, observable entities. Similarly, in suggesting that generated acts are "reducible" to generating acts, one might be suggesting that *statements* describing generated acts are *translatable* into *statements* describing generating acts. More specifically, it might be suggested that for each statement ascribing a generated act, A', to agent S, there is a set of *logically equivalent* statements describing some act or acts of S which generated A'.

It is immediately apparent, however, that this version of the reducibility thesis is not correct. The putative logical equivalence does not obtain; indeed the entailment fails in both directions. Consider a statement describing a generated act, such as "John checkmated his opponent," and one describing a corresponding generating act, such as "John moved his queen to king-knight-seven." Clearly, the former statement does not logically entail the latter statement, since it is logically possible that John could have checkmated his opponent by making a different move with a different piece. Moreover, the latter statement does not logically entail the former. Given only the fact that John moved his queen to king-knight-seven, it does not follow (logically) that John checkmated his opponent. Only when that fact is conjoined with further facts, including the positions of the pieces on the board and the rules of chess, does it logically follow that John checkmated his opponent. In general, statements describing lower-level acts alone do not entail statements describing higher-level acts; some statements describing relevant *conditions*, such as causal effects, circumstances, rules, etc., must be added to get the entailment.[4]

This form of irreducibility has been recognized by some philosophers, such as D. W. Hamlyn,[5] R. S. Peters,[6] and P. F. Strawson.[7] But they have, I think, put a mistaken interpretation on it and drawn unwarranted inferences. Because such "full-fledged" actions as signing a contract or mailing a letter cannot be reduced to bodily movements, they have concluded that there is a *"logical gulf"* between action and movement. From this they have concluded that there can be no causal explanations of actions, only of movements.[8]

---

[4] Compound generation provides an exception to this generalization. A conjunction of statements describing each of two co-temporal acts does entail a statement describing the compound act which is generated by each of them. The peculiarity of this case is due to the fact that each of these co-temporal acts serves as a "condition" in virtue of which the second co-temporal act generates the compound act.

[5] "Behavior," *Philosophy*, XXVIII (1953), 132–45.

[6] *The Concept of Motivation* (London: Routledge and Kegan Paul, 1958), pp. 12–15.

[7] In D. F. Pears, ed., *Freedom and the Will* (New York: St. Martins Press, 1963), p. 66.

[8] Some of their grounds for speaking of a logical gulf are different from the irreducibility under discussion. They include the fact that action characteristically involves intelligence,

The first mistake is to assume that the irreducibility obtains only between *conventional* acts and *bodily movements*. On the contrary, it holds equally between causal acts, such as John's killing George, and other acts which are not bodily movements, such as John's shooting the gun. Secondly, it is a mistake to imply—as the term "logical gulf" implies—that there is no systematic connection between conventional acts, such as signing a contract, and bodily movement acts, such as moving one's hand in a certain way. The phrase "logical gulf" suggests that there is some mysterious, unbridgeable chasm between these different classes of entities. But this certainly does not follow from the irreducibility thesis. Although statements describing higher-level acts may not be logically equivalent to statements describing lower-level acts, there is nevertheless an intimate connection between higher-level acts and lower-level acts. That their relationship cannot be analyzed in terms of logical equivalence hardly implies that they are separated by an unbridgeable gulf. Finally, it is not clear why the falsity of the reducibility thesis should suggest that higher-level acts, in particular conventional acts, should not be susceptible of causal explanations. I defer a discussion of this point, however, to Chapter Three.

We have seen, then, that the notion of level-generation cannot be analyzed in terms of purpose or teleology, nor in terms of the concept of reduction. It is time now to provide, or at least to attempt to provide, a more adequate analysis of generation. Let us begin with a fact that has been noted already: if act A generates act A', then there is a set of conditions C^* which, when conjoined with the performance of act A, ensures that the agent performs act A'. The nature of these conditions varies with the species of generation. In causal generation C^* consists in certain causal effects; in conventional generation C^* consists in the existence of certain rules plus the presence of certain circumstances; in simple generation it consists in the existence of circumstances; etc. Letting "A" and "A'" represent *statements* describing acts (as well as the acts themselves), and letting "C^*" stand for *statements* describing conditions (as well as the conditions themselves), we can say that whenever act A generates act A' there exists a set of conditions C^* such that the conjunction of A and C^* entails A'. To this we may add the further requirement that, although the conjunction of A and C^* entails A', neither A nor C^* alone entails A'. (This requirement immediately implies that S's running at 8 m.p.h. does not generate S's running.)

A further feature of level-generation was noted in our discussion of branching acts. It was pointed out there that when act A generates act A', the following counterfactual assertion is true: *if* S *had not done* A, *then he would not have done* A'. For example, if S's extending his arm out the car window generates his signaling for a turn, then we may say that if he had not extended his arm

---

goals, and reasons, whereas movement, in the sense of "*mere* movement," is devoid of these elements. In the present discussion I am ignoring this issue.

out the car window then he would not have signaled for a turn. Such a counterfactual must be understood subject to the condition that everything else is held "constant"—an assumption which is implicit in almost all counterfactual judgments. Obviously, if S had not extended his arm out the car window, but if he had instead turned on his blinker, then he would nevertheless have signaled for a turn. Thus, in saying "If S had not done A, then he would not have done A'," I do not allow us to suppose that, instead of performing A, S performed some functional equivalent of A.

Unfortunately, the facts that we have produced thus far are not sufficient for act A generating act A'. In particular, what we have said thus far is compatible with A' *generating* A! For example, let A be S's extending his arm out the car window and let A' be S's signaling for a turn. Next suppose that C^* is the (existence of a) rule according to which the *one and only* way to signal for a turn is to extend one's arm out the car window. We can then say that the conjunction of A' and C^* entails A. Moreover, neither A' nor C^* alone entails A. Finally, the counterfactual assertion "If S had not signaled for a turn, then he would not have extended his arm out the car window" is true. Hence, on the criteria suggested thus far, we would be allowed to say that S's signaling for a turn generates S's extending his arm out the car window!

In order to ensure the proper *direction* of level-generation, we need some further condition. And I think that this further condition can be provided by another counterfactual.[9] Whenever act A generates A' the following counterfactual is true: *if the conditions C^* had not obtained, then even though* S *did* A, *he would not have done* A'. For example, let C^* be the existence of the rule that extending one's arm out the car window while driving counts as signaling, plus the circumstance that S was driving when he extended his arm out the car window. Then we can say that if C^* had *not* obtained, then even though S extended his arm out the car window, he would not have signaled for a turn. In making this counterfactual assertion, we again assume everything else held constant. Obviously, if the indicated rule had not obtained, but if a slightly different though substantially similar rule had obtained, then S still would have signaled for a turn. Thus, in imagining that C^* not obtain, we must be sure not to imagine some replacement for C^*.[10]

Our present counterfactual succeeds in identifying the true direction of level-generation. For when one tries to apply this counterfactual in the wrong direction, one gets a false statement, or at any rate one which is not clearly true. Suppose, for example, that we choose our C^* in such a way that when it is conjoined with a statement asserting that S signaled for a turn, it implies that S extended his arm out the car window. Our C^* would here be: there is a

---

[9] On this point I have profited from discussion with John G. Bennett and Jaegwon Kim.

[10] In choosing our C^* we must also be careful to select the *minimal* set of conditions necessary for A generating A'. If we include some additional, inessential elements in C^*, then the negation of C^* does not ensure that act A' would not have been performed.

rule saying that one signals for a turn if and only if one extends one's arm out the car window. Can we now say that if this C^* had not obtained, then even though S signaled for a turn, he would not have extended his arm out the car window? This counterfactual seems to be false. The question of whether or not S extended his arm out the car window (or *would* have extended his arm out the car window) is independent of the existence of such a rule. Even if this rule had not obtained, S's performance of the act of extending his arm out the car window would have been unaffected. Performing an act of signaling for a turn *does* depend on the existence of such a rule; but performing an act of extending one's arm out the car window does *not* depend on the existence of such a rule. Even if it were false that the *only* way to signal for a turn was to extend one's arm, and even if it were true that S signaled for a turn, it might still have been true that S extended his arm.

To complete our analysis of level-generation, the temporal restrictions discussed in the first section must be included. We must also ensure that same-level pairs of acts are excluded. Adding these conditions to the analysis, we wind up with the following.

> *Act-token* A *level-generates act-token* A' *if and only if*
> (1) A *and* A' *are distinct act-tokens of the same agent that are not on the same level;*
> (2) *neither* A *nor* A' *is subsequent to the other; neither* A *nor* A' *is a temporal part of the other; and* A *and* A' *are not co-temporal;*
> (3) *there is a set of conditions* C* *such that*
>   (a) *the conjunction of* A *and* C* *entails* A', *but neither* A *nor* C* *alone entails* A';
>   (b) *if the agent had not done* A, *then he would not have done* A';
>   (c) *if* C* *had not obtained, then even though* S *did* A, *he would not have done* A'.

There is, unfortunately, a remaining difficulty confronting the analysis, which concerns both (3b) and (3c). This difficulty is posed by the possibility of generational "overdetermination," in which act A' is generated by *each* of two independent acts either of which would have sufficed by itself to generate A'. Suppose, for example, that there are two light switches, X and Y, either of which is capable of causing the same light to go on. If S flips both switches at the same time, one with each hand, he performs two switch-flipping acts, each of which generates the act of turning on the light. Now consider one of the two switch-flipping acts, S's flipping switch X. Conditions (3b) and (3c) do not hold with respect to S's flipping switch X and S's turning on the light. It is false to say that if S had not flipped switch X, then he would not have turned on the light, because even if he had not flipped switch X, his flipping switch Y would have sufficed to cause the light to go on. Similarly, it is false to say that if the relevant C^* had not obtained—i.e., if it were not true that S's flipping switch X would result in the light's going on—then even though S flipped switch X, he would not have turned on the light. In our present case the absence of C^* would not imply that S would not have turned on the light.

This "overdetermination" difficulty is a genuine one, I think, and one which I do not know how to circumvent. Some degree of comfort may be taken, however, in two facts. First, generational overdetermination is extremely rare, so that the range of cases covered by the difficulty is extremely small. Secondly, it is somewhat comforting to recognize that the same problem of overdetermination creates an obstacle to the construction of an adequate analysis of causation. Attempted analyses of causation commonly include a condition requiring that a cause, C, be a necessary condition (in the circumstances) for the occurrence of the effect, E. But such a requirement fails in cases of overdetermination. Similarly, conditions (3b) and (3c) of our analysis assert that act A and conditions C^* are, respectively, necessary (in the circumstances) for the performance of act A'. And they too fail in cases of generational overdetermination. Of course the recognition of an analogous difficulty for the analysis of causation does not help us solve our problem; but it does suggest that the concept of level-generation may be no worse off than another concept which is central to our overall conceptual scheme.

4.   The Definition of an Act-Token

Throughout this chapter I have freely made use of the notion of an act-token. No definition of this notion, however, has been presented as of yet. We saw in Chapter One that an act-token is a species of property-exemplification. It is an exemplifying of a property by a person during an interval of time. We also saw, however, that not all property-exemplifications are *act*-tokens. To delineate this special class of property-instances I promised to provide an inductive, or recursive, specification, making use of the notion of a basic act-token plus certain operations to be performed on basic act-tokens. Now the definition of a basic act-token will not be presented until Chapter Three. If I may be allowed to take this notion for granted, however, I can provide the promised recursive definition.

Actually, matters are a bit more complicated. In my recursive definition of an act-token I want to employ the notion of level-generation and of same-levelness. But these notions have been defined while presupposing the concept of an act-token. Thus, if we were to use them in the definition of an act-token, the definitions would be circular. To avoid this circularity, let us rewrite our definition of level-generation (and of same-levelness) in a manner which does not assume that the domain of relata are *act*-tokens. We shall assume only that the relata are property-instances of any kind. The notion of level-generation, then, will be broadened beyond its original, and primary, application.

The new definition of level-generation is as follows.

> *Property-instance* A *level-generates property-instance* A′ *if and only if*
> (1) A *and* A′ *are distinct property-instances of the same subject;*
> (2) *the properties of which* A *and* A′ *are instances do not differ merely in containing different individual concepts of the same object;*
> (3) *neither property-instance* A *nor property-instance* A′ *is subsequent to the other; neither is a temporal part of the other; and they are not co-temporal;*
> (4) *there is a set of conditions* C* *such that*
>> (a) *the conjunction of* A *and* C* *entails* A′, *but neither* A *nor* C* *alone entails* A′;
>> (b) *if the subject,* S, *had not exemplified property* A (*at* t), *then* S *would not have exemplified property* A′ (*at* t);
>> (c) *if* C* *had not obtained, then even though* S *exemplified property* A (*at* t), S *would not have exemplified property* A′ (*at* t).

The definition of same-levelness is easily added.

> *Property-instance* A *is on the same level as property-instance* A′ *if and only if*
> (1) A *and* A′ *are distinct property-instances of the same subject, occurring at the same time; and*
> (2) A *and* A′ *are instances of properties which differ only in containing different individual concepts of the same object.*

Making use of the newly defined notions of level-generation and same-levelness, a recursive definition of an act-token can be proposed. I must remind the reader, however, that the originating clause of the definition contains the notion of a *basic* act-token, the definition of which awaits Chapter Three.

> (1) *If* A *is a basic act-token, then* A *is an act-token.*
> (2) *If* A *is on the same level as an act-token, then* A *is an act-token.*
> (3) *If* A *is level-generated by an act-token, then* A *is an act-token.*
> (4) *If* A *is a temporal part of an act-token, then* A *is an act-token.*
> (5) *If* A *is a temporal sequence of act-tokens, then* A *is an act-token.*
> (6) *Nothing else is an act-token.*

Clauses (2) and (3) are fairly straightforward. They ensure that anything on the same "tree" as a basic act-token is also an act-token. It should be emphasized that not all of these act-tokens need be *intentional* acts; nor need they be acts for which the agent would be held *responsible*. Many of the causally generated acts, for example, will be ones which the agent did not intend to do, and perhaps could not reasonably be expected to foresee that he would do. Nevertheless, they will be regarded as *acts* of his. On this definition of acts, ascriptions of action do not imply ascriptions of responsibility.

Clause (4) is intended to cover cases in which the main intention or goal of an agent is to perform some longish act, which he can accomplish without attention to the segments which make it up. For example, he might play a scale on the piano without carefully attending to each of the notes which he plays. In this case it will be clear that his playing the scale is an act-token; but we also want to say that his playing each note is an act-token. Clause (4) is especially important in cases where a longer act can be done at will, but some of its segments cannot be done at will. A football player may be able to kick his foot in a certain precise manner, but he may be unable to replicate just the middle portion of that kick. That is, if he wants to perform just that middle portion, he will not be able to do so. Since my definition of a basic act-token will involve the ability to do the act at will, this middle segment of the kick will not be a basic act-token. Nevertheless, I think that it should be regarded as an act-token.

Clause (5) is required to cover cases in which an act is *too* long to be either a (single) basic act-token or on the same tree as a (single) basic act-token. S's writing his book, for example, is much too long an act to be generated by any single basic act-token. It should be noted that a "sequence" of act-tokens can be temporally discontinuous, as is clearly illustrated by the book-writing case.

Examination of our recursive definition of an act reveals that at the bottom of any (complete) act-tree will be one or more basic act-tokens. Not all basic act-tokens need be at the *very* bottom of an act-tree, however, since some basic act-tokens will be generated by other basic act-tokens by augmentation generation. S's raising his hand slowly, for example, will be a basic act-token though it is generated by S's raising his hand, another basic act-token.

It should be fairly clear what sorts of things turn out to be act-tokens according to this definition. But let me enumerate a few of the things which, with the help of this definition, will be *excluded* from the class of acts. In many of these cases their exclusion from the class of acts can only be fully confirmed once the definition of a basic act-token is available. Nevertheless, some of these points are worth making now.

First, a person's being in a certain *state*—e.g., his being tall, his having brown eyes, his being a bachelor—will not be an act-token. States will not be generated by or be on the same level as basic act-tokens; nor will they be temporally proper parts of act-tokens, nor sequences of act-tokens. They can, of course, be the *causes* or the *effects* of acts, but that is not sufficient for admitting them into the class of act-tokens.

Secondly, things that *happen* to a person, that he *suffers* or undergoes, will not be acts. This includes S's being hit on the head, S's being pushed downstairs, S's falling asleep, S's getting bald, S's sneezing, S's hiccuping, or S's vomiting. To see that sneezing, hiccuping, or vomiting are not basic acts, we must await the discussion in Chapter Three. But we can see now that these occurrences would not be related in any of the specified ways to basic acts that are already familiar. Admittedly, an agent might perform an act that causes one of these things to happen to him. He might take a sleeping pill which causes him to fall asleep, or he might take an emetic which causes him to vomit. But, as I indicated earlier, this sort of occurrence would not be generated by the corresponding act. The agent's falling asleep would be *caused*, but not *causally generated*, by his taking the sleeping pill, and his vomiting would be *caused*, but not *causally generated*, by his taking the emetic.

Other things that a person undergoes include his heart's beating, his blood flowing, and his arm muscles' contracting. These are not acts, first, because it is not the *agent* that is the subject of the properties, but a *part* of the agent's body: his heart, his muscles, etc. Secondly, if these events are connected in any way with the agent's acts, they are connected either as causes of the acts or (at best) as causal generators of the acts. But neither of these connections justifies their inclusion into the class of acts. In particular, if x generates a basic act, it does not follow that x is an act. Of course we must still make sure that these occurrences are not themselves basic acts, and that will be ensured by the definition of basic acts in Chapter Three.

Thirdly, it should be noted that my definition of acts makes no provision for disjunctive acts, conditional acts, biconditional acts, or other "truth-functional" acts, with the exception of conjunctive (compound) acts and negative acts, which will be discussed shortly. As techniques for forming statements from other statements, the wedge, the horseshoe, the triple bar, etc., are fully appropriate; but they are not appropriate for forming new *acts* from other acts. We can, or course, say that S performed either act A_1 or act A_2, or that S will perform act A_1 only if he performs act A_2. But we need not say—nor do I think it is natural to say—that there was an act-token consisting in S's doing A_1 or A_2 (*at t*) or an act-token consisting in S's doing A_1 only if A_2 (*at t*). Thus, according to my theory of acts no act-tree will have as one of its nodes a disjunctive act, a conditional act, a biconditional act, etc. In a similar way, no act-tree will have acts of the form, "S's doing A_2 by doing A_1." We may speak of S's doing A_2 by doing A_1, but this is to be understood as talk about *two* of S's acts related by generation, not as talk about *one* of S's acts.

Some comments are now in order concerning *negative* acts. It is quite clear that we must commit ourselves to at least some negative act-tokens; things like S's *not* turning his head (at t) or S's *not* raising his hand (at t) have as much claim to be considered basic act-tokens as their positive counterparts, S's turning his head (at t) and S's raising his hand (at t). Moreover, negative basic acts will often level-generate other negative acts, so that we should be prepared to recognize nonbasic negative acts. In addition, negative acts are important because many positive acts are generated by negative acts. *S*'s not moving his body may generate *S*'s sunbathing, and *S*'s not leaving the building may generate *S*'s registering a protest or *S*'s "sitting in." One of the difficulties with negative act-tokens, however, is that their level-relationships with other act-tokens is often very unclear. Perhaps this is largely due to the fact that the *causal* status of negative events in general is relatively unclear.

Another difficulty concerning negative acts is the status of *omissions*. In cases where an agent purposely and consciously refrains from making a certain movement we have clear instances of negative acts. When an agent simply *fails* to do something, however, without conscious intent or prior awareness, it is not so clear whether or not this should be classed as an act. The easy way out would be simply to exclude all such cases from the class of act-tokens. But there are cases in which we would hold an agent responsible for such omissions, and this might incline us to call them acts. I find this a difficult problem indeed, and I do not have any solution to propose. Since I shall not be much concerned with negative acts in the rest of the book, I shall simply leave the matter open.

I have now completed my analysis of the structure of action by exhibiting the variety of ways in which act-tokens can be related. I think that this scheme provides a coherent and systematic account of action. Its ultimate test, however, lies in its usefulness for the study of problems connected with action. In the next chapter I turn to one such problem: the nature of intentional action. I shall try to show that the scheme presented in this chapter, combined with the notions of desire and belief, can help to provide an analysis of intentional acts.

CHAPTER THREE

Intentional
Action

1. Wants

A central feature of human nature is that people do things *intentionally*, or *on purpose*. The nature of intentionality, or purposefulness, has long been the topic of philosophical discussion, and in this chapter I shall attempt to analyze this concept. One of the main notions to be used in my analysis of intentional action is that of *wanting*. A detailed discussion of this notion will be presented in Chapter Four, but some preliminary remarks are necessary here.

Like many words in ordinary language, "want" has various broader and narrower uses or senses. In one of its narrower uses, "wanting" is restricted to mental states that border on strong emotions, possibly accompanied by tension or other body tones. In another of its narrower uses, "want" contrasts with other attitude terms such as "favor," "like," "be attracted by," etc. But I shall use the term "want" in a very broad way. In this use, wants need not be intense or emotion-laden; they need not absorb one's whole consciousness. Secondly, in my use of the term, wanting x is roughly equivalent with "feeling favorably toward x," "being inclined toward x," "being pro x," "finding x an attractive possibility," "finding x to be a 'fitting' or 'appropriate' possibility," etc. My use of the term "want" ignores the subtle difference to which these other phrases can be put. Thirdly, as I understand wanting, one can have wants *vis-à-vis* almost any subject matter. You can want a piece of cake, want to take a walk, want your wife to meet you on time, want to do your duty, and want the war in Vietnam to end. And finally, my sense of "want" allows for the existence of fleeting wants—wants that rise to mind suddenly and fade away just as quickly.

My analysis of intentional action will make use of a certain species of wanting—viz., wanting to do certain acts. Such wants are not essentially different from other wants, like wanting to possess certain objects. Wanting an automobile consists (roughly) in feeling favorably toward the prospect of owning an automobile. Wanting to take a walk consists (roughly) in feeling favorably toward the prospect of one's taking a walk.

All action-wants (as I shall call the latter wants) have implicit time-references, although I shall neglect these references except when necessary. If I want to take a walk, then I either want to take a walk now or an hour from now or some time this afternoon. Clearly, wanting to take a walk now has a different effect on one's action than wanting to take a walk an hour from now. The time-references in wanting are often very indefinite. I want to play tennis some time next week, but no particular day or time of day.

The time of a projected act must be distinguished, of course, from the time when the agent has the want. That is, we must distinguish wanting-to-do-x and wanting-to-do-x_t, where the subscript is attached either to the time of wanting or the time of the desired act. People can have a given want at one time and then cease to have it later. The timing of wants is a complicated matter, and I shall attend to it more fully in Chapter Four.

Wants have various strengths or intensities. S may want to do act A more than he wants to do A'. And his present want to do A may be stronger than it was yesterday. I do not pretend to have a precise procedure for measuring want-intensities. Nevertheless, I assume that comparisons can be made, as they are often made in day-to-day affairs, either by the agent himself or by third persons.

2. A Necessary Condition of Intentional Action

Suppose there is an act-token A of agent S. What are the necessary and sufficient conditions for this act-token to be intentional?

Intentional acts are often acts that the agent *wanted* to do, indeed wanted to do for their own sake. But wanting to do A, in the sense of wanting to do A "for its own sake," is not a necessary condition of doing A intentionally. An act is often done intentionally even though the agent did not think the prospect of performing that act attractive; he may have been indifferent to that act, or even averse to it, at least considered for its own sake. For example, I feel indifferent toward the prospect of waving my hands above my head; nevertheless, in order to attract someone's attention in a crowd I proceed to wave my hands above my head. I am averse to the idea of robbing a bank. Nevertheless, I perform that act (intentionally) because kidnappers of my child compel me to rob the bank and give them the money.

When an intentional act A is not itself desired, there must be some other related act that the agent wanted to do. I wave my hands above my head not for the sake of doing that act, but in order to attract a certain person's attention. I rob the bank not for the sake of robbing the bank but in order to perform thereby a further act—viz., prevent my child from being harmed. In these cases I do not want to do act *A* itself, but I do want to do some act to be *generated* by *A*. (Throughout this chapter I shall use the word "want" in the sense of wanting something "for its own sake." In Chapter Four I shall use the term "want" more broadly, to apply both to intrinsic and to extrinsic wants.)

Now in the bank robbing case it might be argued that the agent acts not because of a (positive) desire, but because of an *aversion*, an aversion to having his child harmed. I admit that there is an important distinction here, a distinction between acting in order to achieve a positively valued end and acting in order to avoid or prevent an aversive occurrence. But for present purposes, we need not make much of this distinction. Whenever an agent acts in order to avoid or prevent an aversive occurrence *x*, there is a sense (or use) of the term "want" in which we can say that he *wants* to *avoid x* or *prevent x*. Thus, it is perfectly correct to say in the bank robbing case that the agent "wants" to prevent his child from being harmed. In this chapter I shall subsume cases of aversion under the broader category of desire in this way, for this will simplify the exposition considerably.

When an agent does *A* intentionally because he wants to do *A'* thereby, he often does not succeed in doing *A'*. But the intentionality of *A* does not depend on there actually *being* an act-token *A'* that the agent wanted. It is only necessary that the agent have believed (to some degree) that his doing *A* would generate *A'*. My waving my hands over my head is intentional because it is done in order to attract John's attention, even if I do not succeed in attracting John's attention. It is not necessary that I actually attract John's attention; it is only necessary that I have believed (to some degree) that my waving my hands over my head would generate my attracting John's attention.

When agent *S* does *A* intentionally, there are three kinds of acts he may have desired. (a) He may have wanted to do a higher act, *A'*. (b) He may have wanted to do a same-level act, *A'*. (c) He may have wanted to do *A* itself. Now if we change our terminology slightly, by regarding every act as being on the *same level* as *itself*, cases (b) and (c) can be compressed. This enables us to give the following necessary condition of intentionality.

> (1) *Act-token* A *is intentional only if there is an act*(*-type*) A' *such that the agent* S *wanted to do* (*exemplify*) A', *and* S *either believed* (*to some degree*) *that his doing* A *would generate his doing* A' *or believed* (*to some degree*) *that his doing* A *would be on the same level as his doing* A'.

Condition (1) says that *S* must believe *to some degree* that his doing *A* would generate, or be on the same level as, his doing *A'*. Why have I made this requirement so weak? In many cases the agent does not firmly believe that act *A* will generate a desired act *A'*. He merely thinks that there is a fair chance, or perhaps only a slim chance, of *A* generating *A'*. However, since he thinks that doing *A* is the only way, or the best way, of doing *A'*, he does *A* with the hope that it will generate *A'*. The degree of belief needed to get *S* to do *A* depends on how much *S* wants to do *A'* and on his other beliefs about how he might do *A'*.

Condition (1) may seem to be violated in several kinds of cases, and the more important of these cases will now be examined. First, there are cases in which the agent's goal in doing *A* seems to be the *possession of an object*, not the performance of an act. I give the automobile dealer a check because I want to own a certain car; but owning the car is not an act. The answer here is simple: the desired act is *gaining* ownership of the car. I give the dealer a check because I believe that this will generate the act of my gaining ownership of the car, an act I want to perform.

Secondly, there are cases in which the apparent purpose of an act is the performance of some future act or the occurrence of some future event, in neither case a *higher* or *same-level* act. I walk to the store because I want to buy bread. And I take a sleeping pill because I want to fall asleep. But my buying bread cannot be generated by my walking to the store, since it would have to be subsequent to my walking to the store. Nor do I believe that my buying the bread would be generated by my walking to the store. Hence, although I want to buy bread, this want does not satisfy condition (1) for the intentional act of walking to the store. Similarly, I want to fall asleep, but this cannot be the want which satisfies condition (1) for the intentional act of taking a sleeping pill; for I do not believe that my taking a sleeping pill would generate an act of falling asleep.

These cases can be handled somewhat like the automobile case. In the first case the want which satisfies condition (1) is not my want to buy bread, but my want to *put myself in a position to buy bread*. If I wanted to buy bread, and if this motivated me to walk to the store in order to buy bread, then I must also have wanted to put myself in a position to buy bread. Since the act of putting myself in a position to buy bread *is* an act I believed would be generated by my walking to the store, my want to perform this act satisfies condition (1). In the sleeping pill case the want which satisfies condition (1) is not my want to fall asleep, but my want to *cause myself to fall asleep*. If an agent wants to fall asleep, and if he acts in order to cause himself to fall asleep, it may be inferred that he wants to cause himself to fall asleep. Since I believe that my taking a sleeping pill would generate the act of causing myself to fall asleep, my want to perform this latter act satisfies condition (1). In general, wants for acts of the form *putting oneself in a position to do x* and wants for acts of the form *causing x to occur* are among the most common wants that satisfy condition (1) for various intentional acts.

A third apparent difficulty for condition (1) concerns intentional acts motivated by feelings of duty or obligation. Suppose Smith hates to visit his aunt, but visits her anyway because he feels he ought to. What is the higher act that he wants to do? Assuming Smith acts out of a genuine concern for his duty, the higher act is that of *doing his duty*, or *fulfilling an obligation*. Smith believes that his visiting his aunt would conventionally generate his doing his duty, and he wants to perform the act of doing his duty. Often, of course, people do what is their duty not because of a genuine desire to do their duty, but because of their fear of the consequences, or their fear of social disapproval. In such a case, the desired act would be *avoiding consequences x*, or *avoiding incurring so-and-so's disapproval*, which the agent believes would be generated by his doing his duty.

Several objections might be raised against this way of handling acts done out of duty. First, it might be asked why we have to invoke Smith's *wanting* to do his duty to explain his visiting his aunt. Why can't we just say that Smith visited his aunt because he believed this would generate the act of doing his duty, but omit any reference to a want? I think that the omission of the want would leave us with an inadequate explanation of why Smith visited his aunt. People often believe that something is their duty but refrain from doing it because they are not, at the time, much motivated to do their duty. They do not especially *want* to do their duty. If, on this occasion, Smith is motivated to visit his aunt because he believes this to be his duty, he must feel positively inclined toward doing his duty. (At the very least, he must have a *negative* feeling toward *failing* to do his duty, which I can re-express as *wanting not to fail* to do his duty.) Wanting to do one's duty, of course, is not phenomenologically the same as other wants. The "attrac-tiveness" of doing one's duty is not that of going swimming on a hot day or of seducing Claudia Cardinale. (But then, the attractiveness of going swim-ming on a hot day is not the same as the attractiveness of seducing Claudia Cardinale, either.) Nevertheless, despite the phenomenological difference, the prospect of doing one's duty (*per se*) is sometimes attractive to people. They find this prospect "fitting" or "appropriate," and this is what I would call wanting to do one's duty.

A second objection might run as follows. "Your handling of the duty cases vitiates the distinction between acting out of desire or inclination and acting out of duty. According to you, all motivated or intentional action is mo-tivated by desires. This doesn't leave room for the relevant distinction."

I admit that my handling of duty cases rules out any distinction between two kinds of motivation: acting from duty and acting from desire. But nothing important is lost, for we can still draw the distinction between acting from duty and acting from *other* desires (or aversions). Clearly we can distinguish, on my analysis, between visiting one's aunt because one likes to visit her and visiting one's aunt because one wants to do one's duty (or is averse to failing to do one's duty). But instead of saying that there are two *kinds* of *motivation* operative here—viz., inclination and duty—I say that there is one mode of motivation, i.e., inclination, and that being motivated by duty consists in having a specific kind of inclination. I thereby avoid multiplying modes of motivation beyond necessity.

A parallel may be found in the problem of altruism. Someone might argue for two modes of motivation by saying that all wants are egoistic, and hence that whenever anyone acts altruistically he is not motivated by desire. Such a theorist might propose two kinds of motivation, inclination and altruism. It is clearly preferable, however, not to postulate a separate "altruistic" mode of motivation, but to say that people sometimes have altruistic desires, that is, desires with altruistic contents or objects. This approach to human behavior has more simplicity, and manages to account both for self-regarding action and other-regarding action.

Although (1) is a necessary condition of an act being intentional, it is not a sufficient condition. To see this, let us examine some cases in which (1) is satisfied for a given act A though A is not intentional.

Suppose S is at a dinner party. S is bent on offending the host, and he knows that if he grimaces as he eats the soup the host will be offended. Meanwhile, however, someone has put some foul-tasting stuff into the soup, and when S eats it he cannot help grimacing. S's grimacing is not an intentional act, then, but merely an automatic reflex response to the foul taste. But S's grimacing does satisfy condition (1), inasmuch as S wanted to perform the act of offending the host and S believed that his grimacing would generate the act of his offending the host.[1]

Consider a second case. S likes to see Mary blush and is very desirous of making her blush at the party. Unable to think of a way to make her blush, however, S gets into a conversation with John, to whom he relates an anecdote about George. Unknown to S, Mary is listening to the anecdote, and, because of the anecdote, is made to blush. Now let A = S's making Mary blush. This act satisfies condition (1), for there is an act(-type) A'—viz., making Mary blush—that S wants to perform, and S has the belief that his making Mary blush would be on the same level as his performing this desired act. But although A satisfies (1), it is clearly not intentional.

These two counter-examples point to an important element in intentional action that is missing from (1). In each of these cases S has a relevant want and belief *vis-à-vis* act A, but his performance of A is unconnected with this want and belief. He does A (or A "happens"), but not *because* of that want and belief. By adding the "because" element to condition (1), we produce a new condition, (2), which is a substantial improvement over (1) viewed as a complete analysis of intentional action.

(2)   *Act-token* A *is intentional if and only if*
    (a)   *there is an act(-type)* A' *such that the agent* S *wanted to*

---

[1] If S had grimaced on purpose, then his grimacing would be an act-token (a basic act-token). But as it actually occurred, S's grimacing was not only not an intentional act, but not even an act at all.

> do (*exemplify*) A', *and*
> (b) *either* S *believed that his doing* A *would generate his
> doing* A' *or* S *believed that his doing* A *would be on the
> same level as his doing* A', *and*
> (c) *this want and this belief caused* S's *doing* A.

Condition (2) is an improvement over (1) because it rules out cases in which act *A* just *happens* to be accompanied by an appropriate want and belief, a want and belief that have no real effect on his performance of the act. According to (2), S's grimacing and S's making Mary blush would not be intentional acts.

Many philosophers would object to the use of the term "cause" in this context, but I wish to contend that wants can properly be understood as causes of acts, and that an adequate theory of human action can be worked out within a causal framework. These contentions will be supported in this chapter and in much of the remainder of the book. The word "cause" itself, however, should not be overstressed. Many other expressions might be substituted for this word, and I shall sometimes make use of these other locutions. Instead of saying that wants and beliefs "cause" acts, one might say that acts "result from" wants and beliefs, or that they "stem from" wants and beliefs, or that they "flow from" wants and beliefs. If a reader finds one of these locutions, or some other locution in the same family, more suitable than "cause," let him substitute it in the relevant places.

As a candidate for a sufficient condition of intentional action, condition (2) is better than (1), but still not fully adequate. It is open to the same sort of counter-example posed by Roderick Chisholm to analyses of purpose like that of C. J. Ducasse.[2] Chisholm's example is this: "Suppose a man believes that if he kills his uncle he will inherit a fortune and suppose he desires to inherit a fortune; this belief and desire may agitate him and cause him to drive in such a way that he accidentally kills his uncle. . . . " Adapting the example to our analysis, we may suppose that *S* wants to perform act *A'*, bringing it about that he inherits a fortune. *S* believes that his killing his uncle will causally generate his bringing it about that he inherits a fortune. Moreover, his having this desire and his having this belief cause him to drive in such a way that he kills a pedestrian that turns out to be his uncle. Thus, S's killing his uncle satisfies condition (2), yet it is clearly an unintentional or accidental act, not an intentional act.

This counter-example shows that (2) is not a sufficient condition of intentionality. But I do not think it shows that the causal element should be

---

[2] See R. M. Chisholm, "The Descriptive Element in the Concept of Action," *The Journal of Philosophy*, LXI (1964), 616, and "Freedom and Action," in K. Lehrer, ed., *Freedom and Determinism* (New York: Random House, Inc., 1966), pp. 19–20. Ducasse's analysis of purpose is in "Explanation, Mechanism, and Teleology," *The Journal of Philosophy*, XXII (1925), 150–55; reprinted in H. Feigl and W. S. Sellars, eds., *Readings in Philosophical Analysis* (New York: Appleton-Century-Crofts, 1949).

eliminated from the analysis of intentionality. Rather, it suggests that the causal factor plays a more complicated role in the pattern of intentional action, a role which I shall now try to trace in greater detail.

3. The Pattern of Intentional Action

Suppose that S wants to do act A'. If A' is a basic act, S may do A' "directly." But most of the acts we want to perform, the acts at which we *aim*, are not basic acts. So let us focus our attention on the more common cases. If A' is not a basic act (nor an act on the same level as a basic act), S must do some other act that will generate A'. Similarly, unless this latter act is a basic act, some further act must be performed to generate *it*. Eventually we must come to some basic act (some *lowest* basic act) or group of basic acts. If S wants to perform A', he must perform at least one basic act that will generate A', and perhaps some intermediate acts which are generated by the basic act and which generate A'.

S's choice of a basic act or acts depends on his level-generational beliefs— i.e., his beliefs about what acts would generate A' in the given situation. Suppose he believes that a particular basic act, A_1, is the best basic act to perform in order to do A'. He believes that A_1 will generate, or has the best chance of generating A_2, that A_2 will generate (or has the best chance of generating) A_3, that $A_3 \ldots, \ldots$ will generate A'.

S's *beliefs* can be represented by an act-tree diagram, in this case the diagram of a *projected act-tree*. Projected act-trees, as opposed to actual act-trees, represent hypothetical acts that the agent, or some other person, *believes* would be performed *if S were to perform a certain basic act. For our purposes, an agent's projected act-tree will be constructed in accordance with the beliefs he has just prior to the time of the proposed action. Of course, the concept of an act-tree is not familiar to many agents. But as I define projected act-trees, an agent need not have the concept of an act-tree, and certainly need not "picture" act-trees in his mind, in order for us to represent his beliefs in terms of them. Act-trees are *our* tool for representing *his* beliefs. To distinguish a diagram of a projected act-tree from an actual act-tree diagram, projected act-trees will be drawn with dashed lines instead of solid lines, as in Figure 7.

The combination of an agent's action-*wants* and his *projected act-tree* I shall call an *action-plan*. In other words, an action-plan consists of a *desire* (a *predominant* desire) to do some act A' and a set of *beliefs* (of greater or less certitude) to the effect that, if one were to perform basic act A_1, this would generate (or be on the same level as) various other acts, including the desired act A'. More generally, an action-plan may consist of desires for two or more acts, all of which are to be generated by a single basic act. But I shall confine my attention to the simpler case where only one act is desired (for its own sake). Calling something an "action-plan" is not intended to suggest that the agent spends time deliberating or reviewing the projected acts in his mind. Action-plans do not require meditation or reflection. The wants and beliefs that constitute action-plans sometimes crop up suddenly and forthwith precipitate the corresponding acts. Thus, even impulsive acts may result from action-plans.

Using the notion of an action-plan, a new analysis of intentional action can be proposed.

(3) *Suppose S has an action-plan which includes acts A_1, A_2, $A_3, \ldots, A_n$, where A_1 is a basic act and $n \geq 1$. S wants to do A_n, and S believes (to some degree) of each of the acts A_1, A_2, $A_3, \ldots, A_n$ firstly, that it will either be generated by A_1 or be on the same level as A_1, and secondly, that it will either generate A_n or be on the same level as A_n. If this action-plan, in a certain characteristic way,[3] causes S's doing A_1, then A_1 is intentional. And if some of the other acts A_2, $A_3, \ldots, A_n$ are performed in the way conceived in the action-plan, then these acts are also intentional. All other acts on the (actual) act-tree are non-intentional.*

Let me illustrate how (3) can be applied to a genuine example. Suppose I am taking an examination for a driver's license. While driving I come to an intersection where, because of "one way" signs, I can only turn right. I am not certain whether I should signal for a turn or whether that should be omitted because of the legal necessity of turning right. I want to perform the act of convincing my examiner that I am a competent driver. Although I am not certain, I think that by signaling for a turn I would perform that act. That is, I believe that an act of signaling for a turn would generate the act of convincing my examiner that I am a competent driver. I also believe, of course, that I would signal for a turn by extending my (left) arm out the window and that this act, in turn, would be generated by the basic act of extending my (left) arm.

My projected act-tree is given in Figure 7. The lowest act on this tree corresponds to A_1 in condition (3), and the highest act corresponds to A_n.

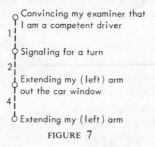

FIGURE 7

<hr>

[3] The reason for the qualifier "in a certain characteristic way" will be explained below.

Of each of the four acts in Figure 7 I have the following beliefs: I believe that it would either be generated by extending my arm or would be on the same level as it, and I believe that it would either generate the act of convincing my examiner that I am a competent driver or be on the same level as it. For example, I believe that signaling for a turn would be generated by extending my arm and would generate the act of convincing my examiner that I am a competent driver. Moreover, the act of convincing my examiner that I am a competent driver is an act that I want to do. Hence, I have an action-plan that satisfies condition (3).

Now suppose that this action-plan *causes* (in the characteristic way) my extending my arm. That is, *because* of my action-plan I proceed to perform this act. Then according to condition (3), my extending my arm is an intentional act. Suppose further that extending my arm actually does generate each of the other three acts that were part of my action-plan. In other words, suppose that my actual act-tree replicates the whole of my projected act-tree. Then each of these other three acts is intentional too.

In order to understand the analysis more completely, let us change the example slightly to see what happens. Suppose now that signaling for a turn is inappropriate in the given situation, and that my signaling for a turn convinces the examiner that I am *not* a competent driver. In other words, suppose now that the actual acts performed are those in Figure 8, not Figure 7. Which of these acts is intentional, and why?

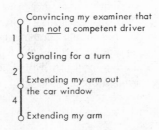

FIGURE 8

The lower three acts in this diagram remain intentional for the same reasons as before. The highest act in the diagram, however, is not intentional. This act does not satisfy condition (3), for it was not one of the acts that formed my action-plan. My action-plan did not include the belief that the act of convincing my examiner that I am not a competent driver would be generated by extending my arm; nor did I believe that the act of convincing my examiner that I am *not* a competent driver would generate the desired act A_n, or be on the same level as it.

On our present supposition only three of the four acts in my action-plan are actually performed, and in particular the desired act is not performed. But condition (3) does not require *all* acts of the action-plan to be performed.

Whatever act is performed, however, as long as it is performed *in the way conceived in the action-plan*, is intentional.[4]

Figure 8 does not represent all the actual acts generated by my extending my arm. Figure 9 reveals some of the additional acts not pictured in Figure 8. Because of the rain, my extending my arm out the window generates my getting my hand wet. Because a pedestrian decides to wait when he sees my signal, I also perform the act of deterring a pedestrian from crossing the street. Finally, the examiner has just examined another bearded driver before me and found him incompetent. So that when I (who am bearded) convince him that I am not a competent driver, he becomes convinced that no bearded men are competent drivers.

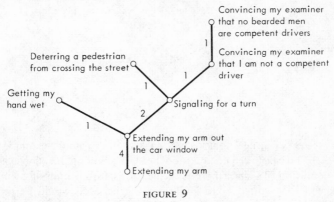

FIGURE 9

Are any of these three additional acts intentional? If we assume, as I have been assuming, that none of these acts were part of my action-plan, then clearly they are non-intentional. True, they were caused by my action-plan, inasmuch as they were generated by a basic act that was caused by my action-plan. But since these acts were not means to my goal of convincing my examiner that I am a competent driver, they are non-intentional. And they would be correctly classified as such by (3).

The situation is slightly different if one of these acts were foreseen. Suppose, for example, that I had realized it was raining when I planned to signal for a turn, and so I knew that I would get my hand wet if I extended my arm out the car window. This means that the act of getting my hand wet was on my projected act-tree, was part of my action-plan, as is shown in Figure 10. This fact might make us think that the act of getting my hand wet would be deemed intentional, but a closer look at condition (3) shows this to be false. Condition (3) requires that each of the acts $A_1, A_2, A_3, \ldots, A_n$ be expected

---

[4] Cf. Chisholm's remark: "an agent performs an *intentional action* provided there is something he makes happen *in the way he intended*." "The Descriptive Element in the Concept of Action," *op. cit.*, p. 619.

by S either to generate the desired act A_n or to be on the same level. Although I believed that I would get my hand wet, I did not believe that getting my hand wet would *generate* the act of convincing my examiner that I am a competent driver, or that it would be on the *same level* as this wanted act. This can be "read off" from Figure 10, which shows that act of getting my hand wet to be *level-indeterminate* with respect to the act of convincing my examiner that I am a competent driver. In other words, I anticipated getting my hand wet as an incidental by-product of my course of action, but not as a means of achieving my goal of convincing my examiner that I am a competent driver.

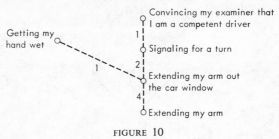

FIGURE 10

Let us see how our new analysis meets Chisholm's counter-example to condition (2). The act-token in question here, S's killing his uncle, satisfies part of condition (3), since there is an act A_n, causing himself to inherit a fortune, which S wanted to do and which he believed would be generated by his killing his uncle. But S's killing his uncle does not fully satisfy (3), for S had no *complete* action-plan for killing his uncle, i.e., a plan that included a relevant *basic* act; or, if he did have a plan, it did not feature the basic acts that actually generated his killing his uncle. The basic act-tokens which generated his killing his uncle were his moving his foot (on the accelerator) and his moving his hands (on the steering wheel). But S did not believe that his killing his uncle would be generated by *these* basic acts. Whatever action-plan he had for these basic acts, it did not include the belief that they would generate his killing his uncle. Hence, S's killing his uncle would be classed by (3) as a non-intentional act.

Let us now consider possible counter-examples to condition (3). The first of these counter-examples can be constructed by elaborating the earlier example in which S grimaced in response to foul-tasting soup. In that example S had a desire to offend his host and a belief that grimacing would offend him. In the original description of the case, there was no causal connection between S's want and belief and S's grimacing. But let us now amend the case, so that there is a causal connection. Oscar, S's practical joker friend, knows about S's desire and S's belief, but he is determined to prevent S from intentionally offending his host. So Oscar puts the foul-tasting stuff in the soup that makes him grimace. Here there *is* a causal connection between S's action-plan (want and belief) and S's grimacing, for his action-plan caused

Oscar to put the stuff in the soup and this caused S's grimacing. Still, S's grimacing is not intentional, indeed, not an *act*-token at all.[5]

One thing to notice about this case is that the time of the grimacing does not correspond precisely to the time at which S *planned* to grimace. S wanted to grimace at time t_1, but S actually grimaced at an earlier time, t_0. Thus, this case could be guarded against by inserting relevant time references into the analysis of intentionality. Troublesome cases would still arise, however, since the time references included in our desires are usually rather vague.

In fact, however, condition (3) already contains a requirement that is intended to handle the grimacing counter-example and similar counter-examples without help from this temporal factor. This is the requirement that action-plans not merely *cause* basic acts, but that they cause the basic acts "*in a certain characteristic way.*" In the grimacing example this requirement is violated, because the agent's want and belief do not cause his grimacing in the characteristic way; rather, they cause his grimacing only via some extremely unusual intermediate factors. Hence, his grimacing would not be classified as an intentional act (nor, indeed, as a non-intentional act).

The requirement that intentional acts be caused by action-plans "in a certain characteristic way" would also rule out two examples proposed by Richard Taylor as counter-examples to the attempt to analyze purposeful action in terms of causation by wants (and beliefs). The first of these examples includes salivating, and the second fidgeting.

> Desires are capable of literally *causing* all sorts of changes in the body, and some of these have, and are believed to have, certain good effects, that is, effects that one wants; but not all such bodily changes qualify as purposeful *actions*. Hunger, for example, which is the desire for nourishment, sometimes causes salivation and other changes which are, moreover, useful to nourishment; but one does not salivate in order to be nourished, or at least, it would be odd to say so. . . .
> . . . Suppose, for example, that a member of an audience keenly desires to attract the speaker's attention but, being shy, only fidgets uncomfortably in his seat and blushes. We may suppose, further, that he does attract the speaker's attention by his very fidgeting; but he did not fidget *in order* to catch the speaker's attention, even though he desired that result and might well have realized that such behavior was going to produce it.[6]

It is obvious that the salivating and the fidgeting are not intentional acts. Yet both of these occurrences are caused by desires, and perhaps by desires that satisfy condition (3)—i.e., the desire to help oneself be nourished and the desire to attract the speaker's attention. But these cases do not constitute counter-examples to (3) because they fail to meet the requirement that the

---

[5] This case is due to Paul Benacerraf. Unlike S's killing his uncle, S's grimacing seems to correspond to his action-plan, because the basic act in his plan was grimacing itself. Thus, the present case cannot be handled like Chisholm's case.

[6] Richard Taylor, *Action and Purpose* (Englewood Cliffs, N. J.: Prentice-Hall, Inc., 1966), pp. 248–49.

behavior be caused by the desire *in the characteristic way*. The fidgeting is not caused "directly" by the desire to attract the speaker's attention, but rather via a state of nervousness or tension that is caused by this desire. And the salivating, though it may somehow be causally related to the desire to eat or the desire to help oneself be nourished, is triggered by automatic mechanisms uncharacteristic of purposeful action.[7]

The difficult question, of course, is: precisely what is this "characteristic" mode of causation by which wants and beliefs cause intentional action? To this question, I confess, I do not have a fully detailed answer.[8] But neither do I think that it is incumbent on me, *qua* philosopher, to give an answer to this question. A complete explanation of how wants and beliefs lead to intentional acts would require extensive neurophysiological information, and I do not think it is fair to demand of a *philosophical* analysis that it provide this information. I think we are aware, intuitively, of a characteristic manner in which desires and beliefs flow into intentional acts. Certainly we can "feel" a difference between a voluntary movement and an involuntary one, and this feeling, I think, is symptomatic of certain causal processes. But a detailed delineation of the causal process that is characteristic of intentional action is a problem mainly for the special sciences. The grimacing case, of course, is very easy to handle, because there the causal chain connecting the want and belief with the physical movement involves an entirely different organism (the practical joker friend). It is obvious that the "characteristic" manner in which action-plans cause acts does not include a distinct organism beyond the organism of the agent himself. But a precise and general specification of the characteristic causal process—one that would rule out the fidgeting and salivating cases—would be quite difficult to give, and certainly is not extractable from our fund of commonsense knowledge.

To help clarify my position, compare the analysis of intentional action with

---

[7] Actually, the salivating and fidgeting cases can be dismissed for other reasons too. The salivating case can be dismissed because, as we shall see in Section 4 of this Chapter, salivating is not a basic act-type for any agent. Hence, the salivating of the agent cannot be a basic act-token. Moreover, both the salivating and the fidgeting cases can be dismissed because the relevant *beliefs* do not have the causal status required by condition (3). Condition (3) requires that beliefs, as well as desires, be *causes* of intentional acts (except where there is a desire to do a basic act). In the salivating case, however, the relevant belief has no real causal role. The agent may have believed that salivating would help him be nourished, but this belief is incidental to his salivating. He would have salivated as a result of hunger and the sight of food even if he had not had this belief. Similarly, the member of the audience may have believed that his fidgeting would attract the attention of the speaker, but this belief was not a crucial causal factor; he would have fidgeted even in the absence of this belief.

Taylor's two examples, therefore, can be ruled out even without appeal to the "characteristic manner of causation." But perhaps slightly different examples can be constructed where appeal to the manner of causation would be necessary.

[8] For further discussion, though, see Chapter Five, Section 5.

the analysis of seeing.[9] An analysis of what it is for someone to see a physical object must, I believe, require there to be a causal connection between the object and the sensory contents of the percipient. But not *any* such causal connection or other will do, for there are some causal processes leading from an object to visual sensory impressions which would *not* count as the person's *seeing* the object. What is needed, then, is a specification of the *appropriate* causal process which constitutes seeing. But is it legitimate to expect a philosophical analysis of seeing to specify this process in detail? I think not. This is a point at which philosophy and the special sciences must collaborate, since a complete delineation of the relevant causal process must include reference to facts that are available only through specialized research, not common sense. Thus, it would be completely legitimate for a philosopher, in analyzing the concept of seeing, to say that S's seeing x involves a "characteristic" causal process connecting x with some visual impressions of S, without specifying this causal process in detail. This is just what I am doing with respect to intentional action.

Definition (3) is not a complete definition of intentional action. It does not give us a means of deciding, with respect to *every* act-token, whether or not it is intentional. This is because it fails to deal with act-tokens which are temporal *sequences* of basic acts (or act-tokens generated by sequences of basic acts), or with act-tokens which are temporal *parts* of basic acts (or act-tokens generated by parts of basic acts), or even with act-tokens that are jointly generated by two or more co-temporal basic acts. Although I shall not attempt to provide an analysis of intentionality which covers all of these cases, many of the requisite changes are fairly obvious. The main elements necessary for a complete analysis of intentionality are presented in definition (3).

4. Basic Acts

The concept of a basic act has played an essential role in our analysis of intentional action, as well as in our recursive definition of an act-token. It is high time, therefore, to provide an explication of this central notion. Actually, its role in the analysis of an *act-token* and its role in the analysis of an *intentional* act-token are closely related. As I shall define the notion of a basic act-token, nothing can be a basic act-token unless it is intentional—i.e., caused in the indicated way by wants (and beliefs) of the agent. Since our recursive definition of an act-token requires every act-token to be related to basic act-tokens, it will follow that every act-token is caused by wants (and beliefs) of the agent. This is not to say that every act-token is intentional; that,

---

[9] See H. P. Grice, "The Causal Theory of Perception," reprinted in R. Swartz, ed., *Perceiving, Sensing, and Knowing* (New York: Doubleday & Company, Inc., 1965), p. 463. My argument is patterned after his suggestions about the analysis of seeing.

we have seen, is certainly false. It is true, however, that the concept of an act-token, as it is defined here, involves the notion of want-and-belief causation.

The notion of a basic act-token presupposes the notion of a basic act-type, for every basic act-token is an instance of (a token of) a basic act-type. Let us begin, then, by explicating the notion of a basic act-type. The central feature of a basic act-type, or basic act-property, is that it is the sort of property that is exemplifiable at will. Raising one's hand is a basic act-property because one can, at will, exemplify the property of raising one's hand. But sneezing, hiccuping, salivating, vomiting, blushing, fainting, etc. are not basic act-properties, because they are not properties that one can exemplify at will. What does it mean to say that one can, or cannot, exemplify a property "at will"? I believe it should be understood in terms of a causal subjunctive conditional. Property A is a basic act-type for S only if it is true that *if* S *wanted to exemplify* A (*at* t), *he would exemplify* A (*at* t). It has been pointed out by J. L. Austin[10] and others that there are many uses of "if"-clauses that are not causal, or even conditional. Austin called special attention to the noncausal "if" in "there are biscuits on the sideboard if you want them," and argued that the "if" in "he can if he chooses" resembles this noncausal "if." But while we may agree that the "if" in "he *can* if he chooses" or in "he *can* if he wants" is noncausal, it does not follow that the "if" in "he *will* if he chooses," or in "he *would* if he chose," or in "he *would* if he wanted" is noncausal. I think that the sentence "He would raise his arm if he wanted to raise it," or the sentence "If he wanted to raise his arm he would raise it" can be used to express a casual subjunctive conditional, and that is the way I shall here use such sentences.

To say that A is a basic act-type for S, or that S has A as a basic act-type, is to ascribe a dispositional property to S, like ascribing the property of being brittle to an object. Something is brittle if it is such that, if it were struck by a hard object, it would shatter. In other words, being brittle consists in a tendency to shatter in response to being struck by a hard object. Similarly, having A as a basic act-type is a disposition to exemplify A as a result of wanting to exemplify it. It is a tendency for one's wanting to do (exemplify) A to cause one's doing (exemplifying) A. I assume here that wanting to do A is the only want the agent has, or the only relevant one he has. Clearly, if S has a stronger and conflicting desire, he would not do A even if he wanted to. In defining basic act-types I restrict my attention to the simple case where A is the only desire. Further complications on this point will be introduced in the next section.

The definition of basic act-types must take into account possible external constraints on the performance of basic acts. If S's arm is tied down, then even if his only current desire is to raise his arm, he will not in fact raise it.

---

[10] "Ifs and Cans," *Philosophical Papers* (London : Oxford University Press, 1961), pp. 153–80.

Similarly, he will not be able to raise his arm if a ceiling is immediately over-head or if the arm is already raised. (Analogous exceptions pertain to being brittle. A brittle object might not actually shatter upon being struck because it is held and supported by soft material that cushions the shock.) Let us say that *S* is in "standard conditions" with respect to raising his arm as long as no such constraints are present—i.e., as long as (a) there are no *external* forces that make it physically impossible for him to raise his arm, and (b) his arm is not already up. Standard conditions do not include *internal* states of the agent's body. Despite the fact that one's arm is paralyzed, therefore, one may be in standard conditions with respect to moving that arm.

The notion of standard conditions can be generalized as follows. *S is in standard conditions with respect to property* A *at* t *just in case* (a) *there are no external forces at* t *making it physically impossible for* S *to exemplify* A *at* t, *and* (b) *if exemplifying* A *involves a change into state* Z, *then* S *is not already in* Z. Given the notion of standard conditions, we may reformulate the neces-sary condition for basic act-types as follows. A *is a basic act-type for* S *at* t *only if: if* S *were in standard conditions with respect to* A *at* t, *then if* S *wanted to exemplify* A *at* t, S's *exemplifying* A *at* t *would result from this want.* On this definition, moving one's arm is not a basic act-type for a man whose arm is paralyzed. Even if he is in standard conditions with respect to moving the arm, it is not the case that if he wanted to exemplify the property of moving the arm he would as a result actually succeed in moving it.

Properties that are not basic act-types for an agent at one time may be acquired as basic act-types at a later time, and properties that are basic act-types at one time may cease to be basic act-types at a later time. Upon learning to wiggle one's ears one acquires a basic act-type one did not possess earlier. And if one's arm becomes paralyzed, one loses a basic act-type formerly in one's repertoire.

The condition I have given is a necessary, but not a sufficient, condition of property *A* being a basic act-type for agent *S*. It is not a sufficient condition because properties such as *imitating Jimmy Stewart* or *making oneself see double* would satisfy this condition, at least for many agents. Many agents are able to imitate Jimmy Stewart at will and are able to make themselves see double at will. If they want to perform the act (exemplify the property) of imitating Jimmy Stewart, their want results in their actually performing this act—they simply proceed to talk in a certain distinctive, halting manner. Similarly, if these agents want to perform the act (exemplify the property) of making themselves see double, their want results in this act—they simply press their eyeballs. But these are not properties we would like to classify as basic act-types.

The difference between these properties and genuine basic act-types, I think, is that one's ability to exemplify *these* properties at will depends on *level-generational knowledge* (or belief). In the case of moving one's hand, simply wanting to do it is sufficient to ensure one's doing it (assuming one is in standard conditions). One does not have to know of any act that will *generate* one's moving one's hand. But in the two examples just considered, simply wanting to exemplify the properties does not ensure that one will actually exemplify them. Relevant level-generational knowledge is also required. To exemplify the property of imitating Jimmy Stewart, one must know *how* to talk; that is, one must know that certain specific ways of talking (which one can exemplify at will) would level-generate an act of imitating Jimmy Stewart. To exemplify the property of making oneself see double, one must know that pressing one's eyeballs in a certain way would causally generate an act of making oneself see double. Without the relevant knowledge, one would not be able to exemplify these properties at will: wanting to exemplify them would not normally result in actually exemplifying them. Thus, the following requirement must be added. A *is a basic act-type for* S *only if* S's *ability to exemplify* A *at will does not depend on level-generational knowledge* (*belief*).[11]

A similar requirement is needed with respect to knowledge of cause and effect. To see the necessity for this additional requirement, consider the property of *vomiting*. There are many people who are able to vomit at will, by putting a finger down their throat. To be sure, their ability to vomit at will does not depend on *level-generational* knowledge, for their vomiting is not *generated* by their putting the finger in their throat. Nevertheless, their ability to vomit at will does depend on their knowledge that putting their finger down their throat will *cause* them to vomit. And for this reason, we do not want to regard vomiting as a basic act-type. The ability to perform basic act-types at will does not depend on any cause-and-effect knowledge. I may be able to raise my hand at will although I have no idea what *causes* the raising of my hand. Perhaps I must know that my *want* causes my raising my hand. But I do not need to know any of the mechanisms that result in my raising my hand. This is not to deny that there *are* mechanisms — indeed a very complex and interesting array of mechanisms—that *do* cause my raising my arm. What is crucial, however, is that my ability to raise my arm at will does not depend on having any *knowledge* (or belief) of these mechanisms. With this point in mind, we may add the following requirements. A *is a basic act-type for* S *only if* S's *ability to exemplify* A *at will does not depend on his knowledge of cause and effect, except possibly the knowledge that his exemplifying* A *would be caused by his wants.*

The complete definition of a basic act-type can now be given.

---

[11] Perhaps there are *some* basic act-types which do involve level-generational knowledge. Consider the property of *raising one's hand slowly*, for example. Presumably, this should be classified as a basic act-type. It might be argued, however, that one's ability to exemplify this property at will depends on one's knowledge that a token of this type would have to be generated by a token of the type *raising one's hand*. To accommodate this point, perhaps we should allow basic act-types to depend on knowledge of *augmentation* generation, though not on knowledge of other kinds of generation.

Property A *is a basic act-type for* S *at* t *if and only if:*

(a) *If* S *were in standard conditions with respect to* A *at* t, *then if* S *wanted to exemplify* A *at* t, S's *exemplifying* A *at* t *would result from this want; and*

(b) *the fact expressed by* (a) *does not depend on* S's *level-generational knowledge nor on* S's *cause-and-effect knowledge, except possibly the knowledge that his exemplifying* A *would be caused by his want.*

This definition, I believe, includes all the cases that we want to include in the class of basic act-types. It includes extending one's arm, moving one's finger, bending one's knees, shrugging one's shoulder, opening one's eyes, turning one's head, etc. Moreover, as we should expect, the negations of most basic act-types are also basic act-types. Extending one's arm is a basic act-type, and so is not extending one's arm. Bending one's knee is a basic act-type, and so is not bending one's knee. A possible exception to this rule is *not sneezing* (i.e., inhibiting a sneeze), which may be a basic act-type even though *sneezing* is not a basic act-type.

Of course, not everyone has the same range of basic act-types. Paralyzed people lack certain basic act-types that normal people have. Moreover, there are certain basic act-types in the repertoire of relatively few people. Not many people have wiggling their ears as a basic act-type. And running at 11 yards per second may be a basic act-type in the repertoire of track stars, but not ordinary men. Certain basic act-types require an agent to be in a "peak" of physical condition, so possession of these basic act-types may come and go with small changes in bodily condition. A high-jumper may have the property of *leaping seven feet* as a basic act-type when he is well rested, but after a hard day's workout this may no longer be a basic act-type for him.

Our definition seems to include things we want it to include. Let us make sure that it also excludes things we want to exclude. First, we would like to exclude *state*-properties from the class of basic act-types—properties such as being six feet tall, being a bachelor, having blue eyes, owning a Jaguar, etc. Happily, it does seem to exclude such properties. Consider the property of being six feet tall, for example. If *S* is not six feet tall at *t*, then his wanting to be six feet tall at *t* will not result in his exemplifying that property at *t*. And even if *S* happens to be six feet tall, and wants to exemplify that property (at *t*), it is false that his exemplifying that property (at *t*) would *result* from his wanting to exemplify it. Now for some state-properties, it is possible for *S*'s wanting to exemplify them to result in his exemplifying them. *S*'s wanting to own a Jaguar may indeed result in his owning a Jaguar. But here there is reliance on cause-and-effect knowledge, for *S* must know that his *doing* something or other will result in his owning a Jaguar. He cannot simply own a Jaguar at will in the way that one can move one's hand at will; he must do something that will *bring about* his owning the Jaguar.

Secondly—and quite importantly—the definition excludes act-properties whose instances are not at (or near) the bottom of act-trees. We have already seen that it excludes the properties of *imitating Jimmy Stewart* and of *making oneself see double*. For the same reason, the properties of *signaling for a turn, checkmating one's opponent, turning on the light*, etc. are excluded from the class of basic act-types. In many of these cases, of course, it is not the case that an agent can exemplify these properties at will. Even if they are exemplifiable at will, however, the ability to exemplify them at will depends on level-generational knowledge, and this excludes them from the class of basic act-types.

It must be admitted that certain problems arise here. There are some properties which I do not want to classify as basic act-types, but which may have to be included, e.g., *typing the letter "s."* An experienced typist, while typing, does not have to think which fingers to move in order to type certain letters; indeed, he may have to perform a mental experiment to discover which finger he uses for a given letter. Thus, his ability to type the letter "s" at will does not seem to depend on his knowing what finger-movement acts would generate his typing the letter "s." It might be denied that he can, in general, type the letter "s" *at will*, on the grounds that special conditions—viz., the presence of a typewriter—must obtain in order for his wanting to type the letter "s" to result in his typing it. On the other hand, at those times when a typewriter *is* present, his wanting to type the letter "s" would result in his doing so.

What this shows, I think, is that the concept of a basic act-type is not as clearcut as I would like. At any rate, it may not be restricted exclusively to "bodily-movement" properties, such as raising one's hand, turning one's head, lifting one's foot, etc. For the sake of simplicity, however, I shall henceforth assume that basic act-types include only bodily movement acts of this sort. This working assumption posits a degree of neatness and uniformity that does not actually exist in the raw data. But such idealizations are often useful in the construction of theories. Once the theory is clearly understood for the idealized conditions, the special assumptions can be relaxed.

A third class of properties excluded from the class of basic act-types are bodily state properties of various kinds, such as sneezing, hiccuping, salivating, blushing, fainting, vomiting, etc. These have been mentioned earlier, but their exclusion bears emphasizing. Most of these properties are excluded by clause (a) of the definition, since most of them cannot be exemplified at will. Those which may be exemplifiable at will, such as vomiting, are precluded by clause (b), which requires that the ability to exemplify them not depend on cause-and-effect knowledge. Clause (b) is also useful in excluding such properties as *making certain muscles move* or *sending certain nerve impulses*. It is clear that we do not want to regard the occurrence of nerve impulses as "acts" of the agent, and hence we do not want to regard them as basic acts.

Similarly, although the flexing of certain muscles might be counted as acts, most of the more minute muscular processes should not be regarded as "acts." Suppose, however, that John is a knowledgeable physiologist, who knows just what nerve impulses will occur or just what muscular movements will take place if he raises his right arm. Then he is in a position to ensure the occurrence of such events whenever he wants them to occur. If he wants them to occur he simply raises his right arm, and these events *will have* occurred. Nevertheless, clause (b) of our definition makes it clear that these occurrence-properties are not basic act-types for John because John's ability to ensure their occurrence depends on cause-and-effect knowledge: his knowledge that his raising his right arm would be the *effect* of these occurrences.

It is an important fact about basic act-types that our ability to exemplify them at will causally depends on certain processes, yet we do not have to *know* about these processes to exemplify the act-types at will. We have *control* over the movement of our hands without knowing the underlying neuro-physiological mechanisms which give us this control.[12] In the case of most events over which we have control, our control depends on cause-and-effect knowledge. Whether or not the window is open, or whether or not the light is on, is under our control. But this is only because we know what acts of ours would cause the window to be open or closed or cause the light to be on or off. The occurrence of such events as the raising of one's hand *also* depends on prior causes; yet we can control *these* events without knowledge of these prior, internal causes. It is this fact which underlies the intuition that the raising of one's hand is "directly" or "immediately" in one's control. If one wants to cause the light to go off, one must select some act as a *means* to this goal. But if one wants to raise one's hand, no selection of a *means* is necessary—one simply raises one's hand.

A word is now in order about the bearing of our definition on mental acts. Although I shall give little attention to mental acts in subsequent discussions, the definition of basic act-types does allow certain mental properties to be counted as basic act-types. Properties like thinking about Vienna, picturing a cow, imagining that I am in Rome, etc. are properties I can exemplify at will. Moreover, my ability to exemplify them at will is not dependent on level-generational knowledge or cause-and-effect knowledge. If I want to think about Vienna, I simply proceed to do so. Not all mental properties, however, are basic act-properties. In particular, neither wanting such-and-such nor believing such-and-such are basic act-properties. It is not the case that if I want to believe a certain proposition, then I simply proceed to believe it. If the evidence is completely against the proposition, I cannot get myself to believe it just by wanting to believe it. Of course, I can employ various tech-

---

[12] It might be argued that we have "tacit" knowledge of these mechanisms. Cf. Jerry A. Fodor, "The Appeal to Tacit Knowledge in Psychological Explanation," *The Journal of Philosophy*, LXV (1968), 627–40. This point would require more extensive discussion than there is room for here.

niques to try to make myself believe it. For example, I might simply recite the proposition to myself over and over, or I might systematically avoid reading any material that I have reason to think would disconfirm that proposition, and systematically seek out material that I think would support the belief in that proposition. But even if these techniques are always successful, it would mean that my ability to have such a belief at will depends on cause-and-effect knowledge—viz., the knowledge that the belief would be caused by these techniques or activities. Similarly, my wanting such-and-such is not a basic act-type because I cannot want something at will. That is, my wanting to want such-and-such does not necessarily result in my wanting such-and-such. Often I am aware of the fact that it would be good for me to have a certain desire—e.g., a desire to listen to good music, or a desire to do my duty. But even though I would like to have these desires, I cannot simply start having them. I cannot control the desires I have by my meta-desires. Again, there are techniques I can use which might succeed in inducing in me the wanted desire, but this is not the sort of control requisite for a basic act-type. Thus, neither particular wants nor particular beliefs are basic act-tokens. Moreover, since they are not generated by any other basic act-tokens, they are not act-tokens at all. We see, then, that our definition of a basic act-type imposes important limitations on what is counted as an act-token.

Having completed the discussion of basic act-*types*, I turn at last to basic act-*tokens*. As I indicated earlier, every basic act-token must be a token, or instance, of a basic act-type. This immediately ensures that S's turning on the light (at t), or S's checkmating his opponent (at t), are not *basic* act-tokens, though they may be act-tokens. However, while every basic act-token is an instance of a basic act-type, not every instance of a basic act-type is a basic act-token. There are two reasons why the converse does not hold. First, there are some properties such as *grimacing* or *coughing* which can be exemplified as *acts*, or, alternatively, as mere *happenings*. Coughing is a property one can exemplify at will—e.g., to signal one's henchmen. Moreover, the ability to exemplify this property at will does not depend on level-generational knowledge or on cause-and-effect knowledge. Nevertheless, *some* instances of the property coughing are not *act*-tokens. When one coughs in a purely spontaneous way, as a consequence of a familiar bronchial irritation, then one has not performed an "act." Similarly, although one *can* grimace at will, when one grimaces as a natural response to foul-tasting soup, one has not performed an "act." Natural coughs and grimaces are events one "suffers," not things one "does." The second reason why not all tokens of basic act-types are basic act-tokens is that it is possible to exemplify a basic act-type in a "nonbasic way." For example, raising one's right hand is a basic act-type. But if one raises one's right hand by *lifting* it with one's *left* hand, then the act of raising one's right hand is not a basic act-token. S's raising his *left* hand is a basic act-token here, and it causally generates the nonbasic act-token, S's raising his right hand.

In order to distinguish natural coughs or grimaces from artificial coughs or grimaces, we must refer to the *causes* of these events. If *S*'s coughing (at *t*) is to be a basic *act*-token, as opposed to something *S* merely *undergoes*, then *S* must cough intentionally. Given our analysis of intentional action, however, this means that *S*'s coughing (at *t*) must be caused by an action-plan of *S*—i.e., by an appropriate set of wants and beliefs. To generalize, *S*'s *exemplifying property* A (*at* t) *is a basic act-token only if it is caused, in the characteristic way, by an action-plan of* S. This requirement is obviously very significant for my theory of action as a whole. Since the recursive definition of an act-token given in Chapter Two ties the notion of an act-token to the notion of a basic act-token, the requirement just introduced concerning basic act-tokens implies that *all* act-tokens, whether basic or not, are at least partially causally related to the agent's wants and beliefs. The plausibility of this claim depends in part on one's conception of wanting and believing. This matter will be explored in Chapter Four.

It should be emphasized that the necessity of introducing the causal requirement is not created by the coughing and grimacing cases alone. Setting aside problems of that sort entirely, there is still the problem of explaining the conditions under which an agent can be said to *exemplify* the property of raising one's hand—as an action. The familiar problem of distinguishing between *raising* one's hand and having one's hand merely *rise* manifests itself here. When shall we say that a person has exemplified the property of *raising* his hand, rather than merely having it rise? To this question I am giving a traditional, though much castigated, answer, which appeals to mental causation. In order for *S*'s raising his hand to be a basic act-token, his raising his hand must be intentional. And in order for it to be intentional, it must be caused by wants and beliefs of the agent.[13]

To complete our definition of basic act-tokens, we must deal with the problem of raising one's right hand by lifting it with the left. The solution to this problem is straightforward. We do not want to consider a property-instance to be a basic act-token if it is *generated* by any other act-token. Formulated slightly differently, we want a basic act-token to be at the bottom of an act-tree. Actually, this must be qualified. We want to allow *S*'s running slowly to be a basic act-token even though it is augmentationally generated by *S*'s running. What we must require, therefore, is that no basic act-token be

---

[13] One might be able to construct a case in which *S* raises the object which *is* his hand without *knowing* that it is his hand. There might be some other description of his hand, "ϕ", such that raising ϕ is a basic act-type for him. He might then want to raise ϕ, and proceed to do it intentionally. If he doesn't realize that ϕ is his hand, then although his raising ϕ is intentional, his raising his hand is not intentional. In that case, his raising ϕ is a basic act-token, whereas his raising his hand is not a basic act-token. On the other hand, since his raising his hand is *on the same level* as his raising ϕ, his raising his hand is an act-token. (Cf. the recursive definition of act-tokens in Chapter Two.) Thus, we need not require that *S*'s raising his hand must be intentional in order to be an act-token. But it must be intentional in order to be a *basic* act-token.

generated by any other basic act-token, except possibly via augmentation generation. Of greatest importance, no basic act-token can be *causally* generated by another basic act-token. This requirement captures Danto's original conception of a basic action, which his own formulation fails to capture. (Cf. Chapter Two, Section 1.)

We can now present the following definition of a basic act-token.

> *S's exemplifying property* A *(at* t) *is a basic act-token if and only if*
> (a)   *property* A *is a basic act-type for* S *(at* t)*;*
> (b)   S's *exemplifying* A *(at* t) *is caused, in the characteristic way*,
>   *by an action-plan of* S*; and*
> (c)   S's *exemplifying* A *(at* t) *is not level-generated by anything*
>   *else satisfying clauses* (a) *and* (b), *except possibly by aug-*
>   *mentation generation.*

5.   Wants and Beliefs as Causes of Acts

In defining basic act-types I said that there is a causal connection between wanting to do a basic act *A* and the actual performance of a token of type *A*. This fact, however, does not exhaust the topic of the causal relation between wanting and acting. First, in defining basic act-types I assumed that *S*'s want to do *A* was the only want he had at the time, or the only relevant want. We must now worry about what happens if *S* has competing wants. Secondly, an agent usually does a basic act *A* not because he wants to do *A* (*per se*) but because he wants to do *A′* and believes that *A* will generate *A′*. In the normal situation, some cluster of wants *and* beliefs cause the performance of a basic act. Thirdly, from the fact that basic act-tokens are caused by an agent's wants, or by his wants and beliefs, it may not be apparent that acts which are *generated* by this basic act-token are caused by those wants and beliefs. These topics require further discussion.

I want to say first that, to my knowledge, no precise, predictively adequate law is known that correlates wants and beliefs with the performance of acts. I think that there are commonsense generalizations which can be formulated and which can sometimes be used for predictive purposes. But nothing has been formulated that compares favorably with certain laws in the physical sciences. It is important to recognize, however, that knowledge of precise laws is not necessary to justify the statement that wants and beliefs *cause* acts. Most of our knowledge of singular causal propositions is not based on knowledge of precise, universal laws.[14] I know that on various occasions

---

[14] See, for example, Davidson, "Actions, Reasons, and Causes," *The Journal of Philosophy*, LX (1963), 697; Michael Scriven, "Causes, Connections and Conditions in History," in W. Dray, ed., *Philosophical Analysis and History* (New York: 1966), section 4, and J. L. Mackie, "Causes and Conditions," *American Philosophical Quarterly*, Vol. II, No. 4 (1965), sections 4, 5, and 9.

flying rocks cause windows to break, but I could not formulate any universal, predictively adequate law that relates the occurrence of rocks flying with windows breaking. Similarly, many centuries before precise measurements for temperature were developed, it was known that cold weather often causes water to freeze. But at that time no one was able to state a universal law that gives precise conditions under which water would freeze. People could have said that water freezes if it gets cold *enough*, but they could not have said how cold is cold enough.

We are in a similar situation, I think, with respect to wants, beliefs, and acts. We certainly know that wants and beliefs result in acts. Indeed, as I shall argue in Chapter Four, this is part of our conception of wanting and believing. But although we can formulate very rough generalizations about wants, beliefs, and acts, we cannot state precise universal laws, using concepts for which we have precise measurement techniques. The absence of measuring techniques is one of the largest obstacles in the way of a precise universal law. Obviously the relative strengths of desires are very important in determining what acts a person performs. But in the absence of fully adequate techniques for measuring these strengths, reliable predictions cannot be made. Perhaps the identification of neuro-physiological states that correlate with wanting and believing might help us achieve techniques for measuring wants and beliefs,[15] but certainly at the present time we do not have this information. The important point for present purposes, however, is that the justification of the belief that wants and beliefs cause acts does not await the discovery of a precise universal law. Many people know that too much water often causes plants to die, but hardly any of these people could state the precise conditions under which a specifiable amount of water will cause a plant to die. Of course, one can be sure that a certain very large amount of water will cause a certain plant to die. But similarly, one can often be sure that a certain very strong desire (and strong belief) will cause a certain agent to perform a certain act. The problem in the plant case is that one cannot predict whether a certain moderate amount of water will cause a plant to die, though *ex post facto* one can say that it did cause the plant to die. Similarly, although we can say *ex post facto* that certain desires and beliefs caused a particular act A_1, we could not have *predicted* that that act would be performed.

Let us look at the vague, rough generalizations about wants, beliefs, and acts that can be constructed from our commonsense knowledge. One such generalization would be *L*.

> *L:* *If any agent* S *wants to do* A′ (*at* t) *more than any other act,*
> *and if* S *believes that basic act* A_1 *is more likely to generate* A′
> *than any other* (*incompatible*) *basic act, and if* S *is in standard*
> *conditions with respect to* A_1 (*at* t), *then* S *does* A_1 (*at* t).

---

[15] See Chapter Five.

L gives us some idea of the relationship between wants, beliefs, and acts, but it has several failings. First, there are cases in which *S* believes that A_1 would generate some act which he very much dislikes, in addition to generating A'. Hence, even though he believes that A_1 is the basic act most likely to generate the desired act A', he will refrain from doing A_1. Secondly, suppose that *S* wants to do A' (at *t*) more than he wants to do A^* (at *t*). However, he does not believe that there is any basic act very likely to generate A'. He thinks that A_1 is more likely to generate A' than any other basic act, but not really very likely. On the other hand, he is sure there is a basic act which would generate his doing A^*. Here, even though he wants A' more than A^*, he may refrain from doing A_1. Thirdly, suppose that *S* believes that basic act A_2 has quite a good chance of generating A', though not quite as good as A_1. On the other hand, A_2 would generate acts he desires in addition to generating A', while A_1 would only generate A' and not these other desired acts. Then *S* might choose to do A_2 instead of A_1.

To avoid these difficulties, we might formulate generalization *L'*.

> *L':*   If any agent S *believes that hypothetical act-tree* A_1, A_2, . . . , A_n (*to be performed at* t) *is more likely, all in all, to achieve more of his desires than any other act-tree* (*that could be performed at* t), *and if* S *is in standard conditions with respect to each of the basic acts of this act-tree* (*at* t), *then* S *performs each of these basic acts* (*at* t).

L' is an improvement over *L*, first, because it takes into account more than one of *S*'s wanted and unwanted acts, and secondly, because it combines the probability factor with the amount-of-desirability factor. But while it is more comprehensive than *L*, *L'* suffers from even greater vagueness. The main vagueness of *L'* lies in the combination of probability and amount-of-desirability. If there are two hypothetical act-trees under consideration, one having a higher probability of achieving lesser desires and the other having a smaller probability of achieving greater desires, which will *S* choose? This depends in part on what sort of decision "criterion" the agent employs, but *L'* tells us nothing about this. Moreover, it cannot be assumed that all people employ the same criterion, nor even that the same person employs the same criterion on all occasions. When this sort of problem is compounded with our inability to make precise measurements of intensities of desire, or to add these intensities, it becomes clear that *L'* cannot be used to make predictions in all cases. It does not mean that *L'* can *never* be used predictively. There are some cases in which one course of action is *clearly* more attractive to *S* than any other course of action, for it clearly combines greater probability of success with greater desirability. Here we can make predictions with substantial confidence. But in the hard cases, *L'* will not be of much help.

Until now I have said that wants and beliefs cause basic act-tokens, but

I wish also to contend that acts which are generated by basic act-tokens are caused by these wants and beliefs. This point seems fairly obvious to me. If something causes *S*'s moving his hand, and if *S*'s moving his hand generates *S*'s closing the door, then that same thing is a cause of *S*'s closing the door. Again, if something causes *S*'s extending his arm, and if *S*'s extending his arm generates *S*'s signaling for a turn, then that same thing is a cause of *S*'s signaling for a turn. Admittedly, the causation of *S*'s closing the door may involve more factors than are involved in the causation of *S*'s moving his hand. But whatever is the cause of *S*'s moving his hand is at least a *partial* cause of *S*'s closing the door.

One might think that those generational conditions that enable a basic act token to generate a higher act token might be counted among the causes of the higher act. But usually it is inappropriate to call these conditions "causes" of the act. Where *S*'s extending his arm generates *S*'s signaling for a turn, for example, it would be odd to regard the existence of the rule about signaling as a "cause" of *S*'s signaling for a turn. Similarly, where *S*'s jumping six feet three inches generates *S*'s outjumping George, it would be odd to regard George's having jumped six feet as a "cause" of *S*'s outjumping George (though it might be a cause in *certain* cases we could imagine). Even in causal generation, this does not seem natural. The light's going on, for example, can hardly be considered a "cause" of *S*'s turning on the light. And even the position of the switch, the condition of the wiring system, etc. would not ordinarily be called "causes" of *S*'s turning on the light. In all of these cases, however, the generational conditions are *causally relevant* to the performance of the higher act, even if they would not ordinarily be called "causes" of the higher act. Their role might be compared to that of "standing conditions" in various causal processes. We would not ordinarily call the presence of oxygen a "cause" of a particular combustion, but it is a causally relevant condition. Similarly, the condition of the wiring system, the position of the switch, etc., are *causally relevant conditions* of *S*'s turning on the light. In general, then, wants and beliefs which cause a certain basic act also cause anything that is generated by that basic act. But these generated acts will always have some causally relevant conditions that were not causally relevant with respect to the basic act.

Some philosophers have sought to deny that what I call "higher-level" or "generated" acts can be governed by causal laws, because they are irreducible to physical movements. P. F. Strawson, for example, writes:

> . . . there are no effective correlations between the two vocabularies for talking about what goes on, the vocabulary of human action and the vocabulary of physical science. If, for example, every case of someone's telling a lie were an instance of one physically specifiable class of sets of physical movements (and vice versa), and every instance of someone's jilting his girl friend were an instance of another such class (and vice versa), then the reign of law in the field

of physical movement would mean that lying and jilting could be deterministically explained. There would, as far as lying and jilting were concerned, be physical laws of human action as well as physical laws of physical movement. But there is no question of any such correlations ever being established.[16]

Strawson seems to think that in order for *S*'s lying (at *t*) to be caused, there must be a correlation between *all* instances of lying and some specific set of physical movements—e.g., bodily-movement acts. Unless lying can be *reduced* to physical movements, he seems to be saying, there is a gulf between acts of lying and physical movements. And hence, although the physical movements may be caused, the acts of lying are not caused. This position is wholly indefensible. There is no reason whatever for requiring *all* instances of lying to be correlated with, or reduced to, some one set of physical movements or bodily-movement acts. Each distinct act-token of lying may be generated by a different bodily-movement act. But if each of these bodily-movement acts is caused, then each act-token of lying would also be caused.

A slightly different reason for thinking that higher-level acts are not caused is that there are no laws dealing with many (perhaps all) of the properties of which higher-level act-tokens are instances. There are no laws saying, "Whenever *x*, *y*, and *z*, then a person checkmates his opponent," or saying "Whenever *x*, *y*, and *z*, then a person turns on a light." It is a mistake to think, however, that an act-token is caused only if the property of which it is an instance is a dependent variable of some universal law. It would indeed be foolish of psychologists or social scientists to try to formulate or discover laws for every act-property, including checkmating one's opponent, turning on a light, or, to take an even more extreme case, pitching one's sixth straight shut-out. But the absence of such laws does not imply that tokens of these properties are uncaused. If John's moving his hand is caused, and if, given the circumstances, this generates John's checkmating his opponent, then we can say that John's checkmating his opponent is caused, despite the absence of laws dealing with checkmates. Similarly, if a baseball's curving in a certain direction is caused, and if, in the circumstances, this generates the baseball's curving *foul*, then we can say that the baseball's curving foul is caused, despite the fact that there are no laws dealing with foul territory. Surely it would be absurd to assert that the ball's curving foul is *uncaused*.

6. Reasons and Causes

Purposive behavior is closely connected with the concept of "reasons." One might, indeed, with Miss Anscombe,[17] define an intentional act as one which the agent does *for a reason*. But what is it to do something for a reason?

---

[16] In D. F. Pears, ed., *Freedom and the Will* (New York: St. Martins Press, 1963), p. 66.

[17] *Intention* (Ithaca : Cornell University Press, 1958), p. 9.

When we explain an act in terms of the agent's reason, what kind of explanation is this? In particular, is this a species of causal explanation, or is it an explanation of quite a different sort? Many recent philosophers claim that reasons-explanations, or motive-explanations, are not species of causal explanations, and some have even claimed that they preclude causal explanations.[18] But I wish to contend that reasons-explanations *are* a species of causal explanations.[19]

To say that S's reason for doing act A was A' is equivalent to saying that S did A *in order to* do A'. In saying that S's reason for extending his arm was to signal for a turn we are saying that S extended his arm in order to signal for a turn. And when we say that his reason for flipping the switch was to turn on the light we are saying that S flipped the switch in order to turn on the light. What, then, is the force of an "in order to" explanation?

When we say that S flipped the switch in order to turn on the light, the explanandum event is obviously S's flipping the switch. But what does the explanans consist of? What events, states of affairs, or facts are being cited as the explanatory factors of S's flipping the switch? At first glance it may seem that the explanans refers to another act of S—viz., his act of turning on the light. A little reflection will show, however, that this is not the case. First, the assertion that S turned on the light cannot be the whole of the explanans. For the fact that S turned on the light is not a sufficient condition for saying that S flipped the switch *in order to* turn on the light. The fact that S *did* turn on the light by flipping the switch does not imply that the *point* of flipping the switch was to turn on the light. He may have had quite a different reason for flipping the switch. Secondly, the fact that S turned on the light is not even a component of the *in order to* explanation, for the *in order to* explanation can be perfectly correct though S did not turn on the light at all. Suppose S

---

[18] Proponents of the view that explanations in terms of reasons or motives are not a species of causal explanations include the following: G. E. M. Anscombe, *Intention* (Ithaca: Cornell University Press, 1958); Isaiah Berlin, "The Concept of Scientific History," in W. Dray, ed., *Philosophical Analysis and History* (New York: Harper & Row, Publishers, 1966); William Dray, *Laws and Explanation in History* (Oxford: Oxford University Press, 1957); Philippa Foot, "Free Will as Involving Determinism," *The Philosophical Review*, LXVI (1957), 439–50; D. W. Hamlyn, "Behavior," *Philosophy*, XXVIII (1953), 132–45; H. L. A. Hart and A. M. Honore, *Causation in the Law* (Oxford: Oxford University Press, 1959); A. I. Melden, *Free Action* (London: Routledge & Kegan Paul Ltd., 1961; New York: Humanities Press Inc.); R. S. Peters, *The Concept of Motivation* (London, 1958); Charles Taylor, *The Explanation of Behavior* (London: Routledge & Kegan Paul Ltd., 1964; New York: Humanities Press Inc.); Richard Taylor, *Action and Purpose* (Englewood Cliffs, N. J.: Prentice-Hall, Inc., 1966); Gilbert Ryle, *The Concept of Mind* (London: Hutchinson and Company Ltd, 1949); J. O. Urmson, "Motives and Causes," *Proceedings of the Aristotelian Society*, Supplementary Volume XXVI (1952), 179–94.

[19] A good defense of this position is Davidson's article, "Actions, Reasons, and Causes," *loc. cit.*, to which I am much indebted. Also see William P. Alston, "Wants, Actions, and Causal Explanations," in H. N. Castaneda, ed., *Minds, Intentionality, and Perception* (Detroit: Wayne State University Press, 1967).

wanted to turn on the light and believed that he would turn it on by flipping the switch. But suppose that, in fact, the switch in question operates the exhaust fan rather than the light. Thus, *S* does not succeed in performing the act of turning on the light. Nevertheless, it is correct to say that *S* flipped the switch *in order to* turn on the light.

What, then, is implied by saying that *S* flipped the switch "in order to" turn on the light? Evidently, this explanation implies that *S wanted* to turn on the light, and it also implies that he *believed* (at least to some degree) that he would turn on the light *by* flipping the switch. Does the *whole* of the explanans consist in the assertion that *S* wanted to turn on the light and that he believed that his flipping the switch would generate his turning on the light? Clearly not. The statement that *S* had this want and had this belief is compatible with the statement that he flipped the switch *for some other reason*, or *not for any reason at all, i.e., accidentally.* Suppose *S* wanted to turn on the light, but decided to fetch his pipe first. While reaching for the pipe, however, he accidentally flipped the switch and thereby accidentally turned on the light. Here it is true to say that *S* wanted to turn on the light and that he believed that he would turn it on by flipping the switch. But it is false to say that he flipped the switch in order to turn on the light, or that his reason for flipping the switch was to turn on the light. Thus, the statement that *S* flipped the switch *in order to* turn on the light implies more than that *S had* the indicated want and *had* the indicated belief. It also implies that his having this want and his having this belief *caused*, or *resulted in*, his flipping the switch. Such an explanation not only implies that he *had* an action-plan that included the indicated want and belief, but also implies that this action-plan *caused* (in the characteristic way) the act of flipping the switch.

Talk about an agent's *reasons* for action, we see, can be analyzed in terms of the *action-plans* which *cause* his action. When I ask why *S* did *A*—i.e., for what reason he did *A*—I presuppose that he had some action-plan that included *A* and that caused his performance of *A*. Of course, that presupposition could be wrong. There may have been no action-plan that both included *A* and caused the performance of *A*. If there was no such action-plan, then *S*'s doing *A* was not intentional; and hence there is no answer to the question *why* (i.e., for what reason) he did *A*. But if there was an action-plan that both included *A* and that caused the performance of *A*, then act *A was* done for a reason. And the point of my inquiry is to find out what that reason was. In other words, the point of my inquiry is to ascertain *what* act it was that *S* both *wanted* to perform and *believed* would be generated by (or on the same level as) act *A*.

In his book *Free Action*, A. I. Melden contends that when we explain a man's action in terms of his motives or reasons, we are simply "*redescribing*" his action. Melden says that "citing a motive is giving a fuller characterization of the action."[20] This statement is potentially quite misleading, however. It is

---

[20] Melden, *Free Action*, p. 88.

true that in answer to the question, "Why was he extending his arm?" we might reply, "He was signaling for a turn." And this reply is properly construed as giving the agent's *reason* for extending his arm. It is a mistake, however, to think that this answer is simply a way of saying *that* the agent signaled for a turn, of saying that he actually performed that action. We have already seen that the mere performance of such an act does not imply that it was the man's *reason* for acting. It is possible that he performed the act of signaling for a turn without its having been his *reason* for extending his arm. (He might not have known that extending one's arm counts as signaling.) Thus, in the context, the reply "He was signaling for a turn" means "He was *aiming* at signaling for a turn" or "His *goal* was to signal for a turn," and not merely "He exemplified the act-property of signaling for a turn." The statement is not concerned with the act-tokens actually occurring, but with the agent's aims or purposes, in short, his action-plan. Normally, when we say "What are you doing?" we are not interested in being told what things the agent is actually doing; we want to know the desires or purposes out of which he is acting. Hence, an answer to such a question is normally taken as a specification of his *desires* or *goals*, not as a description of his actual act-tokens.

This point is underlined by the fact that the performance of *certain* acts implies, or presupposes, that the agent is acting out of specific desires or purposes. The performance of such an act as *hiding from George*, or *hunting rabbits*, or *trying to repair one's watch* implies that the agent has certain goals or purposes, in other words, that he is acting out of certain specific desires. If we want to explain *S*'s reason for crouching behind a car, therefore, we can ascribe to him the further act of hiding from George. The ascription of this act implies that *S* is crouching behind the car *out of a desire* to prevent George from seeing him—that is, that his act of crouching behind the car is caused by a desire to prevent George from seeing him. Similarly, if we want to explain why *S* is playing with certain springs, we can ascribe to him the act of trying to repair his watch. The ascription of this act implies that he is playing with the springs in order to repair his watch—that is, out of a desire to repair his watch. In these cases the performance of the indicated act *presupposes* the presence of a certain desire and its causal role in the agent's behavior. Just as the performance of the act of *re*marrying presupposes that the agent has been married before, so the performance of the act of hiding from George presupposes that the agent has a certain desire, and is acting *from* that desire. Hence, although the agent's action can be explained by referring to these acts, the force of the explanation rests on an appeal to *wants* of the agent and the *causal* force of those wants.

There are many reasons why philosophers have felt that explanations in terms of reasons are not a species of causal explanation. Many of these arguments are connected with the view that wants, or motives, are not causally related to acts. This point will be taken up more fully in Chapter Four. Meanwhile, however, let me mention two other points.

First, it is important to notice that, from the point of view of the agent himself, practical reasoning does not appear as a causal process. When an agent is trying to decide what action to perform, he is trying to select the "best" course of action. A decision of this sort usually requires attention to the probable consequences of alternative acts, and sometimes requires attention to moral principles, etc. Now considerations such as these seem very far from any question concerning the causation of his action. "What will be the consequences of my doing A?" is a very different matter from "What will cause my doing A?" or "Will anything cause my doing A?" Nevertheless, although the agent, while deliberating, does not normally worry about the causes of his action, the process of weighing alternatives, of noticing their probable consequences, etc.—this process itself *constitutes* a causal process culminating in his action. Although the agent's reasoning does not focus on its own causal efficacy, it *has* causal efficacy *vis-à-vis* his action. I shall return to this point in Chapter Four.

Another source of the rejection of the view that human action is explainable by reference to causes is the tendency to assimilate causation in general to *mechanical* causation. In the minds of some philosophers, talk of causation calls up a picture of billiard balls propelling one another or levers pushing and pulling. All causation is assimilated to blind mechanism, to relations between "colorless movements," and this is taken to be incompatible with reasons or rationality. But why should causal relations obtain only between "colorless movements"? Why should all causality imply blind, unreasoning mechanism? Why can't states having intentional objects—e.g., beliefs, thoughts, intentions, desires, etc.—be involved in causal relations?

The notion of reasons and reasoning is intimately tied, I believe, to intentionalistic states. Thus, if intentionalistic states are involved in causal relations, the notion of causation should not be inimical to the notion of reason, should not imply blind, unreasoning mechanism. But from a commonsense point of view, some of the clearest cases of causality involve intentionalistic states. Among the most certain causal propositions we know may be the proposition that S's desire for sleep was caused, at least in part, by his having stayed awake for 35 hours, and that S's thinking of Vienna was caused by his wife reminding him of their trip. Similarly, I think we know that intentionalistic states are sometimes causes of other effects, including acts. One cannot say, therefore, that causality is incompatible with reasons or reasoning. Perhaps some philosophers' attempts to analyze causality have this consequence, but so much the worse, I think, for those analyses.

7. Causality and Agency

The view that acts are caused has often been opposed from another quarter, a line of opposition that centers around the concept of agency. An agent is an entity that originates activity, that makes things happen instead of passively suffering external causes to operate through him. In this sense stones and pieces of wood are not agents, but human beings are; for human beings are the sources or originators of their own activities.

The idea of universal causation, however, seems to be incompatible with this notion of human agency. If every event is caused by prior events, then a person's acts must be caused by events that occurred prior to the agent's birth. But if his acts were caused by such events, how can the *agent* be considered their cause, their source, or their originator? My contention that acts are caused by wants and beliefs opens the door to this dilemma, for it opens the door to causes of acts other than the agent himself. To be sure, I have not yet claimed that every event is caused, nor is this implied by anything said in this chapter. I believe that universal causation is a real possibility, however, as I shall argue in Chapter Six. Thus, I must confront the question of how to reconcile universal causation with the concept of agency.

The problem is twofold. First, there is the problem of agent-causation versus want-and-belief causation. If the acts of an agent are caused by his wants and beliefs, how can *he*, the agent, be considered their cause? Secondly, if an agent's acts are caused by events that preceded his birth, how can we consider *him* to be their source or originator?

In addressing these problems, I wish first to draw a distinction between *event-causation* and *object-causation*, and to contend that these are not *rival* candidates in the search for causes. There is clearly a difference between an *object* (a thing, a substance) causing *x* and an event or state causing *x*. Since Hume, philosophers have paid comparatively little attention to the role of *objects* in causal talk (though Hume himself often used the term "object" in his discussion of causality). Carrying on the Humean tradition, philosophers have reiterated the claim that causes are things that figure in laws or regularities. But it doesn't make any sense to try to place objects in a regularity, even to consider them as "factors" which, together with others, fulfill the antecedent of a causal law. It makes no sense to say, "Whenever Smith, Jones, and Brown, then . . . " or "Whenever this rock, this shoe, and this door, then . . . . " Of course, we might say "Whenever Smith *eats seafood*, then . . . " or "Whenever Smith *has a fever*, then . . . , " but these sentences would correlate something with an *event involving Smith*, or a *state of Smith*, not with *Smith*.

I believe that whenever we say that an *object*, *O*, is a cause of *x*, this presupposes that there is a *state of O* or an *event involving O* that caused, or was a partial cause, of *x*. This seems fairly clear for physical objects. We say that the *brick* was the cause of the broken window when the *impact* of the brick on the window caused the window to break. We say that the *water* caused the building to collapse when the *pressure* of the water on its walls caused its collapse. And when we say that *the masked figure* caused so-and-so to jump, we presuppose that the masked figure's *being seen* by so-and-so caused him to jump, or that the *appearance* of the masked figure caused so-and-so to jump. In none of these cases is there an *incompatibility* between the event-causation and the object-causation. If we accept the proposition that the impact of the brick on the window caused it to break, we are not obliged to *deny* the proposition that the *brick* caused it to break. If we accept the proposition that the pressure of the water caused the building to collapse, we are not obliged to *deny* that the *water* caused it to collapse.

Now agent-causation, I believe, is simply a special case of object-causation, since an agent is simply a particular kind of object or substance. And I contend that in the case of agents, as in the case of other objects, there is no incompatibility between saying that a certain agent was the (object-)cause of a certain event and saying that an event or state involving the agent was the (event-)cause of the same effect. I do not claim that agents are called the cause of an event under the same circumstances that bricks or bodies of water are called causes. I simply wish to assert that there is not always an incompatibility between saying that an agent caused x and saying that some event (or state) *of* the agent caused x. There is room for both assertions because there is room for both object-causes and event-causes; there need be no rivalry between them.

In at least one kind of case the above contention should be uncontroversial. Suppose that the light's going on was caused by an event *of* John, or *involving* John—viz., John's flipping the switch. The fact that this event is the event-cause of the light's going on is clearly not incompatible with the fact that *John* is the agent-cause of the light's going on. We can say, without contradiction, *both* that *John's flipping the switch* caused the light to go on and that *John* caused the light to go on. Similarly, I think, when an act of John's is caused by John's *wants and beliefs*, it would not be incorrect to say that *John* caused his act. (In ordinary language we do not say that people "cause" their own acts, but I see no objection to introducing this locution.) The fact that *John's wanting to turn on the light* caused John's flipping the switch does not preclude the fact that *John* caused John's flipping the switch. There is no contradiction in saying both, since John's having that want is just an *event-* (or *state-*)cause of the act while John is the *agent*-cause of the act.

Richard Taylor writes:

> It is plain that, whatever I am, I am never identical with any such event, process, or state as is usually proposed as the "real cause" of my act, such as some intention or state of willing. Hence, if it is really and unmetaphorically true, as I believe it to be, that I sometimes cause something to happen, this would seem to entail that it is *false* that any event, process, or state not identical with myself should be the real cause of it.[21]

This is precisely the point I am denying. Of course, I am not asserting that wants and beliefs are the "real" causes of acts, as *opposed* to the agent. (I

---

[21] Richard Taylor, *Action and Purpose*, p. 111.

don't know what Taylor means here by "real" cause, anyway.) I am merely asserting that it may be literally and unmetaphorically true that *I* am the cause—the agent-cause—of my act, and *also* true that *my-wanting-such-and-such* and *my-believing-such-and-such* are causes—event-causes—of my act. *I* am not identical with my wants and beliefs, but nevertheless both I *and* these states of mine can be causes of my act.

There are at least two possible reasons why someone might think that *my* being the cause of an act is incompatible with my *wants* or *beliefs* being causes of my acts. First, one might simply fail to draw the distinction between event-causation and object-causation, and therefore fail to see that they are not incompatible. Secondly, one might be led into this error by thinking of mental events or mental states as agents in their own right, like little people ensconced in the heads of regular-sized people. Since there can't be two agent-causes of the same (individual) act—so the argument would run—*I* could not be the cause of an act if my *wants* and *beliefs* were causes of it. But of course wants and beliefs are not little agents or little entities of any sort, so this second line of argument is wholly misguided.

Recently I have been arguing that want-and-belief causation of acts is *compatible* with agent-causation of acts, but I also believe that agent-causation is *explicable* in terms of want-and-belief causation. The idea of performing an *act* (in the fullest sense), as I have argued, is explicable in terms of want-and-belief causation. Similarly, the idea of something being *up to me*, or *within my power*, is connected with the idea of something being dependent on *my desires*. It is up to *me* whether or not there will be a light on in this room, for the light's being on or off is dependent on *my desires*. But it is not up to *me* whether De Gaulle is reelected, since my desires have no effect in the matter whatsoever.

A further test of the relationship between agency and wants-and-beliefs is found in the comparison of the class of things we are inclined to call "agents" or think of as "agents," and the class of things whose behavior is a function of wants and beliefs, or can be interpreted, more or less analogically, as a function of wants and beliefs. These classes are virtually co-extensive. After human beings, they include the higher animals and perhaps some sophisticated machines. The behavior of dogs, for example, is easily interpretable in terms of desires and expectations, so it is not surprising that many people treat dogs as agents almost on a par with humans. The behavior of computers also bears certain resemblances to behavior that is caused by wants and beliefs, and this accounts for the fact that predicates are sometimes applied to them which are typically reserved for human agents. By contrast, it would be almost impossible seriously to regard a rock as an agent, since rocks have no properties which incline us to attribute desires and beliefs to them.

Authors like Taylor, Chisholm,[22] and C. A. Campbell[23] apparently believe

---

[22] "Freedom and Action," *loc. cit.*

[23] "Is 'Free Will' a Pseudo-Problem?" *Mind*, LX (1951), 446–65; and *On Selfhood and Godhood* (London: The MacMillan Company, 1957).

that there are occasions on which agents cause acts without any state or event of the agent being an event-cause of these acts. But it is difficult for me to see how, if they were right, we could ever *tell* that there are such occasions. On my view, a case of grimacing done as an act is distinguishable from grimacing which occurs as a mere reflex because the-agent's-wanting-to-grimace precedes the act but does not ordinarily precede the mere reflex. But on their view, how could the distinction be made? How do I distinguish my grimacing *as an act* from my grimacing *as a reflex*? Or, to pose a slightly different problem, how do I tell that *I* am causing my grimacing and that my grimacing is not totally uncaused? On Taylor's view, acts are not *un*caused; they are caused by *agents*. But how are we to distinguish absence of causation from causation by agents? Normally we identify causes with the help of regularities, but regularities obtain with respect to events, states, processes, and the like, which are precluded *ex hypothesi* by Taylor's view. Thus, the notion of agent-causation *unconnected* with event-causation is bound to be a mysterious and obscure notion. It will be replied that the notion of event-causation is equally mysterious, since it has long eluded philosophical analysis. But the point about *analysis* is not pertinent to my argument here. I admit that I cannot *analyze* the notion of event-causation any more than Taylor can analyze *his* notion of agent-causation. At least in the case of event-causation, however, we have *some* idea of what it comes to since we have *some* idea of the conditions under which certain events can be said to cause others. Mill's methods, for example, are *some* help in this direction. But we have *no* indication, if we use Taylor's notion of agent-causation, of the conditions under which an agent causes an act.

I turn now to the problem raised by the possibility that a person's acts are caused by events which occurred prior to his birth. This would seem to imply that the agent is not the author, source, or originator of his own acts; it looks as if the source of the acts must be traced to quite different things, things which were in existence before the agent himself came into existence. But if I am right in tracing the idea of agency to causation by wants and beliefs, this picture is unwarranted. As long as the act is caused by the wants and beliefs of the agent, then *he* is the author, the source, the originator of the act. The fact that these wants and beliefs were themselves caused by much earlier events does not affect the matter. There is no limit to the number of (event-)causes that a given event may have. Thus, the fact that the act was caused by events of seventy years ago does not vitiate the fact that the act was also caused by the current wants and beliefs of the agent. The events of seventy years ago had their effect on the act only *via* the wants and beliefs, and therefore only *via* the agency of the person who performed it. To paraphrase Hobart's classic discussion of the issue,[24] the past finished its business

---

[24] "Free Will as Involving Determination and Inconceivable Without It," *Mind*, XLIII, No. 169 (1934) 1–27.

when it produced the agent as he is, with his wants and beliefs; it does not stretch out a ghostly hand to *compete* with these wants and beliefs in causing the agent's acts. Nor does it compete with the agent himself, as if it were some *other* agent, trying to overpower the agent in an attempt to achieve its own goals and objectives.

We see, then, that the concept of agency is not threatened by the prospect of universal causation. It remains to be seen whether other concepts, such as ability or decision, are threatened by universal causation. These points will be treated in Chapters Six and Seven.

CHAPTER FOUR

Wanting

1. Occurrent Wants and Standing Wants

John is concentrating on finishing the lawn by six o'clock. He is giving all his attention to mowing it as quickly as possible, with the thought of getting done by six. During this period, whether it be a few seconds or a whole minute, John has an *occurrent* want to finish mowing the lawn by six o'clock. The thought of finishing the lawn by six *occurs* to him, occupies his attention, fills his consciousness. It is a datable event or process. During the same period it would also be correct to say that John wanted to be president of his company. But his wanting to be president of the company is not an *occurrent* want during this time, for John has not been thinking about the company or his future at the company. Nevertheless, we could say that John wants to be president of his company because he has a *disposition* to have occurrent wants to this effect, and this disposition is present while John is mowing the lawn, though it is not being manifested. I shall say that John has a *standing* want to be president of his company.

This example illustrates the distinction between occurrent wants and standing wants.[1] An occurrent want is a mental event or mental process; it is a "going on" or "happening" in consciousness. A standing want, on the other hand, is a disposition or propensity to have an occurrent want, a disposition that lasts with the agent for a reasonable length of time. Though it is perhaps theoretically possible for a person to have such a disposition without ever having any manifestations thereof, we would not ascribe such a disposition to anyone unless the relevant manifestations appeared from time to time. Hence, a standing want for x is ascribed to someone only if he has a number of occurrent wants for x over a period of time.

---

[1] I owe this distinction to William P. Alston. See his article, "Motives and Motivation," in Paul Edwards, ed., *The Encyclopedia of Philosophy* (New York: The Macmillan Company, 1967), where he uses the terms "aroused wants" and "latent wants."

The occurrent/standing distinction is useful for talking about beliefs as well as wants. (Many points in this chapter hold, *mutatis mutandis*, for beliefs as well as wants, but I won't bother to mention this in every case.) There were various times during the past month when John had occurrent beliefs that $7+4=11$—namely when he consciously affirmed or assented to this, e.g. while doing a sum. But at *any* time during this month, not only on those occasions, it would have been correct to say that John believed that $7+4=11$, meaning that he had this standing belief at that time. At any time during the month, *if* John's attention had been turned to the question of whether $7+4=11$, he would have had an occurrent belief to this effect. It is for the same reason that we ascribe a standing want to become company president: at any time during the past year, *if* John's attention had been turned to the prospect of his becoming company president, he would have found that prospect appealing or attractive. Moreover, there were numerous occasions on which he did think of this prospect and found it attractive.

Which kind of want and belief is relevant in intentional action? I said in Chapter Three that intentional acts (indeed, all acts) are caused by wants and beliefs of the agent. But which wants and beliefs function as causes of acts, occurrent ones or standing ones? Generalizations L and L' of Chapter Three say that whenever a person has certain wants and beliefs he will perform certain acts. But do L and L' refer to occurrent wants and beliefs or to standing wants and beliefs?

Consider the following example. Before going to the supermarket I make a mental list of the items I should buy. When first thinking through this list I have an occurrent want to buy each of the items, and as I drive to the supermarket I have further occurrent wants for these items. Of course, I do not have an occurrent want for each of these items at every moment along the way. But at every moment from the time I make up the list until I leave the supermarket, I have a standing want to buy each of these items. At each moment it is true of me that *if* my attention were focused on whether to buy one of these items, I would regard it favorably. Now suppose that I fail to buy one of the items, say cheese, simply because it slips my mind and I forget to buy it. How does this jibe with generalizations L or L'? If L and L' were interpreted as referring to standing wants, this case would be quite anomalous. I certainly had a standing want to buy cheese (and the relevant standing generational beliefs) while I was in the supermarket. Moreover, I was in a position to buy cheese at the time and had no desires incompatible with my desire to buy cheese. Thus, L or L' would lead us to expect that my standing desire (and beliefs) would cause my doing some basic act that would generate my actually buying cheese. Why, then, did I in fact fail to buy cheese? On the other hand, if we intepret L and L' in terms of occurrent wants, the case is perfectly straightforward. Although I earlier had had occurrent wants to buy cheese, when the time for buying cheese arrived (i.e., when I was in the supermarket), I had no such occurrent want. Since the desire to buy cheese did not become occurrent or activated at *this* time, it is not surprising that I in fact failed to buy cheese.

Consider a similar case. Suppose I have been told that in soliciting at a particular house one must be careful about the dog. Whistling three times before entering the yard will keep him friendly, but otherwise he will be very nasty. I repeat this fact to myself numerous times and establish a standing belief to that effect. This standing belief consists in a disposition to recognize this fact consciously from time to time, and in a readiness to assent to it whenever I focus my attention on it. I also have a standing want to keep the dog friendly. But now as I approach this particular house, my attention is caught by something in the sky. I forget entirely about the dog, and enter the yard without whistling three times. Is there anything puzzling about my failure to whistle three times? If we understand *L* and *L'* as dealing with occurrent wants and beliefs, then there is nothing strange here. I failed to whistle three times because I had no *occurrent* want to keep the dog friendly or to ward him off, and I had no *occurrent* belief that the way to keep him friendly is to whistle three times. On this interpretation of *L* or *L'*, the case is perfectly understandable. But suppose *L* and *L'* were construed as referring to *standing* wants and beliefs. Then the case makes no sense. For I certainly had a *standing* want to keep the dog friendly and a *standing* belief that whistling three times was the way to keep him friendly.

These cases indicate that standing wants and beliefs do not by themselves cause acts. Standing wants and beliefs can affect action only by becoming activated, that is, by being manifested in occurrent wants and beliefs. My standing want to keep the dog friendly and my standing belief about the effectiveness of whistling did not result in my actually whistling. But if this standing want and standing belief had become activated at the appropriate time, then I would have whistled. It appears, then, that the role of causing action must be assigned to occurrent wants and beliefs, not standing ones.

A difficulty for the view that acts are always caused by occurrent wants arises in the question of whether there are really enough of these occurrent wants to account for all action. The suggestion that every act is caused by an occurrent want sounds perilously like the old theory of volitions that is now so widely disparaged. It sounds like the view that for each act-tree there is one or more mental occurrences which precede that act-tree and "trigger" it. But is this a defensible contention? Is each of our briefest acts triggered by a mental occurrence?

To elucidate and defend my position, two important points must be emphasized.[2] First, it should be recognized that no temporal restrictions have been placed on the length of basic acts. In particular, no upper temporal limit has been introduced. The examples of basic act-types I have given include such things as raising one's hand, taking a (single) step, turning one's

---

[2] I am indebted here to William P. Alston.

head, etc., all of the tokens of which would be no longer than one or two seconds in duration. The reader may have inferred from this that no act-token of longer duration could be a basic act-token. But this inference is unwarranted. There is no reason why the property of *taking ten steps* (or of *taking enough steps to move from here to there*) could not be a basic act-type, even though an exemplification of such an act-type might occupy a longer interval of time than the basic act-tokens considered until now. If such properties are basic act-types, then it is possible for an agent to have a single occurrent want to exemplify this act-type, and to proceed to exemplify it without further occurrent wants. A desire to take ten steps might cause an act-token of taking ten steps without the necessity of having a different occurrent desire immediately prior to each of the ten steps.

Second, we must recall the clause in our recursive definition of an act-token which stipulated that any temporal part of an act-token is an act-token. Now suppose that S's taking ten steps (from t_1 to t_{10}) is a basic act-token, caused by an occurrent want just prior to t_1. Then each of the ten steps taken during this interval is also an act-token, despite the fact that there was no distinct occurrent want immediately preceding, and directed at, each distinct step. Since S's taking the *ten* steps was caused by an occurrrent want of his, S's taking the *third* step was caused by that same occurrent want. This satisfies the requirement that all act-tokens be caused by occurrent wants. But S never had a distinct occurrent want to take the *third* step. This shows that not every tiny act-token is caused by an immediately preceding occurrent want to do *it*. In other words, an act-token which is a part of a larger act-token must be caused by an occurrent want, but not necessarily by an occurrent want specific to and immediately preceding it.

The range of properties that we can exemplify at will—i.e., as a consequence of a single occurrent want—grows with practice and training. When a sequential course of action is novel or unfamiliar, the agent must concentrate on small temporal parts of it. But when this kind of activity becomes routine, continuous concentration is unnecessary. When first learning to tie a bow, a child will concentrate on each phase of the process; a separate occurrent want will precede each part of the sequence. But once the process becomes habitual, the child forms a single want for the whole activity and does it all the way through without any further occurrent wants. Similarly, when first learning to play a scale on the piano, a child may have to concentrate on finger movement for each separate note. But an accomplished pianist may play an entire scale (or more) as a result of a single occurrent want.

Discovering the precise range of our basic act-types is an empirical matter. Although no conceptual limits can be placed on the temporal length of basic acts, there do in fact seem to be limits, both upper and lower. Lower limits apparently exist, because it does not seem possible to break an activity down into indefinitely smaller parts, *each* of which, when isolated, can be done at will. Though a person can sing a tune through from the beginning, he may not be able to sing any given portion of it starting in the middle. It is equally evident that there are upper limits on the length of basic acts. There are projects that are too lengthy and complicated to be governed by a single occurrent want. They must be subdivided into smaller, manageable parts, each of which must be preceded by an occurrent want. For example, even though I frequently walk from my office to a certain luncheon spot, I cannot execute the entire three-block walk simply as a result of a single occurrent want. I can, perhaps, take ten or twenty steps at a time without concentration, but after each sequence of steps of this sort I must "monitor" my progress to see how far I have come and then form an occurrent want for the next stage of the project. Whenever a desired project is too lengthy for a single occurrent want, it is broken down into successive stages, each of which is preceded by an occurrent want. This is especially necessary when the project must be accomplished over a discontinuous stretch of time. The project of painting my house, for example, takes several weeks for execution, and it cannot be completed through continuous activity. The project is executed by first forming an occurrent want for the entire activity, and then forming occurrent wants for the various stages of the project at various appropriate times. I begin with an occurrent want to do the whole thing—i.e., I want to paint the house. Then I form occurrent wants for subsections of the project—e.g., a want to paint the front of the house today, or a want to paint a particular two-foot area in the next five seconds (approximately). At the outset, when a want for the entire project is formed, the details for executing the project are not yet conceived. The precise manner of it is worked out for each smaller phase by wants and beliefs occurring just prior to that phase. In uttering a long and complicated sentence, I may start with an over-all desire to express a certain thought, without yet wanting to utter any specific words. A want to utter certain specific words to begin the sentence then forms, and additional wants for additional specific phrases are formed once earlier phrases are actually uttered.[3]

Sometimes a project goes haywire because the wrong subplan wants arise after the project is set in motion. I frequently call a certain number in Yonkers, 914 YO 5–3438. Each time I do this, I begin with an occurrent want to dial that whole number. As I proceed, a smaller want is formed to dial each successive digit. On one occasion, however, I want to call a different number in Yonkers, 914 YO 8–7183. Having dialed 9–1–4–Y–O, habit results in my forming an occurrent want to dial 5 instead of 8. And similarly, once I have dialed 5, I form an occurrent want to dial 3. In this manner, I dial the old familiar number instead of the one I originally planned. Here each of the smaller dialing acts—my dialing 9, my dialing 1, my dialing 4, etc.—is in-

---

[3] An elaborate theory of behavior in terms of plans and subplans is given by George A. Miller, Eugene Galanter, and Karl H. Pribram, *Plans and the Structure of Behavior* (New York: Holt, Rinehart & Winston, Inc., 1960).

tentional, since each was caused by an appropriate want. But the act of dialing the entire number, 914 YO 5–3438, is *not* intentional, for I did not plan to dial *that* number.

Sometimes motor habit leads an agent into movement or behavior which he does not plan at all, and which therefore cannot really be considered "action." After eating lunch I feel a piece of food between my teeth and have a desire to remove it with my tongue. I do not plan a course of continuous tongue movement, but I do plan one or two tries at it. Once set in motion, however, the tongue keeps working at the morsel. Fifteen minutes later I find my tongue still going, though I had meanwhile forgotten about it entirely. Here I think it is doubtful whether we should call the latter phase of the tongue activity an "act" of mine at all; perhaps we should say that the *tongue* was moving rather than that I was moving my tongue. This is precisely what my analysis of acts would have us say, since these latter tongue movements were not contained in any action-plan of the agent. In walking to the restaurant for lunch, habit helps me execute certain steps, but these were certainly planned and desired. In the present case habit works overtime, as it were, and leads to movements which were not at all planned.

It must be conceded, however, that the analysis of action I have given is not ideally suited for dealing with habit, nor has it been designed with habitual behavior in mind. The difference between the steps I take in walking to lunch and the movements of my tongue is not really as great as our analysis would suggest. The analysis classifies the former as acts and the latter as not acts at all, but this fails to bring out the fact that there is a continuum on which these cases lie fairly close to each other. Thus, my analysis makes a sharp distinction where the boundary is blurred. Perhaps this result is inevitable, given that the focus of my attention is with maximally purposive action. I think my analysis is compatible with behavior that is ruled by habit, but it is not designed to handle habitual behavior with real subtlety.

2. Wants as Mental Events

Having committed myself to the unfashionable view that acts are caused by mental events, I must now defend myself by discussing the nature of these mental occurrences. Opponents of the view that acts are caused by mental events have usually been concerned with "volitions" or "acts of will," which in the past had been invoked as causes of acts. Since I do not speak of volitions or acts of will, my theory is not directly subject to these criticisms. But since the critics would surely maintain that their points were equally valid for *my* mental events—i.e., wants—their arguments must be met.

To begin my defense, let me dispel some of the misconceptions spread by critics of the mental events view. First, we must not identify wants with bodily sensations or with sensory presentations. The latter two species of mental events are characterized by phenomenal location: they are presented as spatially localizable. A pain, for example, is presented as being in the foot, in the tooth, or in the head, though of course it isn't really *in* one of these parts of the body as blood is *in* the body. Similarly, visual and auditory presentations have apparent locations—to the left of the subject, to his right, behind him, etc. In contrast with sensations and sensory presentations, however, wants have no phenomenal locations. I think of the *object* of my want as being located in a particular place, but I do not think of my *want* as being somewhere in my body, as pains, itches, or throbbings are felt as being in the body. Desires are often *accompanied* by sensation or imagery. A desire to drink may be accompanied by dryness of the palate, a desire to jump seven feet may be accompanied by bodily tautness, and a desire to see one's beloved may be accompanied by an image of her. These sensations and images are incidental to the desires themselves. One can want to drink without feeling dry, want to jump seven feet without feeling taut, and want to see one's beloved without picturing her.

Philosophers who assume that all mental events are sensations, feelings, sensory presentations, and the like, will naturally be disappointed when they try to find wants that answer to these descriptions. In the section of his *Concept of Mind* which deals with enjoying and wanting,[4] Ryle argues that wants are not any kind of feeling.

> Similar considerations, which need not be developed, would show that "dislike," "want" and "desire" do not denote pangs, itchings or gnawings.

And from this he makes the totally unwarranted inference that wants are not any sort of mental episode or event.

> Liking and disliking, joy and grief, desire and aversion are, then, not "internal" episodes which their owner witnesses, but his associates do not witness. They are not episodes and so are not the sorts of things which can be witnessed or unwitnessed.

It is a non sequitur to argue that because wants are not feelings or sensations, therefore they are not (mental) episodes. There is no reason to think that feelings, sensations, and sensory presentations exhaust the list of mental episodes.

A second misconception to be dispelled is the notion that wants are a species of (inner) *acts*. I know of no author who criticizes the view that *wants* are mental events by first assuming that they are acts; but much of the criticism of volitions is concerned with their alleged status as acts, and it is important to realize that these criticisms cannot be applied to wants.

In his discussion of volitions Melden argues as follows:

---

[4] Gilbert Ryle, *The Concept of Mind* (London: Hutchinson and Company Ltd., 1949), pp. 107–110.

Grant for a moment that an event labelled an "act of volition" produces a muscle movement, there is surely a difference between an act of volition occurring and my performing such an act. . . . There is a difference between the occurrence of an act of volition and my performing such an act—who can say that volitions may not occur through no doing of the subject, and in consequence, of interior mental events deep within the hidden recesses of the self? If so, willing the muscle movement is not enough, one must will the willing of the muscle movement, and so on *ad infinitum*.[5]

Melden is right in saying that if every act is caused by an act of volition, then acts of volition must themselves be caused by acts of volition, and we must countenance the existence of an infinite chain of acts of volition. But this problem does not arise for the view that acts are caused by *wants*. Wants simply are not acts, and hence there is no requirement that they be caused by further wants.[6]

The view that volitions are acts would incline one to think that volitions are things we do *in order* to bring about certain physical acts, in the way that we do the act of flipping the switch *in order* to turn on the light. But it would certainly be a mistake to think that in order to perform any physical act, we must first perform a mental act, such as a volition or a want, as a *means* to performing the desired physical act. This picture of things is rightly criticized by Richard Taylor.

To act willfully is not . . . to perform or to undergo some inner, unobservable twitch or convulsion of the soul in the hope or expectation that this will somehow produce a desired twitch or jerk of the body, like the motion of a limb or the tongue.[7]

My contention that wants cause acts, however, does not imply that wants are acts we perform (or events we undergo) *in order* to bring about physical movements, so my position is not susceptible to this sort of criticism. To say that wants are things I do *in order* to produce physical acts suggests that whenever I want to move my hand (or get my hand to move), I must then produce something which will cause my hand to move, and this thing I must produce is a want to move my hand. But obviously if I *already* want to move my hand, I do not have to *produce* such a want as a means to moving my hand. When I want to move my hand, I do not have to cast about for *anything* as a *means* to moving my hand; given the want, I just proceed to move my hand.

Having dispelled two misconceptions about wants, what can be said posi-

---

[5] Melden, *Free Action* (London: Routledge & Kegan Paul Ltd., 1961; New York: Humanities Press Inc.), p. 45.

[6] In Section 3 I shall argue that many wants *are* caused by other wants. But there are two points to remember. First, not all wants are caused by other wants: there are some intrinsic wants. Secondly, wants are never (immediately) caused by *meta-wants*: wanting x is not caused by wanting to want x. (See Chapter Three, Section 4.)

[7] Richard Taylor, *Action and Purpose*, p. 77.

tively about the nature of wanting? As indicated in Chapter Three, to want x is to find the prospect of x attractive, nice, good, appropriate, fitting, etc. To have an *occurrent* want is to have an *occurrent* thought of x as attractive, nice, good, etc., a favorable regarding, viewing, or taking of the prospect of x.[8]

Wanting x is closely related to enjoying x or finding x pleasant. Enjoying x consists in finding the actual occurrence of x nice, good, appropriate, etc. It is a mode of regarding or taking the occurrence of x. Wanting x is distinguished from enjoying x according to the modality in which the agent views x. One enjoys x at t only if one regards x as *actually* occurring at t. One wants x at t only if one regards x as not yet having occurred, or not yet known to have occurred—that is, as a merely *possible* occurrence.

Wanting x should not be identified with believing that you would enjoy x, though it is true that we enjoy most of the things we wanted. It is possible to want something, however, even if you realize, cognitively, that you won't enjoy it when it happens. Conversely, there are things which you know you would enjoy but which you do not find attractive.

Wanting x, like enjoying x, is not essentially language-bound. Enjoying x does not necessarily involve *saying* to oneself: "The occurrence of x is nice." Nor does an occurrent want for x necessarily involve a silent utterance: "The occurrence of x (or my possessing x) would be nice." Animals can enjoy things and desire things though they have no language.

Although the capacity for desire does not require the capacity for language, it is arguable that desire does require the capacity for conceptualization. Being pleased by the prospect of eating does seem to presuppose possession of the *concept* of eating. Moreover, animals can plausibly be said to have at least rudimentary concepts, however one analyzes the notion of having a concept. Dogs certainly have the concept of food, and of being fed, though they do not have a *word* for it. Probably there are certain levels of conceptualization which cannot be achieved without language, but primitive levels of conceptualization, I think, are not language-dependent. Because dogs have the concept of food and of being fed, they can want to be fed and believe that they are about to be fed. But they do not have the complicated concept of playing chess, so they cannot have wants to play chess or beliefs that their master is playing chess.

If occurrent wants and beliefs required private soliloquys it would indeed be difficult to have enough of them to cover all our intentional acts. A single act-tree, after all, normally contains many intentional acts, and corresponding to each of these is a belief. If all of these beliefs necessitated a private utterance, there would not be much time left for overt behavior. I must emphasize, therefore, that having occurrent beliefs and occurrent wants does not imply reciting the content of these beliefs and wants in one's head. Somehow

---

[8] Cf. G. F. Stout, *Analytic Psychology* (London: Allan and Unwin, 1918), I, p. 133: "Both desire and aversion . . . are modes of being attentive."

human beings have the ability to grasp an indefinite number of things in the mind in what seems like a single flash. As I walk down the street, for example, I am aware of all of the following facts in a single stroke: that the curb is to my left; that the street starts to curve a few yards away from me; that there are many people crossing the street, both men and women; that a neon sign is to my right; that a woman with a green hat is walking toward me; that dusk is falling; that it is warm outside; etc. I am *aware* of each of these things during a single moment, and in this sense I have occurrent beliefs of them during this moment. But I certainly do not *describe* these things to myself, nor do I even *concentrate* on them. I simply take them all in effortlessly.

Occurrent wants and beliefs do not come in discrete packages. Not only is there no silent sentence corresponding to each belief or want, there is no other discrete "impulse" or "throb" or "flash" for each want or belief. Such discrete packages would imply that there is a definite number of beliefs or wants that one has during a given interval. But beliefs and wants are not countable in this way. Perhaps this is clearer if we speak of *thoughts*, rather than occurrent wants and beliefs. Normally there is no correct answer to the question, "How many thoughts did you have just now?" Of course, if we ask about a particular proposition *p*, "Did you just have a thought that *p* (or about *p*)?" an answer should be forthcoming, yes or no. But there is no definite number of such propositions for which a yes answer can be given. This is reflected in the study of intentional acts. If we ask an agent whether he had realized he would (or might) perform a certain act, there is normally a yes or no answer forthcoming. But there is no definite number of acts for which there is a yes answer, just as there is no definite number of intentional acts he has performed.

Let me turn now to the problem of the knowledge of one's wants. An understanding of how we know our own wants is an important ingredient in a full understanding of the nature of wanting. The topic has come into special prominence recently with the claim by certain authors that our knowledge of our own wants, intentions, and (derivatively) actions is significantly different from our knowledge of ordinary empirical facts. In their article "Decision, Intention, and Certainty," for example, Stuart Hampshire and H. L. A. Hart write:

> There is a kind of certainty about human actions, wants, likes, and dislikes, which is different from the kind of certainty about these subjects that is based upon empirical evidence: it is a kind of certainty, or knowledge, to which the notion of evidence is irrelevant.[9]

It is true, I think, that we do not normally need *evidence* to know our occurrent wants or beliefs, that we do not have to *infer* them from other sources.

---

[9] *Mind*, LXVII (1958) 1–12; reprinted in Herbert Morris, ed., *Freedom and Responsibility* (Stanford, Calif.: Stanford University Press, 1961).

Nor do we have to focus or concentrate on our wants to have a sort of knowledge of them, because a kind of implicit knowledge is already contained in them, as it were. Compare the case of thinking about x or attending to x. In the process of thinking about x there is already an implicit awareness that one is thinking about x. There is no need for reflection here, for taking a step back from thinking about x in order to examine it and see if it is a case of thinking about x. When we are thinking about x, the mind is focused on x, not on our *thinking* of x. Nevertheless, the process of thinking about x carries with it a nonreflective self-awareness. The same is true for wanting. Wanting x (occurrently) consists in a favorable regarding, taking, or awareness of (the prospect of) x. To be aware of my favorable regarding of x, I do not need to reflect on it; my regarding x favorably already contains self-awareness. Accordingly, if I am currently having a want for a chocolate eclair, and the waitress asks me what I want, I do not have to *examine* my phenomenal field to ascertain what it is that I want. I simply express the content of my want, which I am aware of simply in virtue of *having* the want.

Notice that locutions which are ordinarily used to challenge or deny a statement are interpreted otherwise when a person avows or expresses a want (or belief). This is partly because there is a strong presumption that the utterer could not have been mistaken in simply expressing a want (or belief). Because of this, utterances of the form "I want . . . " are normally dealt with simply as requests, not as statements of alleged fact worthy of investigation. Normally when one person says p and another person replies, *not-p*, the latter is denying the former's statement. But if I said "I want an eclair," and the waitress said, "No, you don't want an eclair," I would not interpret her utterance as denying that I want an eclair. (Of course, if I knew she was a philosophy student, I might interpret her remark as a denial, as an attempt at philosophical humor.) The most natural interpretation of her remark would be as advice—i.e., "Don't get an eclair," implying that the eclairs are not very good, or that I am too fat to be eating eclairs, etc. Similarly, the question "Are you sure that p?" would normally be interpreted as a challenge to my evidence. But if the waitress had said, "Are you sure you want a chocolate eclair?" I would not interpret her as challenging the evidence which underlies my utterance. Rather, I would interpret her as asking me whether my desire for an eclair was firm and settled or shaky and tentative.

If I have an occurrent want for an eclair at the time I am asked by the waitress, I do not have to pause and examine myself in order to answer. But if earlier I had had an occurrent desire, but am now thinking about something else when asked, there may be a significant pause between her question and my answer. Here it may appear that I am "looking about" for my desire, but this is not what actually is happening. In pausing to think before I give an answer, there are two things I could be doing. I may be trying to remember what I wanted earlier, so as to let that earlier occurrent want serve as my decision. Or I may be trying to "activate" or "call up" that desire—that is, on the assumption that the occurrent desire which I had has lapsed into a standing desire, I may be trying to allow that standing desire to manifest itself now in consciousness. Once this standing desire becomes occurrent, however, I do not have to inspect it or reflect on it to know what it is I desire. When the desire is activated, I know what it is and simply proceed to express it to the waitress.

Notice that I do not have immediate knowledge of my standing wants in the way that I have immediate knowledge of my occurrent wants. One reason for this, of course, is that standing wants are just dispositions, not events in consciousness. But a further reason is that a standing want is a *long-lasting* disposition, so that to say I have a standing want is to go beyond the past or present states of my consciousness. There are many times at which I have a certain momentary occurrent want, but am interested in whether this is indicative of a long-lasting want. I may have a momentary desire to marry a certain woman but wonder whether I shall continue to have this desire in the future. Here I might say, "I wonder whether I really want to marry this woman." A slightly different case is where my occurrent wants keep changing. At one moment I want to buy a Ford, at the next moment a Chevrolet, then a Ford again, then a Dodge, etc. Here I am likely to say, "I don't know what I really want." This does not mean that I am ignorant of any of my occurrent wants. What it means is that I don't know what *standing* want I have, what permanent want I have. Or, more likely, it means that I simply have no stable, permanent want on the matter.

I have said that having an occurrent want carries with it a sort of knowledge of one's want. But I do not mean that having an occurrent want carries with it the ability to *say correctly* what it is that one wants. This is for two reasons. First, I may want a certain object that I see but not know what *kind* of object it is. I can point to it, or say where it is, but I cannot say what object I want in any further way. Or I may think that the object is an *F* and say, "I want that *F* over there." But in fact the object over there may not be an *F* at all. In these cases, however, there is still an obvious sense in which I know what I want. Secondly, there are some cases in which a want is itself very indefinite, indeterminate, or vague; a mere craving for I-know-not-what. Here I am unable to express my want in words, but this is not because I am ignorant of something about my want, but rather because the want itself is unclear.

It must also be emphasized that knowledge of one's occurrent wants is only assured during the moment of the want itself; it is easy to forget that one had an occurrent want, especially a fleeting one, once it is gone. Even wants which were occurrent fairly recently are sometimes forgotten, as when I find myself going into the kitchen but no longer remembering why I am going. While in the living room I had an occurrent want to put the butter back into the refrigerator, but in the meantime I have forgotten why I came into the kitchen. In view of these facts, upon remembering an act that you performed but failing to remember an occurrent want that might have caused it, you should not conclude straightaway that there *was* no occurrent want that caused it. You may well have *forgotten* having had that occurrent want.

A person is particularly apt to forget, or somehow to push from recognition, the occurrence of desires or aversions of which he is ashamed or embarrased. Just as we tend readily to forget painful or shameful experiences, we also tend to forget having had, and having acted from, reprehensible or unflattering desires. Though we are aware of these desires as they occur, we quickly forget them or deny to ourselves that they occurred; and if some action resulted from such desires, we try to pretend, to others and even to ourselves, that the action was caused by other desires or aversions instead. In many cases, of course, an act is caused jointly by several motives; so what we do is focus our attention on the ones we find acceptable and gloss over and forget the desires that are shameful.

The possibility of completely unconscious desires—ones which we are *never* aware of —constitutes another challenge to my account of wants and knowledge of one's wants. It is often said that some of our acts flow from desires which we are wholly unconscious of, and this is a hypothesis which I do not want to exclude. What I do wish to maintain, however, is that the notion of an unconscious desire is one that violates one of the main criteria for the ordinary notion of desire, in the way that the notion of a freakish dog violates our ordinary notion of a dog. It is part of our notion of an ordinary (occurrent) desire that an agent is aware of this desire. But there are other aspects of the notion of desire which may be satisfied even if this criterion is violated. These points will be treated in Section 5 of this chapter.

It has become fashionable, particularly since Ryle's work, to regard wants and other similar states as dispositions to act in certain ways, rather than as genuine episodes within consciousness. While I agree that the propensity to give rise to acts is an important dimension of the concept of a want, this dimension does not tell the whole story. One salient failing of a purely dispositional approach is the difficulty it faces in accounting for knowledge of one's own occurrent wants. If a want consisted solely in a disposition to behave overtly in specifiable ways, then it would seem that the only way to tell you want x is to make inferences from your overt behavior. But clearly an agent does not need to infer his wants from his behavior in the way that a third person does. An agent has a sort of "privileged access" to his own (occurrent) wants; his reasons for acting are knowable to him in a way that they are not knowable to others. This fact is left unaccounted for by a purely dispositional analysis of wanting.

While it is important to recognize the fact of non-observational and non-inferential knowledge of one's own wants, we should not allow this fact an exaggerated role in the theory of *action*. From the fact that a person has non-observational knowledge of his own wants it does not follow that he has non-observational knowledge of his own *acts*. Miss Anscombe says that the class of intentional actions is a subclass of the class of things known without observation.[10] But I think that this is a mistake. I know without observation that I *want* to turn on the light, and perhaps that I am *trying* to turn on the light. But I do not know without observation that I *am* turning on the light, though this is an intentional act-token, because I cannot know without observation that I am succeeding in turning on the light. Perhaps I can know without observation that if I am turning on the light, then I am turning it on intentionally; still, I do not know without observation that I am intentionally turning on the light. Again, it is true that I can know my action-plan without observation, but this does not entail that I can know my *action* without observation.

Other writers, such as Hampshire and Hart,[11] have argued that there is a non-inductive knowledge, or even certainty, of one's own future actions, based on the non-inductive or non-observational knowledge of one's own wants or intentions. But this too is a mistake. I cannot have completely non-inductive knowledge of what I shall do in the future, first, because I cannot know non-inductively what I shall be *able* to do in the future, and secondly, because I cannot know non-inductively what I shall still want or intend to do in the future. I may know non-inductively what I want *now* to do in the future, but there is always a possibility that I shall change my mind, and this possibility must be handled with inductive or empirical information. Admittedly, there is a non-inductive or non-observational *component* in my knowledge of what I shall do in the future, for I know non-inductively what I *now* want to do later, and this is some grounds (depending on the act) for believing that I *will* do it later. The claim that there is a non-inductive *component* is much weaker, however, than the claim that I have non-inductive knowledge of my future acts. And it does not justify thinking of human action as in a non-empirical realm, quite distinct from purely physical events. For, notice, if sense-datum propositions or other basic propositions are the foundation of all empirical knowledge, and if these propositions are known immediately and non-observationally, then there is a non-observational *component* in our knowledge of all physical facts.

3. Practical Inference

If a man believes that *p* and believes that *p* implies *q*, then, characteristically, he will believe that *q*. I say "characteristically" because men usually but not always make inferences that are warranted—at least in the case of fairly obvious inferences. Similarly, if a man wants *x* and believes that *y* is a means to *x*, then, characteristically, he will want *y*. The term "characteristically" is inserted for the same reason as before, but for a further reason

---

[10] G. E. M. Anscombe, *Intention*, p. 14.

[11] *Op. cit.*; also see Hampshire's book, *Freedom of the Individual* (London: Chatto and Windus Ltd, 1965).

too. Although *y* may be a means to *x*, the man may also think that *y* will lead to undesirable consequences, so that, on the whole, he does not want *y*. This is similar to nondeductive inference, in which a certain body of evidence makes it likely that *p*, while the addition of further evidence to the original body of evidence makes it unlikely that *p*.

The term "inference" is commonly applied to cases in which a person comes to believe one proposition on the basis of his belief of one or more other propositions. We may further use the term "inference" in cases where a person comes to have a certain want on the basis of some combination of other wants and beliefs. The former kind of inference I shall call "*cognitive inference*" and the latter kind "*practical inference.*" A study of practical inference is important for an understanding of wants and their relation to action.

In studying cognitive inference, we must distinguish between the propositions believed by the agent and the believings of those propositions. The importance of this is illustrated by noticing two senses of "because" that pertain to cognitive inference, one pertaining to the propositions, the other to the beliefs.

Suppose that from the propositions that all men are mortal and that Socrates is a man, *S* infers that Socrates is mortal. The content of this inference—i.e., the propositions involved—is as follows.

(p):   All men are mortal.

(q):   Socrates is a man.

(r):   Socrates is mortal.

In making this inference *S* says to himself (as it were) that (r) is true *because* (p) and (q) are true. Here "because" signifies a *logical* relationship, holding between the conjunction of (p) and (q), on the one hand, and (r). Put another way, to say that (r) is true "because" (p) and (q) are true is to say that (p) and (q) constitute a *reason* for accepting (r). In this case, of course, we have a logically sufficient reason for accepting the conclusion, but in nondeductive inference the premises constitute a reason, though not a logically sufficient reason, for accepting the conclusion.

There is a second sense of "because" that might be used in describing *S*'s inference. This can be brought out by considering propositions $B_S(p)$, $B_S(q)$, and $B_S(r)$.

$B_S(p)$:   *S* believes that (p).
$B_S(q)$:   *S* believes that (q).
$B_S(r)$:   *S* believes that (r).

Since *S* inferred (r) from (p) and (q), we can say that *S* believes (r) *because* of his believing (p) and his believing (q). The "because" in this case is *causal* rather than logical. There is no causal relation between Socrates being a man, all men being mortal, and Socrates being mortal. But there is a causal relation between S's *believing* (p) and (q) and S's *believing* (r). The process in which S sees that (p) and (q) are a good reason for accepting (r), and thereupon accepts (r), is a causal process. Philosophers who deny that inference is a causal process may be led to their position by attending only to the relationship between propositions such as (p), (q), and (r), not to the relationship between propositions such as $B_S(p)$, $B_S(q)$, and $B_S(r)$. (Of course, the latter three *propositions* are not causally related, but the *events* they describe are causally related.)

Practical inference has the same structural features as cognitive inference, with the same twin senses of "because." There are two special problems associated with practical inference, however. First, there is no set of rules of practical reasoning which correspond to rules of deduction. This problem should not be overemphasized, though, since there is a similar lacuna in inductive reasoning. In any event, I shall not make any proposals in this area. The second problem is that there is no standard way to distinguish between the content of a want and the want itself. To assert that S has a certain belief, we say, for example, "S believes that the sun is rising." To express the content or object of S's belief we simply delete the first three words and obtain, "The sun is rising." But the case is different with wants, as there is no standard way of dealing with wants and their contents or objects. We may say, "S wants to win the game," but if we delete the first part of this sentence, we only obtain the phrase "to win the game," an incomplete form of speech.

There are several ways one might try to formulate the content of a desire. An evaluative phrase, like "x would be good," might be employed. Thus, if S wants the Tigers to win the pennant, the content of his want could be expressed as, "The Tigers' winning the pennant would be good." An alternative formulation would make use of the imperative mood. Thus, the content of this same want would be rendered, "Tigers, win the pennant." The imperative mood is clearly inadequate, however, for it is inapplicable where the desired event involves no agent, such as the desire for it to rain. The evaluative locution also has disadvantages. There is something a bit too stand-offish about "x would be good"; it sounds more like a mere appraisal than an aroused interest. It is possible to think that something would be good without actively desiring it, without feeling really attracted by it.

I shall select a locution that employs the optative mood rather than the declarative mood, for the optative mood, despite its lack of use in English, is naturally suited to express desires. Unfortunately, the phrase "let such-and-such happen" will have to be avoided, because it is too easily understood as a request. Instead, I shall adopt the formula, "let it be the case that such-and-such." The content of S's desire for the Tigers to win the pennent would be expressed by: "Let it be the case that the Tigers win the pennent." The content of S's desire to own a Porsche would be expressed by: "Let it be the case that I own a Porsche." And the content of S's desire to buy some bread would be expressed as: "Let it be the case that I buy some bread." (Contents of wants will always be expressed from the agent's point of view; hence the first person pronoun.) This formula is somewhat lengthy and a bit artificial, but otherwise, I think, fairly satisfactory. I shall call the content of a desire an "*optative proposition*," and what philosophers usually call a "proposition" (*simpliciter*) I shall call a "*declarative proposition*." To have a belief, then, is to assent to a declarative proposition, while to have a want is to "assent" to an optative proposition.

We are now in a better position to examine practical inference. When a person makes a practical inference, the content of the inference consists in a combination of optative propositions and declarative propositions. Suppose that S wants to eat some pizza and believes that he can obtain some pizza by calling Domino's and ordering one. S then forms a further desire—viz., to call Domino's and order a pizza. The content of this practical inference consists in these propositions.

(k):   Let it be the case that I eat some pizza.

(l):   If I call Domino's and order a pizza, I will be able to eat some pizza.

(m):   Let it be the case that I call Domino's and order a pizza.

In making this inference, S says to himself (as it were) that (m) is acceptable *because* of (k) and (l). This is analogous to saying that (r) is acceptable *because* of (p) and (q). In both cases the "because" signifies a sort of logical relationship. Proposition (m) is "logically" related to (k) and (l) in the sense that acceptance of (k) and (l) constitutes a *good reason* for accepting (m).

The fact that (k), (l), and (m) are logically related does not imply that practical inference is not a causal process, just as the fact that (p), (q), and (r) are logically rather than causally related does not imply that cognitive inference is not a causal process. That practical inference is a causal process can be supported by attention to propositions $W_S(k)$, $B_S(l)$, and $W_S(m)$.

$W_S(k)$: S wants that (k).

$B_S(l)$: S believes that (l).

$W_S(m)$: S wants that (m).

These declarative propositions describe events which are causally related. S's wanting to eat some pizza and his believing that calling Domino's and ordering one is a means to that end *resulted* in S's wanting to call Domino's and order a pizza. Thus, we can say that S came to want (m) *because* he wanted (k) and believed (l); and this "because" is a causal because.

In studying practical inference it is appropriate to look at the matter from the agent's point of view, to see how (k) and (l), for example, constitute good reason for accepting (*m*). But it is a mistake to look at the matter *only* from the agent's point of view. When a person is engaged in practical inference, his attention is focused on propositions such as (*k*), (*l*), and (*m*), not propositions such as $W_S(k)$, $B_S(k)$, or $W_S(m)$. Although he is implicitly aware of his wanting and believing, the object or content of his thought is not his wanting or believing. He is not thinking *about* his own mental states. Now, since the successive objects of his thought—viz., (*k*), (*l*), and (*m*)—are not causally related, one would be apt to conclude that the inference process is not a causal one. But while (*k*) and (*l*) do not cause (*m*)—indeed, such an idea would be utter nonsense—*S's accepting* (*k*) and *S's accepting* (*l*) do cause *S's accepting* (*m*). The process in which *S* finds good reason for accepting (*m*), and thereupon accepts it, is a causal process. While *S* is going through this process he is not thinking *of* or *about* the process he is going through, and hence does not think of it as a causal process. Nevertheless, it is a causal process.

What is ordinarily called *deciding* or *deliberating* is a process of practical inference and therefore a causal process. But practical inference is called "deliberation" only in special cases—namely, where the agent begins with doubt or indecision about what to do. Deliberation commences when he asks himself whether or not he should do act *A* and finds himself unsure. He proceeds to weigh various factors in an attempt to settle the matter, and finally ends his deliberation by firmly accepting either the optative proposition, "Let it be the case that I do *A*," or the optative proposition, "Let it be the case that I do not do *A*." This is what we call a *decision*.

In some cases of deliberation the agent "recites to himself" the considerations for and against doing *A*. But most practical inference does not consist in silent verbalization. Consider, for example, the following practical inference.

(*t*):   Let it be the case that I eat that apple.

(*u*):   I could put myself in a position to eat that apple by taking it from the fruit bowl with my hand.

(*v*):   Let it be the case that I take that apple from the fruit bowl with my hand.

I do not *recite* these propositions to myself as I assent to them; things happen much too quickly for that. But I do have occurrent wants and beliefs for these propositions during the brief time interval in question.

In a complicated practical problem there are too many factors to be considered for them all to be entertained simultaneously. For this reason, the agent gives conscious attention to certain of the factors while "storing" the others in memory. In this way both occurrent wants and beliefs and standing wants and beliefs play a part in deliberation. During the initial stage of his deliberation, the agent has an occurrent belief that his doing *A* would have consequence x plus an occurrent aversion to the occurrence of x. During the second stage he turns his attention to factor y. He assents to the proposition that his doing A would cause y and he has an occurrent desire for the occurrence of y. During this second stage, his belief and aversion *vis-à-vis* x are stored as a standing belief and aversion, ready, as it were, to be recalled when necessary. What fills his consciousness during this stage are thoughts about y, not x. Often, in the course of a long drawn-out deliberation, a person will repeatedly have a certain occurrent desire, then focus on other matters, then have another occurrent desire of the same sort, etc. Thus, the form in which we transcribe practical inference on paper does not correspond exactly to the temporal process of the deliberation, for although a given desire is listed once, there may be several occurrent desires for the same optative proposition.

Near the beginning of Chapter Three, I distinguished between action-wants, object-wants, and event-wants. But most of my attention in that chapter was paid to action-wants. In practical inference, however, object-wants and event-wants are involved as well as action-wants. Frequently one begins with some object-want or some event-want and these lead, via practical inference, to action-wants. For example, an initial want for an apple (an object-want) leads to a want to reach out and take that apple (an action-want), or a desire for the Vietnam war to end (an event-want) leads to a desire to join a protest demonstration (an action-want).

Once an action-want has been formed, the problem is how to perform the desired act. Often the agent must perform a sequence of acts in order to put himself in a position for performing the desired act. To put himself in a position to perform the desired act of buying bread, he must perform the sequence of acts that constitutes going to the store. Once he is in a position to perform the desired act, he must still know what *lower* acts to perform, including certain basic acts. Thus, there will be a chain of practical inferences leading from a desire to perform the original act to a desire to perform some basic act. This is illustrated by the chain of inferences below, where the original action-desire (for our purposes, at any rate) is the desire to convince the examiner that the agent is a competent driver.

(a):   Let it be the case that I convince my examiner that I am a competent driver.

(b):   If I signal for a turn, I will convince my examiner that I am a competent driver.

(c):   Let it be the case that I signal for a turn.

(c):   Let it be the case that I signal for a turn.

(d):   If I extend my arm out the car window, I will signal for a turn.

(e):   Let it be the case that I extend my arm out the car window.

> (e): Let it be the case that I extend my arm out the car window.
>
> (f): If I extend my arm, I will extend my arm out the car window.
>
> (g): Let it be the case that I extend my arm.

Of course, a series of inferences of this sort may take place in a split second, without one's uttering any of the above sentences. Nevertheless, the above sentences capture the content of those inferences.

When one assents to an optative proposition concerning a basic act, such as (g), one arrives at a "limit" of desire. Having formed a desire to do a certain basic act, there are no further decisions about means that need be made. According to our definition of a basic act, an agent is able to perform a basic act at will, without needing any information about other things as means to its performance. Thus, the natural consequence of a desire to perform a basic act is not any *further* desire, but the performance of the basic act itself. There is a sense in which the continuation of the series from (a) to (g) is simply the extending of one's arm. This is probably what Aristotle had in mind when he wrote that the conclusion of a practical syllogism is not a proposition but an action.

In the course of moving from (a) to (g) the agent does not think of himself as being involved in a causal process, for he is not thinking about the fact that his wants and beliefs are causing new wants. His moving from (a) to (g) constitutes that causal process, however, even if this movement is not the content of his thoughts. Similarly, in the course of moving from (g) to actually extending his arm, the agent does not think about the fact that this is a causal process. The focus of his attention is on (g), and (g), of course, does not cause his extending his arm. But although (g) does not cause his extending his arm, *his assenting to* (desiring) (g) *does* cause his extending his arm.

Throughout this section I have been using the term "want" slightly differently than I used it in Chapter Three. Here I have been using the term to include both *intrinsic* and *extrinsic* wants, while in Chapter Three it was used only for (more or less) *intrinsic* wants. Both uses, the broader one and the narrower one, are legitimate, but the different uses must be explained in order to clarify just what I wish to maintain. In Chapter Three I would have refrained from saying what I have just said in the foregoing discussion— namely, that the agent "wanted" to extend his arm out the window. And in Chapter Three I would not have said that the agent "wanted" to extend his arm, which I did say in the preceding paragraph. I would not have said this in Chapter Three because these wants are merely extrinsic wants, extrinsic to the desire to convince the examiner that one is a competent driver. In Chapter Three it was explicitly denied that S "wanted" to visit his aunt, because, considered for its own sake, the agent was averse to visiting his aunt. In this section, however, I am willing to say that he "wanted" to visit his aunt, because, after considering the fact that it was his duty to visit his aunt, his over-all attitude toward visiting his aunt was positive. Intrinsically he was averse to visiting his aunt but he still formed an extrinsic desire to visit his aunt.

Even in Chapter Three, however, I included cases of wants which were not *absolutely* intrinsic. First, I was interested in wants which occurred to the agent just prior to his action and which were operative in producing the action. Perhaps some further wants had once been a cause of this kind of want, but that did not matter. S's desire to brush his teeth would have been considered intrinsic at time t_n even though he originally came to have teeth-brushing desires because of desires to avoid the displeasure of his parents. (When he was a child, at t_o, his desires to brush his teeth were extrinsic to the desire to avoid displeasing his parents. But now, at t_n, the prospect of brushing his teeth in the evening strikes him as "appropriate" or "fitting" without being mediated by any further desire. Similarly, S may originally have been motivated to do his duty only as a means of obtaining social approval, which was intrinsically desired. But later in his development S has occurrent desires to do his duty which are not mediated by the thought of social approval.)

Secondly, the wants included in Chapter Three were not "absolutely" intrinsic since they may have been extrinsic relative to some object-wants, event-wants or wants for subsequent acts. My policy in Chapter Three was to focus on action-wants that were not extrinsic relative to action-wants for acts on the same act-tree. In other words, I used the word "want" for the *most* intrinsic want in a given (single-tree) action-plan. But this did not ensure that the want in question was absolutely intrinsic, for it meant that I was willing to say that S "wanted" to *make himself* fall asleep, even though this want was extrinsic relative to the want to fall asleep.

Let me return now to the sequence of practical inferences from proposition (*a*) to (*g*), followed by the performance of the act of extending one's arm. This sort of sequence lies at the basis of generalizations L and L' that were presented in Chapter Three. L is based on the presupposition that if S wants to do A' more than any other act (at t), then a sequence of practical inferences will lead S to have an extrinsic want to do whichever basic act he believes is most likely to generate A'. Beginning with a desire to do A'—say, convincing the examiner that he is a competent driver—the agent must choose an act that will generate A'—say, signaling for a turn—and he must continue in this way until he arrives at a basic act—say, extending his arm. The situation is more complicated if more than one intrinsic desire (or aversion) is relevant. Suppose that the agent realizes that he would get his hand wet if he extended his arm out the window and that he is (intrinsically) averse to getting his hand wet. Then his practical inferences might proceed as follows. His desire to convince the examiner that he is a competent driver results, *for a moment*, in an extrinsic desire to extend his arm out the window. But then he notices that this act would generate getting his hand wet, and he has an occurrent aversion to getting his hand wet. If his aversion to getting his hand wet is greater than his desire to convince the examiner that he is a competent driver, his over-all (extrinsic) attitude toward extending his arm out the window becomes negative. Hence, he also forms a negative (extrinsic) attitude toward extending his arm.

In choosing whether or not to extend his arm out the window, the agent is choosing between two competing possible act-trees: one which contains *both* the act of convincing the examiner that he is a competent driver and the act of getting his hand wet, and one which contains *neither* of these acts. If he is more averse to getting his hand wet than he is desirous of convincing the examiner that he is a competent driver, and if no other intrinsic desires or aversions are involved, then an act-tree with neither of these acts would have more "total utility" than an act-tree with both of them. Generalization L' was introduced to help summarize what happens where competing possible act-trees are compared for "total utility" and where competing possible basic acts are compared for the act-trees that each is likely to generate.

The reader will recall my remark in Chapter Three that neither L nor L' is a very precise generalization, capable of being used to make reliable predictions. The reason for this, as we can now see, is that L and L' are summaries of people's propensities to make practical inferences, but unfortunately, we have no precise knowledge of when people will make specific practical inferences. Two of the problems were indicated in Chapter Three. First, it is difficult to measure the strength or intensity of the agent's various wants. Secondly, where there is a larger probability of achieving a less desired end and a smaller probability of achieving a more desired end, will the agent seek to maximize his possible gain, or to be more sure of achieving a smaller gain? This varies from agent to agent and from mood to mood of a given agent.

Now that we have seen some of the complications involved in practical inference, we can see even further difficulties in trying to make predictions of an agent's acts. For one thing, it cannot be assumed that the agent has a fixed intensity of desire for a given act throughout the course of a decision. In deciding whether to extend his arm out the car window, the agent may have several occurrent aversions for getting his hand wet, but the intensities of these may be different. Thus, the problem for prediction is not merely the problem of measuring the intensity of any single occurrent desire, but of knowing whether there will be any change in the intensity prior to a decision.

Another problem is that of ascertaining whether or not an agent will take the time to imagine the consequences of an act to which he is momentarily attracted. A man feels a sudden impulse to throw a rock at a window. At that moment he has no other relevant occurrent desires or aversions. Shall we predict that he *will* throw it? Such a prediction could not reliably be made unless we could tell if further occurrent desires or aversions would crop up *before* he performed the act. If the man gives himself time to think of the consequences, occurrent aversions and beliefs might arise that would cause him not to throw the rock. He might realize that he will be caught and that this will prove humiliating. But there is a possibility that the desire to throw the rock will precipitate that act right away, before reflection or hesitation set in.

It is evident, then, that despite some commonsense knowledge of the manner in which wants and beliefs cause acts, and despite some degree of success in predicting people's action, we do not have fully adequate predictive laws or fully adequate knowledge of the relevant antecedent conditions of behavior.

As a final note on this topic, I wish to allay one sort of fear the reader may have about generalization L'. This generalization seems to ensure, if true, that agents always do whatever will "maximize their expected utility." Since, according to many theorists, maximizing one's expected utility is the hallmark of rational action, L' would seem to ensure that no one ever acts irrationally. Yet this clearly runs counter to everyday experience and everyday language. In fact we do have occasions to say that people are acting irrationally.

The first point to be made in reply is that L' may well not be true, especially if interpreted in certain ways. Suppose that a man is concluding a complicated bit of deliberation, and tries to bring together all the factors he has considered. He brings before his mind what he thinks were all his considerations, and makes a decision on those factors. But in fact he forgets a very important consideration, one which, if he had not forgotten it, would have led to the opposite decision. Does his actual behavior accord with L'? Well, in one sense it does, since his behavior results from those occurrent wants and beliefs which he had *just prior* to the action, and it results from these occurrent wants and beliefs in accordance with L'. But if we take into consideration the *standing* wants and beliefs which he had, or if we take into consideration some occurrent wants and beliefs which arose during deliberation but which were *forgotten* in the final stages of deliberation, then his behavior does *not* accord with L'. Whichever interpretation we choose, however, we can certainly say that this man's action was not fully rational. A similar case is that of rash and unreflective action. Consider the man who throws the rock at the window. If this act results from a sudden impulse, there is a sense in which it accords with L' but also a sense in which it does not. In terms of his *occurrent* wants and beliefs immediately preceding the act, it accords with L'. For, *ex hypothesis*, he did not pause to think of the consequences. But in terms of his *standing* wants and beliefs—or what we might call his "best interests"—this act did not accord with L'. Surely the man had a standing belief that he might well get arrested and a standing aversion to the prospect of being arrested and fined. There just was no time for this belief and this aversion to become occurrent and operate on his decision. In either case, however, we can say that the man acted irrationally. Even if we say that his action was in accord with L', it can be called irrational precisely because the man did not take time to call forth his other relevant beliefs and desires.

There are other cases too where a man's action may accord with L' but still be termed irrational. In ordinary language we call an act (or the agent) irrational if the act is based on desires which it is irrational, foolish, or silly of the man to have, or if it is based on unfounded or merely wishful beliefs. Some people continue to have desires for a certain kind of thing even though things of that kind never satisfy them or make them happy; indeed, they may make them quite miserable. (Cf. the man who continues to like "hard" women though they always make him miserable.) Or we might consider a man irrational whose short-term desires are always stronger than his longer-term desires—e.g., the man who has a stronger desire to smoke now than to avoid getting cancer later. When a man's action is predicated on a belief for which he has little evidence, here too we might say that he is acting irrationally. But in none of these cases is there a violation of L'. Thus, even if L' is completely true (interpreted in a specific way), it does not follow that men are never irrational or never act irrationally.

4. Wanting and Acting

I turn now to the much discussed question of the logical status of the relation between wants and acts: is this a *logical* connection or is it a *contingent* connection? Numerous philosophers contend that the connection between wanting and acting is logical, and *therefore* there can be no *causal* connection between them. Since I maintain that wants are causes of acts, this contention must be examined.

A. I. Melden, who has argued the above contention most vociferously, writes as follows:

> As in the attempt to construe the difference between mere bodily movements and actions in terms of acts of volition, so here in the case of wanting when this is identified with some Humean cause of doing, we are faced with a manifest contradiction. Construed as an internal impression which is thought to function as a cause that issues in some items of so-called overt behavior . . . , the impression must be describable without reference to any event or object distinct from it. It must be possible to characterize that internal impression without invoking any reference to the so-called object of the desire, no less than the action that consists either in getting or in trying to get that object. But as a desire, no account is intelligible that does not refer us to the thing desired. The supposition, then, that desiring or wanting is a Humean cause, some sort of internal tension or uneasiness, involves the following contradiction: As Humean cause or internal impression, it must be describable without reference to anything else—object desired, the action of getting or the action of trying to get the thing desired; but as desire this is impossible. Any description of the desire involves a logically necessary connection with the thing desired.[12]

---

[12] Melden, *Free Action* (London: Routledge & Kegan Paul Ltd., 1961; New York: Humanities Press Inc.), p. 114.

What does Melden mean in saying (in the last sentence of the passage) that any *description* of a desire involves a logically necessary connection with the thing desired? Does he mean that any linguistic expression which can be used to designate a desire must mention the object of the desire? This is surely false. We can refer to any desire by a definite description of the form, "the desire that S had at time t_1," or some similar definite description which makes no mention of the object of the desire.

Melden probably means something slightly different, however. I think that what he means is that a desire necessarily has an intentional object, and that the intentional object of the desire makes it the desire that it is. The intentional object of the desire, then, is "logically related" to the desire. But does this mean that a desire is logically related to a physical object, or to an actual act (an act-token)? The intentional object of a desire cannot be construed as an actual physical object or an actual act, for then the desire for a unicorn would not have any intentional object at all, nor would the desire for me to hit a home run in Yankee Stadium. The intentional object of a desire, then, must be a *concept*, or something like a concept, rather than an actual object or act. The intentional object of wanting a unicorn is the concept of a unicorn and the intentional object of wanting me to hit a home run in Yankee Stadium is the concept of my hitting a home run in Yankee Stadium. But from the fact that a desire is logically related to the concept of x it does not follow that it is logically related to x. From the fact that my wanting to raise my hand (at t) is logically related to the concept of my raising my hand (at t) it does not follow that my wanting to raise my hand (at t) is logically related to the actual act of my raising my hand (at t). Hence, there is no reason to deny that my wanting to raise my hand (at t) is a *cause* of my raising my hand (at t).

Another argument often given for the contention that wants and acts are logically related is that acts are our *criterion* for the ascription of wants. Richard Taylor, for example, writes:

If ... we ask, in the case of any such hypothetical [e.g., "I will if I wish" or "I will if I intend"] that is seriously proposed as an expression of the relation between a cause and its effect, what might be the criterion for deciding whether it is true, we find this criterion to be the very occurrence of that event which is supposed to be regarded as the effect, rendering the relationship embodied in the hypothetical not the empirically discoverable one of a cause to its effect but a logical relationship of entailment between concepts. The fact, however, that a given event occurs can never entail that another wholly different one will occur, or has occurred, if the relation between them is that of cause to effect. ... Suppose, then, that someone moves his finger and we propose as a causal explanation for this that he wanted to move it. How shall we, or the agent himself, decide whether this was in fact the cause? ... Our entire criterion for saying what he wanted ... to do, is what he in fact did; we do not infer the former from the latter on the basis of what we have in fact found, but we regard the former as something entailed by what we now find, namely, just his moving his finger.[13]

It is simply false to say that *S*'s doing *A* is our *criterion* for *S*'s wanting to do *A*. First of all, for most act-types *A*, *S*'s doing *A* does not *entail* that *S* wanted to do *A*, either intrinsically or extrinsically. The fact that *S* did *A* does not entail the presence of a want to do *A* because *S* might have done *A uninten- tionally*. *S*'s turning on the light, for example, does not entail that *S* wanted to turn on the light. He may have flipped the switch thinking that it controlled the exhaust fan which he wanted to turn on. Secondly, it is wrong to say that *S*'s doing *A* is our *entire* criterion for deciding that *S* wanted to do *A*. Certain- ly it is part of our evidence for thinking that *S* wanted to do *A*, but it does not exhaust our evidence. Included in our range of possible evidence are such items as (1) other acts of the agent, including verbal avowals in particular; (2) antecedent events that may be causally relevant to wanting to do *A*, including, for example, other wants of the agent; and (3) want-manifestations that are not acts—e.g., facial expressions. Such items of evidence will be discussed more fully later in this section. Finally, it is certainly a mistake to say that *S*'s doing *A* is the only criterion that *S* himself has for saying that he wanted to do *A*. An agent need not infer his wants from his behavior.

Another possible line of argument is to contend, not that action entails desire, but that desire entails action. It is, of course, obviously false that wanting to do *A* entails doing *A*, for there are many wants that do not issue in corresponding acts. A weaker thesis, however, is the thesis that wanting to do *A*, *ceteris paribus*, entails doing *A*. As Raziel Abelson puts it:

> Assume that Jones wants, intends, desires, or in some sense has a motive to open the window. What does this entail about what he will do? Well, it entails that he will open the window, but it does not entail this *tout court*. It entails that he will open the window *provided* that no reason arises for his not doing so (e.g., a hurricane is not blowing outside) and provided nothing prevents him (e.g., he is not paralyzed, and the window isn't stuck). The provisos here con- stitute the contextual limitation I spoke of on the entailment between motive and act. To say "I want to open the window; nothing prevents me, and I have no reason or motive not to, not even the motive of laziness; but still, I won't open the window" is senseless. What on earth could I mean by "want"? In this contextually limited way, a motive is indeed logically connected to an ac- tion. . . .[14]

---

[13] "I Can," *The Philosophical Review*, LXIX (1960); reprinted in S. Morgenbesser and J. Walsh, eds., *Free Will* (Englewood Cliffs, N. J.: Prentice-Hall, Inc., 1962), p. 88.

[14] "Review of Richard Taylor, *Action and Purpose*," *The Journal of Philosophy*, LXVI No. 6 (March 27, 1969), 183–84. Also cf. Charles Taylor, *The Explanation of Behavior* (London, 1964), p. 33: " . . . this is part of what we mean by 'intending X,' that, in the absence of interfering factors, it is followed by doing X. I could not be said to intend X if, even with no obstacles or other countervailing factors, I still didn't do it. Thus my inten- tion is not a causal antecedent of my behavior."

This is a more plausible interpretation of the claim that wanting is logically related to action. There is no reason to conclude from this, however, that wants are not *causally* related to acts. Consider the following analogy. To say that *S* imbibes poison does not entail that *S* dies soon thereafter. However, together with the further provisos that *S* does not take an antidote, that *S* has not developed an immunity to this poison, etc., it perhaps *does* entail that *S* dies shortly afterward. Even if we grant this entailment, however, it does not follow that *S*'s imbibing the poison does not *cause* his dying. On the contrary, if *S* dies soon after imbibing the poison, we would immediately conclude that it was imbibing the poison that *caused* his death.

The concept of a poison provides a good analogue for the concept of a want. The concept of a poison is the concept of something that tends to have certain effects, viz. death. Similarly, I think, the concept of wanting is the concept of something that tends to have certain effects, viz. acts. In other words, it is a logical truth about poisons (or imbibing poisons) that they tend to cause death. And, I suggest, it is a *logical* truth about wants that they tend to *cause* actions. Thus, there is a logical relationship between wants and acts. Far from precluding a causal relationship between them, however, this logical relationship *ensures* a causal relationship. More precisely, the logical relationship ensures that *if* there are any wants and *if* any of these wants have consequences which are typical of wants, then some wants cause some acts.

We have, in effect, already established a logical/causal relationship of another sort between wanting and acting. On my definition of an act-token, it is a logical truth that an act-token is caused by some want or other. In other words, it is part of the concept of an *act* that an act is caused by a want, just as it is part of the concept of *boiling* that boiling is caused by heat. In addition to the claim that the concept of an act includes the idea of being caused by a want, I wish to make the further claim that the concept of a want includes the idea of tending to cause acts.[15]

On my view, then, the concept of an occurrent want is the concept of a mental event that tends to result in behavior. It is, therefore, a logical truth that wants tend to cause action. Having said this, I wish immediately to qualify it. Philosophers have learned from (sometimes bitter) experience that it is far from easy to know when a certain concept is "built into" or "contained in" another concept; there is no sharp line between analytic statements and synthetic statements, if there is any line at all. Thus, I would not claim that the tendency to cause acts is *unquestionably* logically tied rather than

---

[15] In *A Materialist Theory of the Mind* (New York: Humanities Press, 1968), D. M. Armstrong takes such a view not only of the concept of wanting, but of mental state concepts in general. He writes: "The concept of a mental state is primarily the concept of *a state of the person apt for bringing about a certain sort of behavior.*" (p. 82) The notion that mental state concepts are defined in terms of causal roles is also defended by David K. Lewis, in "An Argument for the Identity Theory," *The Journal of Philosophy*, Vol. LXIII, No. 1 (1966), 17–25.

contingently tied to the notion of a want. As with many words in ordinary language, it is difficult at best to say what they imply by virtue of their "meanings" as opposed to what they imply by virtue of constant conjunction. Nevertheless, I think the statement that wants are mental events which tend to result in behavior is quite a good candidate for being a logical truth. Moreover, it is instructive to adopt this assumption here in order to make sure that its being a logical truth is not *incompatible* with the claim that wants cause acts. Many philosophers would admit that there could be a causal connection so long as the relationship were *contingent*. It will be helpful to establish, therefore, that wants can be causes of acts *even if* the above-mentioned statement is *logically* true.

Consider the properties of being a magnet, being an acid, and having a negative charge. Like wanting, these properties have causal notions built into them. It is a logical truth, for example, that anything which is a magnet tends to attract small ferrous metal objects—i.e., tends to *cause* ferrous metal objects to move toward it. Similarly, it is a logical truth that anything which is an acid has a tendency to cause litmus paper to turn red.[16] Again, it is a logical truth that anything having negative charge tends to repel (cause to move away) other objects with negative charge.

In all these cases I have used the word "tend" to qualify the statement. This is for two reasons. First, although magnets have a *tendency* to attract ferrous metal objects, no attraction will in fact take place unless a ferrous metal object is in the vicinity. Something could be a magnet, therefore, without ever attracting anything. Secondly, and more importantly, other forces exerted on a ferrous metal object that is near a magnet will prevent it from moving toward the magnet. It is not literally true that *whenever* a small ferrous metal object is near a magnet it will move toward the magnet; that depends on other forces too. Thus, the causal propensities of a magnet are interconnected with the causal propensities of other objects. The same is true in the case of wanting. The fact that S wants to do A does not entail that this want *will* cause S's doing A; nor does it entail that it will cause S's doing some basic act. There are many occasions on which an action-want does not cause any action at all, because some stronger want is present which "overrides" the former one. We may say, then, that wants have a *tendency* to cause acts, but we cannot say that every want causes some act or other.

In addition to the fact that a given want may fail to produce any act because of competing wants, the acts which a given want does have a tendency to produce depend on factors other than the want itself, specifically on the agent's *beliefs*. True, in the case of wanting to perform a basic act, there is a single determinate act which the want has a tendency to produce—viz., that

---

[16] More precisely, this was *once* a logical truth. Contemporary chemists would probably define an acid a little differently than eighteenth-century chemists. But for illustrative purposes it is sufficient that this *once* have been a logical truth.

basic act. But if we consider other wants, say wanting to win the next point (in a tennis match), it is not clear which acts tend to result. We cannot say, in general, that wanting to win the next point tends to cause an actual act of winning the next point. But nor can we even say what *basic* acts such a desire will lead to unless we know what *beliefs* the agent has. Given certain beliefs, the desire to win the next point will lead to certain basic acts; given other beliefs, the desire to win the next point will lead to other basic acts. And similarly for most wants.

We see, then, that wanting is a *system-dependent* notion: the effects of a given want depend on a variety of other factors at work in the system, in particular, different wants and beliefs. The nature of this system has already been explained. Wants lead to basic acts via a series of practical inferences, in which the agent's beliefs and perhaps additional wants come into play. This entire system, I suggest, is part of a conceptual structure which forms our notions of wanting and believing. In other words, our concepts of wanting and believing include a presupposition that wants and beliefs combine in this way to cause action. Our notions of wanting and believing presuppose, as it were, a commonsense model of the manner in which action is caused.[17] Of course, this model is not only not explicitly formulated, but it is also extremely vague. The vagueness of L', which was discussed in Chapter Three and in Section 3 of this chapter, is a reflection of the vagueness of our model. Nonetheless, it resembles to some extent genuine theories in the exact sciences.

It is a logical truth that wants are mental events which tend to cause action in the ways I have indicated. But it is a contingent truth that human beings, or any other animals, ever *have* any wants. (*Ipso facto*, it is a contingent truth that human beings ever *act*, that is, act purposively.) Now to say that it is a contingent truth that human beings ever want anything is not to say that this fact is discoverable by some simple method of correlating certain observable facts about human beings with other observable facts about human beings. It is an empirical fact about human beings, but not one that can be immediately inferred from observational data. The justification for thinking that *other* human beings have wants is based on the fact that a variety of observable events they are involved in, including their verbal utterances, can be *explained* by the *hypothesis* that they have wants (and beliefs). The inference from observable facts concerning human beings to the proposition that they have wants is not a deductive inference, nor an inference by enumerative induction nor an analogical induction; rather it is an inference to the best explanation.[18]

Although I maintain that wants and acts are logically related (in a sense), it should be evident that my view is very different from the Wittgensteinian

---

[17] The notion of a commonsense model which is presupposed in our concept of wanting is suggested by Richard Brandt and Jaegwon Kim, "Wants as Explanations of Action," *The Journal of Philosophy*, LX (1963), 425–35.

[18] Cf. Gilbert Harman, "The Inference to the Best Explanation," *The Philosophical Review*, LXX (1965), 88–95.

position which also posits a logical, or at least noncontingent, relationship between mental states and behavior. Wittgenstein thought that certain behavior (in certain circumstances) logically or criteriologically implied the presence of a certain mental state. I deny that any amount of behavior is logically sufficient for ascribing any particular (intrinsic) want to the agent. It is always possible, at least theoretically, to account for his behavior by the postulation of some *other* (intrinsic) want. But while I deny that behavior is ever a *criterion*, in Wittgenstein's sense, for the presence of a particular want, I also deny that behavior is merely a *symptom*, in Wittgenstein's sense, of a particular want. According to Wittgenstein, a symptom is something which we find by observation to be correlated with the kind of thing of which it is a symptom. On my view, however, we do not find that behavior is *correlated* (empirically) with certain wants (and beliefs). Rather, it is a logical truth that certain wants (together with certain beliefs) will lead to certain behavior. An analogue of the relationship between behavior and wants is the relationship between the movement of two small pieces of paper and the hypothesis that they are both negatively charged. On the one hand, the fact that these pieces of paper move in opposite directions at time *t* is not a *criterion* for their having negative electrical charge, since their movement does not logically imply anything whatever about electrical charge. On the other hand, their movement is not a *symptom* of electrical charge either, since we have not discovered the relationship between electrical charge and repulsion by *observed correlations* of electricity and repulsion.[19] Rather, we introduce the notion of electrical charge in such a way that it is a logical truth that negatively charged objects tend to repel one another. It follows from this that one plausible hypothesis to account for the movement of the pieces of paper is that they are both negatively charged. But their movement is not a logically sufficient condition, or a criterion, of their being negatively charged.

I maintain that it is a logical truth that wants tend to cause acts. This does not entail that it is a logical truth that a particular act-token was caused by a particular want. Of course, if *A* is an *act*-token, *A* must have been caused by *some* want or other. But *S*'s performing *A* does not entail *which* particular want caused *A*. The fact that John flipped the switch does not entail that John wanted to flip the switch. First, it does not entail that John had an intrinsic desire to flip the switch, that this was the *point* or *reason* for his flipping the switch. Secondly, it does not even entail that he had an extrinsic desire to flip the switch, since the act may have been unintentional. If the performance of a certain act *entailed* that the agent had had a specific want, especially a specific *intrinsic* want, then any explanation of the act in terms of

---

[19] An excellent critique of the assumption that behavior must be related to mental states either as criteria or as symptoms is given by C. S. Chihara and J. A. Fodor, "Operationalism and Ordinary Language: A Critique of Wittgenstein," *American Philosophy Quarterly*, II (1965), 281–95. Also see Hilary Putnam, "Dreaming and 'Depth Grammar,'" in R. J. Butler, ed., *Analytic Philosophy*, First Series (Oxford: Basil Blackwell, 1962).

that want would be completely trivial. But explanations in terms of the agent's wants need not be trivial because there is normally a range of various possible (intrinsic) wants that might have caused the given act. John may have flipped the switch because he wanted to turn on the light; or because he wanted to turn on the exhaust fan and thought that this switch would turn it on; or because someone asked him to flip it and he wanted to be obliging; or because he wanted to see what was written on the underside of the switch; or he may have wanted to adjust a picture on the wall and accidentally flipped the switch as he moved his hand toward the picture; etc. We *explain* his act by citing *which one* of a range of possible wants was *actually* the cause of his act. It is a logical truth that certain sets of wants and beliefs (e.g., wanting to turn on the light and believing that flipping the switch would generate this) *would*, if the external conditions were right, tend to cause an act of flipping the switch. But it is an empirical matter to ascertain *which* of these different sets of wants and beliefs was *in fact* the cause of this act.

A condition of adequacy for any account of the nature of wanting is that it be compatible with the actual epistemic status of wants. A purely dispositional account of wanting fails this test of adequacy by failing to account for the privileged access of a person to his own wants. The Wittgensteinian account fails the test because it attributes too strong an epistemic position to third persons; it implies that a third person can have logically sufficient grounds for ascribing a specific want to someone, but this, I think, is not correct. Let us now examine my own account to see if it can pass this condition of adequacy.

I have already discussed first-person knowledge of one's own wants in some detail, and further discussion is not necessary. It is because a person has privileged access to his own wants, moreover, that his avowals or expressions of desire are, for a third person, particularly good evidence of his wants. But there are two important reasons why a discussion of third-person knowledge should neglect this kind of evidence, at least to a certain extent. First, one often has extremely good evidence for another person's wants without his making any avowal. Secondly, there is no reason to rely on someone's avowal of a want as good evidence for a want unless we presuppose that he uses the word "want" correctly in his own case. But this presupposition cannot be justified unless we have an independent way of telling what his wants are.

The problem of third-person knowledge can be divided into two parts: how do we know that other people ever have any wants? And how do we know which wants a person has at a particular time? The first of these questions is tantamount to the general problem of the existence of other minds. A want, on my view, is a mental event that has a tendency to cause acts. How do we know that other people *ever* have such mental events? This is a problem I shall not examine in detail, for it would take me too far from my central concerns. My general view is that the hypothesis of mental events in others—in particular the sorts of mental events which have a tendency to cause action—is the best of the competing hypotheses to account for their observed movements, their physiology, their facial expressions, and their speech—especially the speech which is ordinarily interpreted as expressions of mental states or descriptions of mental states. But this is too large an issue to deal with here.

Let us assume, then, that we are justified in saying that a particular person S *sometimes* has wants. What justifies us in saying that he has a particular want at a particular time? The most important evidence, of course, is the action S performs at that time. By this I do not mean a single act that he performs at the time or even a group of acts on a single act-tree. A single act, or even a group of acts on a single act-tree, can be interpreted as resulting from any number of (intrinsic) wants. John's moving his hand, flipping the switch, and turning on the light (all on a single act-tree) can be the result of his wanting to turn on the light, his wanting to turn on the exhaust fan, his wanting to oblige a request, his wanting to see the underside of the switch, his wanting to adjust a picture on the wall, etc. Our evidence is not usually confined to a single act or even a single act-tree, however. We usually can observe a number of *co-temporal* acts and a number of *sequential* acts, and these are extremely helpful in narrowing down precisely what the agent's goals or purposes are.

One of the most important kinds of co-temporal acts consists in the agent's turning his head, or looking, in a certain direction. This sort of act is most helpful in letting us identify his goals. If, for example, John was looking at the picture while he moved his hand, this supports the hypothesis that he wanted to adjust that picture. If, on the other hand, he was looking at the lamp while flipping the switch, that tends to support the hypothesis that he wanted to turn on the light. If he was peering at the switch, that would suggest that he wanted to see what was written on the underside of the switch. To take another case, suppose we see someone waving a pen wildly in the air, and wonder whether he wants to get someone's attention, or to shake some ink out of the pen, or to practice conducting an orchestra. The third hypothesis would be strongly supported by observing him perform two other co-temporal acts—viz., humming and tapping his foot rhythmically.

Observing a sequence of acts is equally valuable in assessing the agent's desires. If we see John open a book and look at it, then squint, then get up and go over to the light switch, and finally flip the switch, we have substantial reason for saying that he wanted to turn on the light (rather than turn on the exhaust fan, for example). On the other hand, if he had walked to various parts of the room looking all the while at the picture, and then, after walking to the wall, flipped the switch and moved the picture in one movement of the hand, this would tend to substantiate the hypothesis that he just wanted to adjust the picture and flipped the switch accidentally. Sequences of acts are important in identifying an agent's purpose because one often engages in an extended program of action all aimed at a single goal. (Each of the smaller action-plans will contain a desire to *help bring about x*, where *x* is the ultimately desired event.) An observer can attribute a prolonged sequence of action to a specific goal with more reliability than any single temporally proper part of that sequence of action.

Acts are not the only observable manifestations of desires. There are observable events or characteristics of an agent, such as facial expressions, which result from his desires or aversions though they were not the object of these desires. Such events or characteristics can help an observer determine the agent's wants. An interesting example of this concerns dilation of the pupils. According to a study by Eckhard H. Hess, the pupils of a person's eyes tend to dilate when he is looking at a thing which he desires or for which he has a strong positive attitude.[20] (This fact is known to Chinese jade dealers, who watch a buyer's pupils to know when he is impressed by a specimen and is likely to pay a high price.) Moreover, there is evidence that all of us have a nonconscious or implicit awareness of pupil dilations in others, that we react more favorably to someone with enlarged pupils though we are unaware *why* we find them more appealing. Hess presents two photographs of an attractive girl which seem to be identical, but which in fact differ in that the pupils of her eyes in one photograph have been enlarged. He reports that male subjects responded more favorably to this photograph, although they were unable to identify any difference between the two photographs. This suggests that we use pupil dilation as a cue without consciously recognizing it as such.

It is very likely that our ability to discern emotional states of others, and perhaps desires as well, depends heavily on cues of which we are not consciously aware. One can tell when a friend is sad, irritated, angry, excited, etc., without being able to specify *how* one knows it.[21] It is quite likely, in fact, that our propensity to attribute mental states *in general* is heavily dependent on facial cues of which we are largely unconscious, and on tones of voice which we could not describe in detail. The use of such cues is probably innate, since babies seem to react to emotions of their parents almost as readily as grownups. The role of such innate and largely unconscious tendencies is probably of great importance in understanding why people think of humans and animals as having mental states. It might also help account for the fact that we are unwilling to regard machines as having consciousness though they are able to "perform" complicated maneuvers. An animal with certain facial features and certain tones of voice seems to us to be *conscious* and *sentient* while a metallic machine that can execute much more sophisticated maneuvers does not seem to us to be conscious. The difficult question is to say whether, and why, such innate predispositions can be considered strong evidence in a philosophical justification of the existence of other minds.

---

[20] "Attitude and Pupil Size," *Scientific American*, CCXIL (April 1965), 46–54.
[21] Such cases have been stressed by Michael Polanyi. See *The Tacit Dimension* (Garden City, N. Y.: Doubleday & Company, Inc., 1966).

Thus far I have mentioned only observable *effects* of wants which can be used as evidence for their presence. But since we also have some information about the *causes* of wants, this too can be used in trying to identify an agent's wants. Instead of inferring from effect to cause, we infer from cause to effect. Certain wants are normally caused by physiological states. Hunger, for example, normally results in a want to eat, and a lack of sleep results in a want to sleep. Hence, if I observe that S has not eaten for 16 hours, I have strong evidence that he will want to eat; and if I know that S hasn't slept for 40 hours, I can infer that he (probably) wants to sleep.

Information about an agent's likes and dislikes and about his personality traits can be used to help determine his current wants. If I know that S likes chocolate ice cream, then I might guess that he will want to buy a chocolate ice cream cone at the ice cream parlor he has just entered. And if I know that S is a vain or boastful person—i.e., someone who frequently wants to impress others—then I might surmise that he will want to impress the strangers he has met at a cocktail party. Information about such personality characteristics can often be obtained by observation of *previous* behavior and then used to help diagnose his *present* desires. Of course, this sort of information is very weak evidence *by itself* for the presence of any particular want at this particular time, but it can be quite helpful when *combined* with information about the agent's current behavior.

Knowledge of an agent's beliefs is valuable in determining his wants. If I know that John believes that this switch turns on the exhaust fan, then when I see him flip the switch I could infer that he wanted to turn on the exhaust fan. Beliefs, perhaps even more than wants, have causes with which we are quite familiar. One of the most common causes of believing p is simply *perceiving p* to be the case. Since our commonsense knowledge of what normal human beings are able to perceive is fairly reliable, if we see S looking directly at a chair, we have reason to infer that S believes that there is a chair in front of him. We can also assume quite generally that adult human beings understand the language of their culture, which also helps us identify an agent's beliefs. If George said to John, "Please turn on the light for me," we may infer that John believes that George has asked him to turn on the light, and probably believes that George wants him to turn on the light. When we see John immediately proceed to the switch and flip it, we may combine this with our assumption about his beliefs and infer that John wanted to oblige George's request (or something like this).

There is, then, a variety of evidence a third person may have for identifying the wants of an agent, even without want avowals by the agent. To be sure, we do not always have all the relevant information for making a want ascription with confidence. But there are some cases, probably many cases, in which our grounds for ascribing a particular want to an agent are as good as one gets in many empirical matters. In other words, we have "adequate evidence." But while our evidence may be adequate, it never *entails* that the agent has that want. Avowals by the agent are of further help in justifying our want ascriptions, but here too we do not get logically sufficient evidence since the agent may be lying. The reason why our evidence never entails the presence of a certain want is that it is always *compatible* with the postulation of some other set of desires and beliefs. It is always *possible* to explain the observed behavior, even avowal behavior, by more than one set of wants and beliefs; and usually more than one set is compatible with the other observable evidence of the kinds I have indicated. A variety of evidence, including co-temporal acts, sequential acts, etc. may make one hypothesis far more likely and plausible than any competing hypothesis; but it never logically precludes the competing hypotheses.

This discussion shows that the epistemic status of third persons *vis-à-vis* the wants of others can correctly be accounted for by my analysis of wanting. A third person can *know* what wants another person has, but not with "logical certainty." The epistemic status of first persons has already been discussed, and it was indicated that a person can know his own (occurrent) wants without recourse to evidence of the sort required by third persons. The agent himself, then, is in a better position to know his own present occurrent wants than anyone else. It does not follow, though, that in *all* respects the agent is in a better epistemic position *vis-à-vis* his own wants. First, a third person may be a better judge of an agent's *standing* wants than the agent himself. Second, a third person may remember that an agent had a certain occurrent want once though the agent himself may have forgotten it. Thirdly, another person is sometimes better at *formulating in words* what an agent wants than the agent himself. Finally, the agent may have *unconscious* wants which a trained psychologist, for example, can identify more readily than he can—a point which will be elaborated in Section 5.

One final topic of interest concerns the acquisition of the concept of wanting (or the use of the word "want"). The Wittgensteinian critique of earlier accounts of mental concepts or mental words was based on the argument that no one could *learn* to use the words properly if those accounts were correct. It is fair to expect, therefore, that any account of the notion of wanting should at least be compatible with the possibility of acquiring and using that concept correctly, both in first-person and third-person cases. How does my analysis of wanting fare in this respect?

A detailed examination of language learning and concept acquisition is the province of empirical psychology and linguistics, not armchair philosophy. But a couple of possible ways in which children might learn to use the term "want"—both compatible with my analysis of wanting—can be suggested here. First, since it is possible for us to know when others have particular wants, it is possible for adults to tell when a child has a certain want and to say, "Johnny wants to play with the ball," or "Johnny wants a candy," etc. (Notice: it is unnecessary for the adults to know with "logical certainty" that the child has a particular want; it is only necessary that they be right enough of the time.) The child notices the occasions on which adults ascribe these wants to him and correlates their words with the state he is in. He comes to recognize that when he is attracted to playing with the ball, or attracted to the candy, then the adults say he "wants" to play with the ball, or "wants" the candy. Thus, he learns to say of *himself* that he wants the ball or the candy in the right circumstances.

A second possible way in which the child might learn first-person uses of the word "want" is this. When he is attracted to the ball and wants to reach it, he is likely to *mention* the object that he wants. (I assume that he has reached the stage of naming kinds of objects.) In general, if one is thinking of *x* or attending to *x* it is natural to express one's thought by naming *x*. Thus, when the child wants the ball or wants some candy, he will say, "ball" or "candy." Gradually he acquires the idea of making a *request*—i.e., of uttering words in order to obtain a certain object. The word "want" is taught to him (or simply learned by him) as part of request behavior. Thus, he learns to say "I want the ball" or "I want some candy," instead of simply "ball" or "candy." At this point he need not think of "I want" as describing a mental state he is in or a mental event he is having, but simply as a prefix used in making requests. Although he *has* these mental events, he has not yet *reflected* upon his consciousness to notice them *as* mental events. Later, however, he comes to recognize that his reaching for the ball, or his asking someone to give him the ball, results from a *felt attraction* for the ball. At this stage he recognizes wanting as a mental event that tends to cause his behavior.

The child's understanding of the third-person use of "want" probably parallels his understanding of the first-person use. Just as he learns to say of himself that he "wants" the ball either when he reaches for it or asks for it, so he learns to say of another child that *he* "wants" the ball either when he reaches for it or asks for it. If the concept of wanting as a "mental" event is acquired somewhat later in his own case, perhaps it is also acquired later for the case of others. When fully grasped, however, the term "want" is seen to apply in the same sense both to himself and to others—viz., to a mental event which tends to lead to action.

5.   Unconscious Wants

I have said that a person always has a sort of implicit knowledge of his own occurrent wants. How does this jibe with the widespread opinion that there are desires or motives of which the agent is unconscious or unaware? These desires cannot be dismissed as mere standing desires, for they are said to activate behavior. But they diverge from the notion of an occurrent want as I have explained it inasmuch as they are not events occurring in consciousness.

I wish to maintain that the notion of an unconscious want is a tenable one, since certain important elements of the ordinary notion of wanting can be satisfied even if the agent is not conscious of having a want. At the same time, I wish to maintain that an unconscious want is a nonstandard form of want, since it violates one of the normal criteria for wanting. An unconscious want is related to a normal want in the way that a sweet lemon is related to a normal lemon. One of the usual criteria of lemonhood is a sour taste, but we can decide to call fruit which is not sour but which is otherwise like a lemon a "sweet lemon." Similarly, one of the usual criteria of (occurrent) wanthood is that of being in consciousness, but we can decide to call a nonconscious state which is otherwise like a want an "unconscious want."

What is the relevant respect in which unconscious wants are *like* normal wants? The relevant similarity is the tendency for unconscious wants, like normal wants, to cause other wants by practical inference. An unconscious want is a state which is postulated as the cause of certain conscious wants, the presence of which would otherwise be surprising. Upon the death of his father, a man who hasn't attended a synagogue for twenty years begins attending every day to recite the mourner's prayers. He avers that he simply "wants" to attend every day, but this is rather surprising given the considerable inconvenience of daily attendance plus the absence of any other religious convictions in this man. We hypothesize, therefore, that the man has guilt feelings associated with his father, and that his attending synagogue daily is a way of punishing himself. In other words, we postulate that the man has an unconscious desire to punish himself, or an unconscious desire to expiate his sins (*vis-à-vis* his father), and this desire causes him to have the conscious desire to attend synagogue regularly, which he views (unconsciously) as a means of punishing himself or expiating his sins.

Notice that this method of interpreting talk of unconscious desires does not imply that his conscious desire is not at all a cause of his action. We do not have to deny that he attended synagogue because he wanted to attend synagogue. Rather, we say that this conscious desire is not the whole of the explanation, or the most interesting part of the explanation, since this conscious desire was itself caused by an unconscious one. Hypothesizing the unconscious desire implies that the conscious one was simply an extrinsic desire—extrinsic relative to the hidden one—and since an intrinsic desire normally gives the agent's "real" reason for acting, it is the unconscious desire that is of greatest interest.

The postulation of unconscious desires is most common when a conscious desire is anomalous, or at least when a recurrent pattern of such desires is anomalous. A recurrent conscious desire to take everything in sight whenever one enters a store is anomalous, especially if one has no further purpose concerning these objects, such as to sell them or use them for some project. So we are likely to postulate the presence of some unconscious desire (and belief) to account for these conscious ones—e.g., the desire to get caught and thereby cause embarrassment to one's parents.

Unconscious desires tend to be postulated particularly when the conscious ones are *compulsive*. A want is compulsive when it retains its strength or intensity despite apparently strong counter-forces. The kleptomaniac continues to feel a powerful desire to take objects in stores despite the fact that he has a strong conscious desire to avoid getting caught and a conscious realization that it is likely he will get caught. Normally, a strong desire to avoid getting caught and a belief that he is likely to get caught would cause a man to stop wanting (on the whole) to take the merchandise. But a kleptomaniac's desire to filch things is uncontrollable precisely in the sense that it does not respond to ordinary influences from other desires or aversions. Hence, we are likely to postulate the presence of an unconscious desire which is causing the conscious one and keeping it "in strength" against conscious countervailing forces.

When an unconscious desire is postulated, an unconscious belief must be presupposed to accompany it (if a conscious belief of that sort is not present). If we think that the kleptomaniac's behavior is caused by an unconscious desire to cause embarrassment to his parents, we must assume that he believes, unconsciously if not consciously, that his getting caught stealing *would* cause them embarrassment. Thus, the want-and-belief model is carried over from the ordinary cases to cases where the wants and beliefs are unconscious.

In the cases considered thus far behavior is caused by unconscious desires, but only via the intermediary of conscious wants. The synagogue-goer does not act in the absence of any conscious wants whatsoever, for he does have a conscious want to attend the synagogue and a conscious want to recite the mourner's prayers. It is clear, then, that his act of attending synagogue and his act of reciting the prayers are *intentional* acts, in spite of the fact that they are ultimately to be explained by unconscious desires. We may now raise the question of whether behavior is ever caused *directly* by unconscious desires without any intermediate conscious desires, and if so, whether acts resulting from these unconscious desires could be called intentional.

I am uncertain how to answer either of these questions. To begin with the second question first, it seems that we are inclined to call acts *un*intentional if there is no corresponding *conscious* desire present. Even if we grant that a certain "slip" of the tongue was unconsciously desired by the agent, we might continue to consider it unintentional. I am not completely certain on this point, however. For as soon as we admit that there was an unconscious desire, we are tempted to put "slip" in scare quotes, suggesting that it wasn't *really* a slip at all, but rather an intentional act.

The first question, whether action is ever directly caused by unconscious desires, is also very difficult, as well as important. It is common to interpret Freudian theory as demonstrating that much of our behavior is not controlled by conscious thoughts at all. This seems to be a rival to the view that all our behavior—at least all our *action*—has conscious causes. It is not evident, however, that this interpretation of Freudian theory is correct. We can admit that unconscious desires are among the causal factors of action without committing ourselves to the view that, in this range of cases, conscious desires play no role whatever. Whenever it is admitted that an action is caused by an unconscious desire, two possibilities remain. Either the action was caused "directly" by the unconscious desire, or the unconscious desire caused one or more conscious desires which in turn caused the action. In the case of the kleptomaniac, for example, one possibility is that the kleptomaniac *blindly* takes things from the shoprack, with no conscious awareness of what he is doing, as if in a trance. A second possibility is that he has a conscious desire to take these items from the shoprack, a desire which he would prefer not to have and which he cannot comprehend. This desire does play a causal role in his behavior, but since it is (allegedly) caused by a further, unconscious desire, the latter desire is of primary interest. I do not know whether all cases involving unconscious desires are of the second sort. On the other hand, it should not be assumed—as I think it sometimes is assumed—that they are all of the first sort.

An unconscious want, I have said, is not a conscious event or a conscious state, but this does not imply that unconscious wants do not manifest themselves in consciousness in some manner or other. According to Freudian theory unconscious desires emphatically do manifest themselves, in dreams and possibly in waking thought as well. But in such manifestations, the thought content is disguised, usually by some form of symbolism. The agent does not have an explicit thought of having intercourse with his mother, for example, but has thoughts in which various objects symbolically represent intercourse with his mother. The symbolic disguise ensures that the agent is not consciously aware of having the desire which the psychoanalyst postulates him to have. Of course, he might come to learn of these unconscious desires in the same way that the psychoanalyst learns of them—i.e., by inference from his behavior, conscious desires, dreams, etc. Or he might learn that he has these desires by being told so by his psychoanalyst. But he does not have the sort of *non-inferential*, *unmediated* knowledge of these wants as he has of his normal, conscious wants.

I have already indicated the necessity of postulating unconscious beliefs in cases where unconscious desires are postulated. But the plausibility of postulating unconscious beliefs is suggested by quite different sorts of cases as well. I suggested in Section 4 of this chapter that there are many cases in which a person uses cues of which he is not explicitly aware in making judgments of various sorts, including judgments about the attitudes or emotional states of other people. Here it might be plausible to talk about the presence of unconscious, or perhaps better, *pre*conscious beliefs. If someone forms the belief that his wife is irritated about something, and this belief is traceable to facial cues of which the believer is not consciously aware, we might still say that he has nonconscious beliefs about these cues. Such terminology would be justified by the fact that (a) he obviously *perceives* these cues (in some sense of "perceive"), and (b) his perception or recognition of these cues is responsible for his believing that she is irritated. This seems very like a case in which one comes to believe (consciously) that q is true because one perceives that q and then *infers* from q that p is true.

A similar case of the nonconscious use of cues occurs in experiments originating with Lazarus and McCleary.[22] A person is presented with a large number of nonsense syllables, and after seeing certain of the syllables, an electric shock is administered to him. Presently he comes to anticipate the shock at the sight of the "shock syllables," yet he is unable to say what makes him expect the shock. Here it is plausible to say that he is unconsciously, or at least preconsciously, aware of the syllables as portents of the shock, that he *believes*, albeit nonconsciously, that these syllables will be followed by a shock. The hypothesis of such a belief would be based on two considerations. First, a plausible explanation of his believing that he will receive a shock at certain junctures is that he believes (nonconsciously) that these syllables are followed by shocks. Secondly, these syllables are in his visual field and indeed are the objects of his attention; moreover, they were in his visual field on the other occasions when he subsequently received shocks. These two considerations are the sorts we would normally use in ascertaining that a person has a certain belief (setting aside his belief avowals). First, he has other (conscious) beliefs which could well be the *effect* (via cognitive inference) of this belief, and secondly, the appropriate sort of *causal* (i.e. perceptual) conditions are present to lead to this sort of belief. The only thing missing is the conscious awareness.

We see that the notion of belief, like the notion of desire, can be extended to cases devoid of conscious awareness. These extensions of our ordinary notions depend on the fact that desires and beliefs have specific cause-and-effect relationships, first, with other (conscious) wants and beliefs, and ultimately with the agent's behavior and his environment.

---

[22] R. S. Lazarus and R. A. McCleary, *Journal of Personality*, XVIII (1949), 191, and *Psychological Review*, LVIII (1951), 113; cited by Polanyi, *op. cit.*, pp. 7–8.

CHAPTER FIVE

Explanations
of Action
in the Behavioral
Sciences

1. Compatibility or Incompatibility

The nature of commonsense explanations of action in terms of wants and beliefs has now been examined. I call such explanations "commonsense" explanations for two reasons. First, they require no specialized knowledge or intensive study either to understand or to employ; every mature human being of normal intelligence uses such explanations frequently. Secondly, their legitimacy is taken for granted in everyday life and everyday conversation. Explanations of action in terms of wants and beliefs, or in terms of aims, purposes, goals, reasons, etc., are so widespread that they normally occasion no comment or criticism. A particular explanation might be challenged on the grounds that the act was performed for a different reason, or different purpose, than the original explanation cites. But we do not challenge a reason explanation or purpose explanation on the grounds that there are no such things as reasons, wants, or purposes. We take it for granted that people have wants and purposes which cause their behavior; the only question that arises is which particular wants or purposes caused a man's action in a specific case.

While want-and-belief explanations go unquestioned in everyday life, there is no reason why they should go unquestioned by science or by philosophy. And indeed criticisms have come from both of these quarters, especially from the group of psychologists called "behaviorists." They have called into question the legitimacy and adequacy of putative explanations in terms of conscious or subjective events; purposes and desires have been held to have no value for the scientific explanation of behavior. One of the founders of behaviorism, J. B. Watson, writes as follows.

> Behaviorism claims that consciousness is neither a definite nor a usable concept. The behaviorist . . . holds, further, that belief in the existence of consciousness goes back to the ancient days of superstition and magic. . . .

126

One example of such a religious concept is that every individual has a *soul* which is separate and distinct from the *body*. This soul is really a part of a supreme being. This ancient view led to the philosophical platform called "dualism." This dogma has been present in human psychology from earliest antiquity. No one has ever touched a soul, or seen one in a test tube, or has in any way come into relationship with it as he has with the other objects of his daily experience. Nevertheless, to doubt its existence is to become a heretic and once might possibly even have led to the loss of one's head. . . .

Wundt . . . substituted the term *consciousness* for the term soul. Consciousness is not quite so unobservable as soul. We observe it by peeking in suddenly and catching it unawares as it were (*introspection*). . . .

To show how unscientific is the main concept behind this . . . school of psychology, look for a moment at William James' definition of psychology. "Psychology is the description and explanation of states of consciousness as such." Starting with a definition which *assumes* what he starts out to prove, he escapes his difficulty by an *argumentum ad hominem*. Consciousness—Oh, yes, everybody must know what this "consciousness" is. When we have a sensation of red, a perception, a thought, when we *will* to do something, or when we *purpose* to do something, or when we desire to do something, we are being *conscious*. . . .

In his first efforts to get uniformity in subject matter and in methods the behaviorist began his own formulation of the problem of psychology by sweeping aside all mediaeval conceptions. He dropped from his scientific vocabulary all subjective terms such as sensation, perception, image, desire, purpose, and even thinking and emotion as they were subjectively defined.[1]

A more recent behaviorist psychologist, B. F. Skinner, writes:

An even more common practice is to explain behavior in terms of an inner agent which lacks physical dimensions and is called "mental" or "psychic." The purest form of the psychic explanation is seen in the animism of primitive peoples. From the immobility of the body after death it is inferred that a spirit responsible for movement has departed. The *enthusiastic* person is, as the etymology of the word implies, energized by a "god within." It is only a modest refinement to attribute every feature of the behavior of the physical organism to a corresponding feature of the "mind" or of some inner "personality." The inner man is regarded as driving the body very much as the man at the steering wheel drives a car. The inner man wills an action, the outer executes it. The inner loses his appetite, the outer stops eating. The inner man wants and the outer gets. The inner has the impulse which the outer obeys. . . .

The fictional nature of this form of inner cause is shown by the ease with which the mental process is discovered to have just the properties needed to account for the behavior. When a professor turns up in the wrong classroom or gives the wrong lecture, it is because his *mind* is, at least for the moment,

---

[1] Reprinted from *Behaviorism* by John B. Watson by permission of W. W. Norton & Company, Inc. Copyright 1924, 1925 by John B. Watson. Copyright 1930, Revised Edition, by W. W. Norton & Company, Inc., and renewed (c) 1958 by John B. Watson., pp. 2–6.

absent. If he forgets to give a reading assignment, it is because it has slipped his *mind* (a hint from the class may re*mind* him of it). . . . In all this it is obvious that the mind and the ideas, together with their special characteristics, are being invented on the spot to provide spurious explanations. A science of behavior can hope to gain very little from so cavalier a practice. Since mental or psychic events are asserted to lack the dimensions of physical science, we have an additional reason for rejecting them.[2]

Here it is argued that explanations of behavior in terms of inner events or states, such as desires, will, purpose, etc., are "spurious," that the events invoked are "fictional." We are urged therefore to dispense with explanations in terms of mental events and instead seek explanations in terms of the publicly observable events that impinge on the organism.

Confronted with this attack, it appears that one is forced to make a choice. Shall one accept commonsense explanations of behavior in terms of purpose, desire, belief, and similar mentalistic notions? Or, on the other hand, shall one dispense with these explanations in favor of the ones to be offered by the science of psychology? One seems to be obliged to choose one of the modes of explanation, but not both.

That we are confronted with mutually exclusive options has been argued explicitly by Charles Taylor:

> The upshot of this discussion has been that the account of our behavior implicit in our ordinary language is teleological in form. And this must be taken in a strong sense. It is not just that such notions as "action" and "desire" are teleological notions; it is also that *their use carries the implication that no non-teleological account is valid.*[3]
>
> . . . to say that a being is purposive is to say that his behavior can be accounted for in terms of purpose, and this in turn implies that the basic level laws are teleological in form. Again, in the second chapter, we saw that the form of explanation implicit in our ordinary language was *incompatible* with a more basic level explanation of a non-teleological type, so that, if this latter were shown to hold, we should have to undertake a far-reaching conceptual revision. Our ordinary notions of behavior require that this be accounted for by laws governing action. Thus the thesis that living beings are purposive is the thesis that their behavior is to be explained on the most basic level by that form of teleological laws which we have called laws governing action. And the thesis of mechanism, *directly negating this,* is to the effect that the most basic level laws are non-teleological laws governing movement. What is at issue, then, is the form of the laws and the concepts used in them.[4]

Taylor's view is that explanations in terms of desire or purpose, properly

[2] B. F. Skinner, *Science and Human Behavior* (New York: The Macmillan Company, 1953), pp. 29–31.

[3] Charles Taylor, *The Explanation of Behavior* (London: Routledge & Kegan Paul Ltd., 1964; New York: Humanities Press Inc.), p. 54; italics mine.

[4] *Ibid.*, pp. 100–101; italics mine.

understood, are incompatible with stimulus-response explanations, or neurophysiological explanations. It is an empirical question, according to him, which of these forms of explanation is valid or correct. But they cannot both be valid. And if, indeed, the nonteleological forms of explanation were correct, a widespread conceptual revision about human behavior would be necessary, for we would be forced to abandon our teleological explanations in terms of purposes, desires, intentions, etc.

Taylor's incompatibility thesis is seconded, at least with respect to neurophysiological explanations, by Norman Malcolm:

> ... a mechanistic explanation of behavior rules out any explanation of it in terms of the agent's intentions. If a comprehensive neurophysiological theory is true, then people's intentions never are causal factors in behavior.[5]

The purpose of this chapter is to examine the extent to which scientific explanations of behavior are compatible or incompatible with purposive explanations of behavior—i.e., explanations in terms of wants and beliefs. There are a variety of models and theories of behavior (or relevant *to* behavior) proposed by behavioral and social scientists. Are these really incompatible with our commonsense model of wants and beliefs, as Taylor and Malcolm imply? Or might our commonsense model and some of the various scientific models *jointly* be valid? Do the findings of behavioral science really require us to overthrow our commonsense conceptual scheme? Or can we retain our commonsense scheme even if the hypotheses of psychologists and sociologists turn out to be correct?

I shall defend the thesis that most of the prominent studies and theories of behavior in the social sciences are not really incompatible with the commonsense model elucidated in Chapters Three and Four. On my view, much of the work done in the behavioral sciences either presupposes concepts quite similar to those of wanting and believing or frames hypotheses which are compatible with the operation of wants and beliefs. The fact that an hypothesis *makes no reference* to wants and beliefs does not entail that its truth would *preclude* the causal role of wants and beliefs. Hence, even those theories in the behavioral sciences which ignore mentalistic or teleological factors need not be incompatible with commonsense explanations which rely on such factors.

Needless to say, there is no room in a single chapter to discuss all or even a significant proportion of the relevant literature in the behavioral sciences. The best I can do is select representative studies to illustrate the points I wish to make. These studies fall into four main categories. First, I wish to call attention to the widespread use in the behavioral sciences of concepts quite similar to wanting and believing. Many investigators either presuppose the importance of wants and beliefs in the causation of behavior, or use such

---

[5] "The Conceivability of Mechanism," *The Philosophical Review*, LXXVII (1968), 63.

concepts in trying to develop a more precise and empirically satisfying theory of behavior than our vague commonsense model gives us. Illustrations of such work will be given in Section 2. If the role of wants and beliefs in the causation of action is granted, it becomes important to understand the causes of wants and of beliefs. In Chapter Four it was mentioned that there are rough, commonsense ways of telling some of the factors that cause wants and beliefs. Many of the investigations in the behavioral sciences can be viewed as attempts to gain a firmer understanding of these factors. Examples of such investigations will be discussed in Section 3.

Theories in the behavioral sciences which employ wants and beliefs to explain behavior and which identify the causes of wants and beliefs are obviously not incompatible, at least not seriously so, with our commonsense model. But stimulus-response theories of behavior and neurophysiological theories of the causes of behavior might be expected to be diametrically opposed to our commonsense model. An attempt to explain behavior in terms of histories of conditioning or an attempt to explain behavior in terms of neuron firings might look like challenges to the commonsense model that threaten to unseat it. If theories of conditioning are correct, then what *really* causes behavior are stimuli and reinforcements, not wants and beliefs. And if neurophysiological theories can be made broad enough to account for all purposive action, then neuron firings are *really* the causes of behavior, not wants and beliefs. These apparent rivals to the want-and-belief model will be examined in Sections 4 and 5 respectively. I shall argue that there need be no conflict between the want-and-belief model, on the one hand, and either the stimulus-response approach or the neurophysiological approach, on the other hand. On the contrary, it may turn out that *all* of these models can validly be used to (help) explain human action.

2. Use of the Want-and-Belief Model in Behavioral Science

I begin with material in the behavioral sciences which makes use of schemata very similar to our commonsense model of wanting and believing. Actually, the use of such schemata is fairly common among behavioral scientists, though different terminology sometimes obscures this fact. Such terms as "motive," "need," "goal," "attraction," and "utility" often mean roughly the same as "want"; and such terms as "cognition," "expectancy," and "subjective probability" take the place of "belief." In a typical textbook of social psychology, Krech, Crutchfield, and Ballachey list *cognition* and *motivation* as the first two (of three) "basic psychological factors."[6] Men's

---

[6] D. Krech, R. S. Crutchfield, and E. L. Ballachey, *Individual in Society* (New York: McGraw-Hill Book Company, 1962).

"motivation," they write, are their "wants" or their "goals."[7] These are the "initiating and sustaining forces of behavior." About cognition they say: "The responses of the individual to persons and things are shaped by the way they look to him—his *cognitive world*."[8] More explicitly, "Man acts upon his ideas. His irrational acts no less than his rational acts are guided by what he thinks, what he believes, what he anticipates." Krech, Crutchfield, and Ballachey do not try to state precisely the relationship between motives, cognitions, and action. Instead, they seem to assume that this connection is fairly well understood and not in need of clarification. In their chapters on motivation and cognition, therefore, they devote most of their time discussing what affects people's wants or beliefs—i.e., the causes of wants and beliefs.

The procedure of Krech, Crutchfield, and Ballachey is not uncommon in psychology. They acknowledge and presuppose the centrality of wants and beliefs in the determination of behavior, but do not attempt to state the nature of this determination in great detail. This procedure is certainly not true of all psychologists, however. Many have attempted to formulate systems or theories which employ notions similar to wanting and believing, but which are far more precise and hence more easily testable than our vague commonsense assumptions about the operation of wants and beliefs.

Edward C. Tolman is a clear example of a theorist who works with concepts akin to wanting and believing, but seeks to make their scientific status more secure. Tolman begins his important work, *Purposive Behavior in Animals and Men*, by affirming the presence of purpose and cognition in behavior.

> Behavior as behavior, that is, as molar, *is* purposive and *is* cognitive. These purposes and cognitions are of its immediate warp and woof. It, no doubt, is strictly dependent upon an underlying manifold of physics and chemistry, but as a matter of first identification, behavior as behavior reeks of purpose and cognition.[9]

Although Tolman defends the notions of purpose and cognition, he wishes to strip them of their mentalistic associations. As a behaviorist, he is anxious to justify their use on purely behavioristic grounds.

> The mentalist is one who assumes that "minds" are essentially streams of "inner happenings." Human beings, he says, "look within" and observe such "inner happenings" . . . .
>   Contrast, now, the thesis of behaviorism. For the behaviorist, "mental processes" are to be identified and defined in terms of the behaviors to which

---

[7] *Ibid.*, p. 69.

[8] *Ibid.*, p. 17.

[9] (Berkeley: University of California Press, 1932), p. 12.

they lead. "Mental processes" are, for the behaviorist, naught but inferred determinants of behavior, which ultimately are deducible from behavior. Behavior and these inferred determinants are both objectively defined types of entity. There is about them, the behaviorist would declare, nothing private or "inside."[10]

Tolman views purposes and cognition as "intervening variables" that are inferred from behavior and from environmental and physiological states.

> We have sought to show that immanent in any behavior there are certain immediate "in-lying" purposes and cognitions. These are functionally defined variables which are the last step in the causal equation determining behavior. They are to be discovered and defined by appropriate experimental devices. They are objective and it is we, the outside observers, who discover—or, if you will, infer or invent—them as immanent in, and determining, behavior. They are the last and most immediate causes of behavior. We call them, therefore, the "immanent determinants."
>
>   But these immanent determinants, it must now briefly be pointed out, are, in their turn, caused by environmental stimuli and initiating physiological states. Such environmental stimuli and such organic states we designate as the ultimate or "initiating causes" of behavior. The immanent determinants intermediate in the causal equation between the initiating causes and the final resultant behavior.[11]

We saw in Chapter Four how third persons infer the presence of wants and beliefs from the agent's action and from certain probable causes—viz., from physiological states which cause wants and from features of the environment which cause beliefs (via perception). Thus, Tolman's view of wants and beliefs as "functionally defined variables" is not at all distant from our commonsense employment of these notions.

The bulk of Tolman's book is devoted to the examination of experimental evidence supporting the postulation of purpose and cognition and to the elaboration of their role in determining behavior. Most of the experiments are done with animals, but Tolman presupposes, I think, that if the presence of purposes and cognitions can be demonstrated for rats or monkeys, the case for men will not be difficult. Let us look very briefly at one such discussion of experimental data.

In Chapter Four Tolman cites experimental evidence to support the postulation of at least certain kinds of beliefs, namely "expectations." In previous chapters he had adduced evidence for wants, or what he calls "demands for goal-objects." Here in Chapter Four he says:

> It has been shown that different types of goal-objects, given one and the same physiological drive, are demanded with different strengths. But it must now

---

[10] *Ibid.*, p. 3.
[11] *Ibid.*, pp. 19–20.

also be pointed out that such differences in demand can, to use the vernacular, "get in their licks" only by virtue of some sort of accompanying "cognitive expectations" as to the character of such coming goal-objects. Thus, if . . . a change be made from a "good" reward to a "poor" one, or vice versa, it seems obvious that this change can induce a corresponding change in behavior only after the new reward has had a chance to be experienced one or more times— only after, that is, it has had a chance to induce a new cognitive expectation. . . .

Let us turn now to the specific experiments which justify this concept of an immediate, immanent, cognitive expectation as to the coming goal.[12]

In one of the experiments cited by Tolman, rats were kept thirsty and then run through a maze at the end of which they found water. Their performance in the maze was measured by the "errors" in making turns and the time taken. After many days of this kind of situation, suddenly they are made hungry but not thirsty and then sent through the maze at the end of which is now food rather than water. Their performance drops (gets worse) considerably. On the very next trial, however, their performance immediately returns to its previous level. Tolman explains this as follows.

In other words, on the first day of the change, when the animals were for the first time hungry, and before they had as yet experienced food in the maze, though they had experienced water, their behavior was apparently directed, to some extent, by something to be designated as the "old" cognitive expectation of water. But water is not so satisfactory, so demanded a goal, given hunger, as was the old goal of food. Hence there appeared on this day some disruption in the performance. Upon getting to the goal-box at the end of this day, however, the rats actually found not water, as they had expected, but food. And *one* experience of this new goal-object was, it seems, enough to change their expectation to the new one of food. For, on the next subsequent day, their behavior dropped [improved] to the normal level. That is, the rats again now expected a goal satisfactory to their new drive.[13]

In another experiment described by Tolman, a monkey's behavior was studied in a situation where his "expectations" are disappointed. The experimenter, while in view of the monkey, puts a piece of banana under a cup, a procedure familiar to the monkey. Then, unobserved by the monkey, he substitutes for the banana some less desirable food, say lettuce. Tolman quotes a description of the monkey's behavior:

She jumps down from the chair, rushes to the proper container and picks it up. She extends her hand to seize the food. But her hand drops to the floor without touching it. She looks at the lettuce but (unless very hungry) does not touch it. She looks around the cup and behind the board. She stands up and examines it thoroughly inside and out. She has on occasion turned toward observers present

[12] *Ibid.*, p. 71.
[13] *Ibid.*, pp. 72–73.

in the room and shrieked at them in apparent anger. After several seconds spent searching, she gives a glance toward the other cup, which she has been taught not to look into, and then walks off to a nearby window. The lettuce is left untouched on the floor.[14]

Tolman takes this "disruptive behavior" to be evidence for the presence of an "immanent expectation," or belief, in the monkey.

Because of his terminology, it is easy to see that Tolman invokes wants and beliefs as determinants of behavior. In the case of another important psychologist, Kurt Lewin, the terminology of the theory hides the fact that factors very much like wants and beliefs are invoked. Nevertheless, examination of Lewin's work reveals, I think, that these purposive concepts lie at the heart of his theory.

Lewin's theoretical constructs are borrowed, quite deliberately, from topology and physics. The central constructs include *life space*, *regions*, *force*, *valence*, *locomotion*, and *tension*. An individual's life space is not the actual physical environment but rather his psychological environment or psychological field. Such a field or life space is divided into regions, which represent possible situations (or perhaps activities) that the agent might find himself in. Each of the regions in the life space has a positive or negative valence, that is a positive or negative force on the individual. The state of tension of the individual also is a determinant of the force exerted on him. The resultant of the forces exerted on him determines his locomotion from one region to another (or his remaining in the same region), which signifies his behavior or activity.

Precise interpretation of the indicated constructs is extremely difficult, since Lewin says slightly different things about them in different places. There is definite textual evidence, however, which supports an interpretation of certain of these crucial constructs in terms of wants and beliefs. And I certainly think that this interpretation would clarify Lewin's theory while helping to make it plausible.

Consider, for example, the notion of a psychological field. We have seen that it does not comprise the *actual* physical and social environment of the individual. What, then, does it comprise? The clearest answer Lewin gives, I believe, is this:

> . . . I do not consider as a part of the psychological field at a given time those sections of the physical or social world which do not affect the life space of the person at that time. The food that lies behind doors at the end of a maze so that neither smell nor sight can reach it is not a part of the life space of the animal. If the individual knows that food lies there this *knowledge*, of course, has to be represented in his life space, because this knowledge affects behavior. It is also necessary to take into account the subjective probability with which

14 *Ibid.*, p. 75.

the individual views the present or future state of affairs because the degree of certainty of expectation also influences his behavior.

The principle of representing within the life space all that affects behavior at that time, but nothing else, prevents the inclusion of physical food which is not perceived. This food cannot possibly influence his behavior at that time under the conditions mentioned. Indeed, the individual will start his journey if he thinks the food is there even if it is actually not there, and he will not move toward the food which actually is at the end of the maze if he does not know it is there.[15]

It is clear from this passage, especially the last sentence, that the individual's psychological field is constituted by his *beliefs*. What he *thinks* exists or obtains must be represented in his field even if it does not exist or obtain; and what does exist must not be represented in his field if he doesn't *think* or *realize* that it exists. This is because the individual's behavior (at least his *attempted* behavior) is not a function of the way the world *actually* is, but the way the individual *believes* it to be.

The behavior of the individual is determined by the forces exerted on him by the various regions of his life space, and these forces are called "*valences*."

A region G which has a valence (Va(G)) is defined as a region within the life space of an individual P which attracts or repulses this individual.[16]

Valences can be either positive or negative, depending on whether the force on the individual is *toward* the region or *away* from the region. The idea of a region "attracting" or "repulsing" a person, or exerting a (psychological) force on him, is strongly suggestive of wants and aversions. And a close look at Lewin's explanation of the concept of force or valence confirms this suspicion. Speaking of a certain experimental arrangement involving an obstruction box, he writes:

The basic idea of the obstruction box is to measure one force, namely, the tendency to go to G, by another force, namely, by the tendency to avoid entering B. The food possesses what we call a "positive valence" . . . , that is, it corresponds to a region which the individual *wants* to enter. The grill B corresponds to a "negative valence" . . . , that is, to a region the individual does *not like* to enter.[17]

It is quite clear here that the notions of positive and negative valences correspond to that of desire and aversion. To say that a certain region in an individual's life space has a positive valence is to say that the prospect (or

---

[15] Kurt Lewin, *Field Theory in Social Sciences*, edited by Dorwin Cartwright (New York: Harper & Row, Publishers, Incorporated, 1951), pp. 57–58.

[16] *The Conceptual Representation and the Measurement of Psychological Force* (Durham, North Carolina: Duke University Press, 1938), p. 88.

[17] *Ibid.*, p. 73 (italics mine).

thought) of that activity or state of affairs is desired by the individual. These valences, both positive and negative, determine what the individual actually *does*—i.e., they determine his "locomotion."

The importance of *occurrent* wants and beliefs in the determination of action was stressed in Chapter Four. Lewin's principle of "contemporaneity," I think, is his way of stressing the same point. As Lewin puts it: "Any behavior or any other change in a psychological field depends only upon the psychological field *at that time*."[18] Since the psychological field is comprised by (or is a function of) the agent's desires and beliefs, the principle that behavior at a given time depends only on the psychological field at that time implies that the behavior is determined by the desires and beliefs which the agent has at that time. This view is very similar to that expressed in the preceding chapters where I tried to explicate the commonsense account of action in terms of wants and beliefs.

Still another example of the use of concepts akin to wanting and believing can be found in decision theory and related fields, e.g., game theory. The central concepts here include *utility* (or *preference*) and *subjective probability*. The degree to which an agent *wants* a certain event or state of affairs is represented by a utility number. If he wants an apple, for example, more than he wants a pear, we might represent his desire for an apple with the utility number 50, and assign the utility number 20 to represent his desire for a pear. John von Neumann and Oskar Morgenstern developed a technique for making numerical utility assignments unique up to a linear transformation.[19] To illustrate this technique, suppose that the agent we were just considering, in addition to preferring an apple to a pear, also prefers an apple to a banana but a banana to a pear. Having arbitrarily chosen the numbers 50 and 20 for the apple and the pear respectively, we proceed as follows to ascertain a utility assignment for a banana. We offer the agent tickets to various lotteries with a specified chance of winning an apple and a specified chance of winning a pear. We try to find a lottery ticket such that the agent is *indifferent* between getting that lottery ticket and getting a banana. For example, suppose our agent is indifferent between getting a banana and getting a lottery ticket which offers 1/3 chance of winning an apple and 2/3 chance of winning a pear. Then we assign a utility number for a banana which is 1/3 of the distance between the number assigned to a pear and the number assigned to an apple, in other words, 30. This ensures that the probability of winning an apple times the utility of getting the apple plus the probability of winning the pear times the utility of getting the pear is just equal to the utility of getting a banana.

In the foregoing the agent was told precisely what were his chances of winning an apple in a specific lottery, and it was assumed that he formed a

---

[18] Lewin, *Field Theory in Social Science*, p. 45.
[19] John von Neumann and Oskar Morgenstern, *The Theory of Games and Economic Behavior* (Princeton, N. J.: Princeton University Press, 1944).

belief about his chances of winning an apple accordingly. In other words, we assumed that his *subjective probability* was the same as the specified objective probability in the lottery. But in general, when studying the actions a person is likely to perform or the actions it would be rational for a person to perform, we must be concerned with his *subjective probability* assignments, or his *beliefs*.

Decision theorists study various criteria for making choices under various conditions, but of special importance is the rule of *maximizing expected utility*. To illustrate this rule, suppose S is choosing between acts A and *not-A* (henceforth written $\bar{A}$). For example, suppose S is a dinner guest who is to provide the wine but has forgotten whether chicken or beef is to be served.[20] Let A be the act of bringing white wine and $\bar{A}$ the act of bringing red wine. There are four possible outcomes of his action: O_1—he brings white wine and chicken is served (so he brings the *right* wine); O_2—he brings white wine and beef is served (the *wrong* wine); O_3—he brings red wine and chicken is served (an *odd* wine); O_4—he brings red wine and beef is served (the *right* wine). S's utility assignments for these various outcomes are as follows: $u(O_1) = 10$, $u(O_2) = -10$, $u(O_3) = -4$, and $u(O_4) = 10$. Moreover, although S doesn't *know* what will be served, he estimates the probability of chicken being served as .4 and the probability of beef being served as .6. To calculate the expected utility of each act, we multiply the probability (given that act) of one of the outcomes times the utility of that outcome and add the probability of the other outcome times the utility of that other outcome. Thus, the expected utility of act A (bringing white wine) $= p(O_1)u(O_1) + p(O_2)u(O_2) = .4(10) + .6(-10) = 4 + (-6) = -2$. Similarly, the expected utility of act $\bar{A}$ (bringing red wine) $= p(O_3)u(O_3) + p(O_4)u(O_4) = .4(-4) + .6(10) = -1.6 + 6 = 4.4$. Since the expected utility of $\bar{A}$ (bringing red wine) is 4.4 and the expected utility of A (bringing white wine) is -2, the rational thing for S to do is act $\bar{A}$ (bring red wine).

The social sciences exhibit many theories in which the concepts of utility (or preference) and subjective probability play a central role. Models of "rational decision" or "rational choice" figure widely in psychology, economics, sociology, and political theory. Although social scientists often disclaim any connection between their concepts and psychic states, it is nonetheless clear that their models presuppose our commonsense want-and-belief model of human behavior as their underlying intuitive foundation.

3. Studying the Causes of Wants and Beliefs

In everyday explanations of action we are often interested not simply

---

[20] The example is borrowed from Richard Jeffrey, *The Logic of Decision* (New York: McGraw-Hill Book Company, 1965).

in the wants and beliefs which cause a given act, but in the factors which cause those wants and beliefs. We are not satisfied with the "immediate" causes of the act, but wish to inquire into some of the prior links in the causal chain. Often an explanation of an act will mention such factors, even when there was no specific request for them. If I ask you, for example, "Why did Jones go to the concert tonight?" you might reply, "Because Smith told him they were going to play the Trout Quintet." The only event explicitly mentioned in this reply is Smith's telling Jones something. How does this explain Jone's act? Obviously, the reply implies that Smith's telling Jones that they were going to play the Trout Quintet caused Jones to believe that they were going to play the Trout Quintet. And this belief, presumably in conjunction with Jones' desire to hear the Trout Quintet, caused Jones to go to the concert. Thus, Jones' act is explained by implicitly indicating certain beliefs and desires and explicitly indicating the *cause* of the relevant belief.

Behavioral scientists have similar reasons for inquiring into the causes of wants and beliefs. They want to know not merely the most immediate causes of behavior, but also its more remote causes. Inquiry into the causes of wants and beliefs is especially important for behavioral science because of its frequent concern with the prediction or control of behavior. Wants and beliefs cannot be directly observed; hence, to predict behavior which is caused by wants and beliefs one must first ascertain those observable events which cause wants and beliefs, for these events will help one make predictions. Similarly, wants and beliefs cannot be directly manipulated; hence, if one wishes to control behavior, one must ascertain which manipulable events or factors cause wants and beliefs.

For all these reasons, inquiry into the causes of wants and beliefs is a common phenomenon in the behavioral sciences. Very often, however, the task is not stated precisely in these terms. As we have already seen, talk about wants and beliefs often occurs in rather different terminology. Secondly, since the presence of a want or a belief is usually inferred from behavior, there is normally some correlation of the behavior with the factors which cause a want or belief. Often an investigator will talk more explicitly about the behavior than the want or the belief. Nevertheless, it may be quite clear that the immediate effect of the causal factors under investigation is to bring about some want or some belief which in turn causes the behavior.

Let me begin by reviewing a few of the approaches to studying the causes of wants, including the causes of the relative strength or intensity of a want. Physiological investigation is one of the most salient ways of studying the causes of wants. At present, however, the physiological causes of only the most basic wants, such as the want for food or the want for sex, are understood at all well. Experiments on rats indicate that the desire for food seems to be controlled largely by regions in the hypothalamus, called the "hunger center" and the "satiation center." Sexual and maternal desires in rats seem also to be controlled by regions of the hypothalamus, for stimulation of one region produces male mounting behavior and stimulation of another region produces female maternal behavior. This sort of information, however, tells us only about *generic* wants; it tells us about the cause of wanting food *in general,* but nothing about the desires for specific foods—e.g., for a slice of roast beef or for a malted milk. Even less is known about the (neuro-)physiological causes of desires not directly related to biological needs, such as a desire to listen to the Brandenburg Concertos or a desire to read poetry.

Many psychologists try to account for nonbiological desires in terms of desires, drives, or needs which have a biological basis. Here the attempt is not to find the immediate physiological causes of desires, but to show that primary or basic desires, via some process of learning or conditioning, bring about certain secondary or nonbasic desires. This approach is formulated by Neal Miller and John Dollard:

> Social scientists are keenly aware of the role of primary drives, such as hunger, which are met by the distinctive conditions of learning characteristic of each society. . . . As time passes in the life of the child, these crude drive tendencies become less visible . . . and are replaced by various *social* motivations. These social motivations are variously called *secondary drives, acquired drives,* or *social attitudes.* Upon the primary drive of pain is built the . . . secondary drive of anxiety. Upon the crude hunger drive are built appetites for particular foods. All of these secondary drives are derived by the joint operation of psychological variables under the pressure of social conditions. It is these secondary drives which particularly interest the social scientist, because they form such a large and obvious part of social motivation. In an analogous though more complex manner, there arise also acquired drives toward gregariousness, social conformity, prestige seeking, desire for money, and most important here, *imitativeness.* It is necessary to notice that once these social drives have been generated, they operate exactly as do the primary drives; but it is also crucial that they never lose their acquired, or dependent, character.[21]

Assuming it is correct to translate the term "drive" here as "desire," it is obvious that Miller and Dollard seek to account for the various social desires in terms of certain other, more primary, desires and aversions—e.g., desires for food and aversions for pain.

Another theory which tries to account for certain desires in terms of other desires is Freud's theory of *displacement* or *substitution.* When a certain desire is frustrated or incapable of being satisfied, a substitute desire often crops up in its place. Thus, a worker who desires to hit his boss, but whose prudence forces him not to do so, may form a desire to lash out at some fellow worker, or perhaps to kick the proverbial cat. Freud theorized that the frustration of sexual desires often leads to the formation of other, sometimes more socially acceptable, desires.

---

[21] Neal Miller and John Dollard, *Social Learning and Imitation* (New Haven: Yale University Press, 1941), pp. 9–10.

. . . the component-instincts of sexuality, as well as the united sexual impulse which comprises them, show a great capacity to change their object, to exchange it for another—i.e. for one more easily attainable; this capacity for displacement and readiness to accept surrogates must produce a powerful counter-effect to the effect of a frustration. One amongst these processes serving as protection against illness arising from want has reached a particular significance in the development of culture. It consists in the abandonment, on the part of the sexual impulse, of an aim previously found either in the gratification of a component-impulse or in the gratification incidental to reproduction, and the adoption of a new aim—which new aim, though genetically related to the first, can no longer be regarded as sexual, but must be called social in character. We call this process SUBLIMATION. . . . [22]

The idea of displacement has been widely used by psychologists studying the phenomenon of aggression.[23] The aggressive behavior of a boy in school, for example, might be explained by the presence of frustration in the home. When the boy's hostile desires at home are inhibited by threats of force, he may form hostile desires at school by way of displacement of the original desires.

The study of the causes of desires can focus on one of two separate questions: how a person develops a certain *standing* want and how he comes to have a certain *occurrent* want at a given moment. The attempt to derive acquired or secondary desires from primary drives is probably an attempt to deal with standing wants; it is not really designed to explain why a person has a specific occurrent want at a specific time. To deal with occurrent wants it is important to consider the perceptual cues of the agent at the time in question. Very often a standing want is aroused or made manifest in an occurrent want by things that the agent notices in his environment. This is made explicit by Krech, Crutchfield, and Ballachey:

> The particular set of wants which is activated at any one moment is also determined by specific cues in the environmental situation. Such situational cues may instigate a latent want; they may also serve to strengthen a want already active.
>
> The situational cues which are most powerful in arousing and intensifying wants are the *goal objects* actually present in the situation. Both genetic factors and learning are responsible for the want-arousing power of goal objects. A man's hunger for food may be aroused if he smells the odor of broiled steak emanating from his neighbor's barbecue; his sexual want may be aroused if he sees his neighbor's comely wife; his acquisitive want may be aroused if he catches a glimpse of his neighbor driving up in a new Mercedes Benz 300 SL.
>
> The situational cues may also take the form of *symbols* and other indirect

---

[22] From *A General Introduction to Psychoanalysis* by Sigmund Freud, published by Liveright Publishers, New York. Copyright 1920, 1935, by Edward L. Bernays, p. 354.

[23] For example, see John Dollard, Leonard Doob, *et al.*, *Frustration and Aggression* (New Haven: Yale University Press, 1939).

cues pertaining to the goal and its achievement. The man's hunger may be activated by hearing the noon whistle; his acquisitive want by opening the pages of the *Wall Street Journal*.[24]

Another illustration of a theory designed to deal with occurrent wants is that of approach-avoidance conflict theory. But here the concentration is not so much on *which* desires an agent has at a given time, as on the *intensities* of these desires at a given time. The central hypothesis of approach-avoidance theory is that an agent's desire for a goal-object and his aversion for a feared object increase in intensity as he comes closer to them. Thus, the relative position of the agent to the object is a determinant of the relative strength of his desire or aversion for the object. Neal Miller, who has developed approach-avoidance theory in some detail, states his hypotheses as follows:

(A)   The tendency to approach a goal is stronger the nearer the subject is to it. This will be called the *gradient of approach*.

(B)   The tendency to avoid a feared stimulus is stronger the nearer the subject is to it. This will be called the *gradient of avoidance*.

(C)   The strength of avoidance increases more rapidly with nearness than does that of approach. In other words, the gradient of avoidance is *steeper* than that of approach.

(D)   The strength of tendencies to approach or avoid varies with the strength of the drive upon which they are based. In other words, an increase in drive raises the height of the entire gradient.

(E)   When two incompatible responses are in conflict, the stronger one will occur.[25]

Having looked at a handful of examples of how behavioral scientists study the causes of wants, let us now turn to some ways in which they study the causes of beliefs. One of the interesting questions in this area is the nature of the development of concepts and beliefs in the maturing child. The most important work in this field has been done by Jean Piaget.[26] Piaget studies the ages at which children typically acquire a more or less clear grasp of the conception of physical objects, of time, of space, and of causality. He also studies the growth of the ability in children to reason and make inferences. All of this work is obviously relevant to understanding the sorts of *beliefs*

---

[24] Krech, Crutchfield, and Ballachey, *op. cit.*, p. 85.

[25] "Comments on Theoretical Models Illustrated by the Development of a Theory of Conflict," *Journal of Presonality*, (1951–52), XX 90.

[26] Cf. *The Construction of Reality in the Child*, trans. Margaret Cook (New York: Basic Books, 1954), and *Judgment and Reasoning in the Child*, trans. Marjorie Warden (London: Routledge and Kegan Paul, 1928).

children can have at different ages, inasmuch as the ability to have beliefs about spatial or temporal relations, for example, presupposes a conception of space and time. Piaget's work is not directed at discovering the causes of a particular belief being acquired at a particular time, so much as discovering the nature of the growth, over time, of the sorts of cognitive capacities which adult human beings have.

When it comes to the causes of occurrent beliefs, there are two obviously important topics of inquiry by behavioral science—viz., *perception* and *memory*. Many of the occurrent beliefs which a person has at a given time are caused by his seeing, hearing, or otherwise perceiving facts about his environment. Many other of one's occurrent beliefs are caused by past beliefs or past experiences which one brings to mind or recalls. Hence, a thorough understanding of the operation of perception and memory is extremely helpful in understanding the circumstances which bring about one's beliefs.

Much of the investigation of perception and memory focuses on the physiological and neural processes which underlie them. I shall not attempt to review any of the literature on these matters. But some of the other investigations of perception and memory focus on factors such as social influence, the influence of one's desires, and the influence of previous activities by the agent. These are interesting enough to warrant brief discussion.

It is a matter of common experience that a mental *set* or *desire* influences the sorts of things in the environment that one notices. A hungry person is much more likely to notice the presence of restaurants than someone who has no current interest in eating. The effects of set or preoccupation on sensitizing the perceptual mechanism has been experimentally demonstrated by L. Postman and D. R. Brown.[27] They arranged for some subjects to succeed and others to fail on a certain experimental task. Then each of these groups of subjects were examined for their recognition threshold of words exposed briefly in a tachistoscope. The "success subjects" had a lower threshold for success words (e.g., "excellent," "perfection," "winner") than the "failure subjects"; and failure subjects, correspondingly, had a lower threshold for failure words (e.g., "unable," "obstacle," "defeat").

A second sort of investigation of the causes of perceptual beliefs, leading to a theory of the causes of attitudes as well, was conducted by Muzafer Sherif. Sherif performed experiments designed to establish the effect on a person's beliefs of his being in a group situation. In these experiments the so-called "autokinetic effect" was employed.

> In complete darkness such as is found in a closed room that is not illuminated, . . . a single (stationary) small light seems to move, and it may appear to move erratically in all directions. If you present the point of light repeatedly to a

---

[27] "The Perceptual Consequences of Success and Failure," *Journal of Abnormal and Social Psychology*, XLVII (1952), 213–21.

person, he may see the light appearing at different places in the room each time, especially if he does not know the distance between himself and the light.[28]

Subjects were studied first when alone, and asked to state the distance they believed the light moved. Subjects were then studied in a group situation to discover modifications in their estimates (beliefs) brought about by membership in the group. Two interesting results were obtained. First, subjects tested individually tended to establish subjectively a range of extent of movement and a point which served as a reference point with which each successive experienced movement was compared. The ranges and references were peculiar to each individual. Secondly, in the group experiments each group tended to converge toward a standard of its own. The members of the group tended to change their own previous ranges or norms and to approximate more closely to the estimate of the rest of the group. Obviously, each member's beliefs about the movement of the light were affected by the estimates made by the other members. On the basis of these experiments, Sherif advanced the hypothesis that a group of people, in an unstable situation, will always tend to establish a collective frame of reference or a common set of attitudes.

In the investigation of memory one of the interesting discoveries is the so-called "Zeigarnik effect," so named for the experimenter, Bluma Zeigarnik.

> She devised a number of different tasks (puzzles, problems, etc.) for student subjects to perform. During the experimental session, each student was invited to work at the tasks. The subject was allowed to continue some of the activities until they were clearly completed. For example, work at a puzzle might continue until the solution was clearly attained. But some of the activities were informally interrupted before they were finished. The experimenter interrupted by simply asking the subject to work at some other task instead. After the subject had worked on all of the tasks for a while, finishing some of them but not finishing others, the various tasks were collected and put out of sight. Then Zeigarnik asked the subject in an informal way if he could recall some of the activities he had worked on. Typically the subject described a number of the tasks immediately. Then, however, he would have to pause and think carefully before being able to recall any more. Zeigarnik found, as she had expected, that the number of *unfinished* tasks which were recalled (particularly during the "spontaneous" period before the pause) greatly exceeded the number of completed tasks that were recalled. In fact, the ratio of recalled unfinished tasks to recalled completed tasks . . . for a sizable number of subjects averaged about 1.9.[29]

Evidently, the fact that the subject failed to complete a certain task made it more likely that he would remember, or think of, that task. In other words,

---

[28] Muzafer Sherif, *The Psychology of Social Norms* (New York: Harper and Brothers, 1936), p. 91.

[29] J. W. Atkinson, *An Introduction to Motivation* (Princeton, N. J.: Van Nostrand, 1964), p. 83.

it made it more likely that he would be *aware* of his having worked on that task, or that he would have occurrent *beliefs* of his having worked at that task.

We have mentioned perception and memory as two of the most important causal processes leading to (occurrent) beliefs, and we have seen some selected investigations of the factors which affect these processes. A third manner in which beliefs are affected—as is obvious from everyday experience—is when the agent hears or reads information. This too is fertile soil for scientific investigation, and many behavioral scientists, especially sociologists, have investigated the factors which contribute to belief in the context of oral or written communication. Sociologists have studied the effects of radio and newspaper advertising on the beliefs and attitudes of consumers, and they have studied the effects of mass media campaigning on the opinions of voters.[30] Lazarsfeld, Berelson, and Gaudet, for example, were interested in whether the opinions and beliefs of individuals were more affected directly by mass media, or whether they were more influenced by face-to-face communication. They write:

> We are led, first of all, to study opinion leaders. In every social group there are some individuals who are particularly active and articulate. They are more sensitive than others to the interests of their group, and more anxious to express themselves on important issues. It is relatively easy to locate these individuals, and thus to study how they differ from the majority of their group.
> In the present study we found that one of the functions of opinion leaders is to mediate between the mass media and other people in their groups. It is commonly assumed that individuals obtain their information directly from newspapers, radio, and other media. Our findings, however, did not bear this out. The majority of people acquired much of their information and many of their ideas through personal contacts with the opinion leaders in their groups. These latter individuals, in turn, exposed themselves relatively more than others to the mass media. The two-step flow of information is of obvious practical importance for any study of propaganda.[31]

I have now mentioned the investigation of perception, memory, and verbal communication as factors in the causation of beliefs. A further important element in the causation of beliefs, or changes of beliefs, is the presence of certain other beliefs. One approach to this field current among psychologists bears the generic name "balance theory." This is a kind of theory which states that systems of belief have a tendency to be "in balance," and that

---

[30] Cf. Paul Lazarsfeld, Bernard Berelson, and Hazel Gaudet, *The People's Choice* (New York: Columbia University Press, 1948), and Elihu Katz and Paul Lazarsfeld, *Personal Influence* (Glencoe, Ill.: The Free Press, 1955).

[31] Lazarsfeld, Berelson, and Gaudet, *The People's Choice*, Preface to Second Edition (New York: Columbia University Press, 1948), Reprinted by permission of the publishers. pp. xxii-xxiii.

there is a tendency for beliefs to change or new beliefs to form whenever a belief system is unbalanced. Probably the most influential specimen of "balance theory" is that found in the work of Leon Festinger. In his book, *A Theory of Cognitive Dissonance*, Festinger explains the core of his theory as follows:

1. There may exist dissonant or "nonfitting" relations among cognitive elements.
2. The existence of dissonance gives rise to pressures to reduce the dissonance and to avoid increases in dissonance.
3. Manifestations of the operation of these pressures include behavior changes, changes of cognition, and circumspect exposure to new information and new opinions.[32]

In general outline, then, this theory says that inconsistent beliefs will tend to give rise to changes in the belief system; systems of belief which are in consonance will tend to move toward consonance. Actually, Festinger's theory is not really prepared to predict *what* belief changes will occur, or what behavior will occur, when a belief system is in dissonance. But presumably some changes in belief can be said to have been caused by the present of dissonance.

Another author, Dana Bramel, has used balance theory, in conjunction with other assumptions about self-esteem, to try to make predictions about beliefs and to test these predictions. Bramel has tried to show how these assumptions, together with the hypotheses of balance (or dissonance) theory, suggest that a man will "project" certain characteristics on others if he has certain beliefs about himself. Specifically,

If a person is exposed to information strongly implying that he possesses an undesirable characteristic, he is more likely to attribute that trait to others, if the information is dissonant with his level of self-esteem: the greater the dissonance, the more likely it is that projection will occur.[33]

In other words, given a set of beliefs about oneself relative to others—which constitutes one's "self-esteem"—if a new belief about one's own characteristics is introduced which is dissonant with this set, there will be a tendency to "project" these characteristics—i.e., to form a belief that other people have these characteristics too. Such projection will tend to maintain one's level of self-esteem. Bramel tested this hypothesis by inducing a (false) belief in a subject to the effect that he has homosexual tendencies. Those subjects for whom this belief was dissonant with their self-esteem formed beliefs that their experimental partners also had homosexual tendencies; and the greater

---

[32] (Stanford: Stanford University Press, 1962), p. 31.

[33] "A Dissonance Theory Approach to Defensive Projection," *Journal of Abnormal and Social Psychology*, LXIV (1962), 122.

the dissonance, the higher was the degree of homosexual tendency attributed to (believed to be true of) the partner.

Another fertile area for the study of the causation of beliefs is the study of how people formulate and test hypotheses. Many of our beliefs are formed by first framing a proposition which one thinks may be true, and by then gathering evidence which supports it. The procedures used in framing and testing such hypotheses are obviously important for understanding the formation of belief. Some of the most important work in this area has been done by Jerome Bruner. In *A Study of Thinking*,[34] co-authored with Jacqueline Goodnow and George Austin, Bruner identifies a variety of different strategies that might be used in formulating and testing hypotheses and studies the conditions under which these strategies tend to be used. When presented with a problem the solution of which requires a variety of tests, a person may choose different kinds of tests to perform and different orders in which to perform them. Different strategies of testing have different advantages and disadvantages. One strategy may enable a person to gain substantial information relevant to his problem from a small number of tests but may at the same time impose considerable cognitive strain in assimilating this information. Another strategy may decrease the cognitive strain involved in assimilating information but require a larger number of tests to get an equivalent amount of information. One strategy may involve quite a bit of risk in whether or not one will get the requisite information quickly, but with luck the information can be acquired in a short time. With another strategy, the needed information cannot be acquired in a very short time but the amount of risk involved may be less. Having explained the advantages and disadvantages which different strategies might conceivably have, Bruner shows which advantages and disadvantages would be possessed by specific strategies in a particular problem-solving situation. He then proceeds to provide experimental evidence about the conditions under which a person will tend to choose one of these strategies over others. His delineation of the variety of possible strategies and his examination of the circumstances which prompt a choice of one strategy over others sheds considerable light on the nature of hypothesis-making and hypothesis-testing, and thereby sheds light on the manner in which some of our beliefs are acquired.

4.   Stimulus-Response Theories of Behavior

In the preceding two sections I have examined investigations of behavioral scientists that lend support to the want-and-belief model of behavior. But not all behavioral scientists are committed to theories or ex-

---

[34] Jerome Bruner, Jacqueline Goodnow, and George Austin, *A Study of Thinking* (New York: John Wiley & Sons, Inc., 1956). Cf. Chapter Four.

planations of action which make use of, or presuppose, anything like wants or beliefs. Indeed, as we saw in Section 1 of this chapter, some behavioral scientists have explicitly disavowed any reference to, or reliance on, such mentalistic notions. So-called "stimulus-response" theorists, or "behaviorists," have introduced theories of behavior or schemes for explaining behavior which make no use whatever of mentalistic or purposive notions. It cannot be said that *all* psychologists dubbed "behaviorists" are averse to purposive notions like wanting and believing. We have seen that E. C. Tolman, who styles himself a "behaviorist," explicitly embraces purposive notions. Nevertheless, many other behaviorists eschew the use of purposive notions in psychology, and try to account for behavior exclusively in terms of such notions as "stimulus," "drive," "conditioning," etc. One of the most prominent psychologists of this persuasion—perhaps even more extreme than most—is Burrhus F. Skinner. I shall use Skinner's work as the focal point of my discussion of stimulus-response psychology.

Skinner seeks to systematize the vast majority of behavior in terms of *operant conditioning*.[35] Operant conditioning occurs when a certain kind of behavior is followed by reinforcing events. For example, a person undergoes operant conditioning if food is presented to him whenever he hums a certain tune. The function of such reinforcement is to "strengthen" the response of humming the tune—i.e., to increase the probability of emission of that response. Having been reinforced by food whenever one hums the tune, the probability of humming the tune is greater than it was prior to this conditioning. The probability of a given response at a given time is a function not only of previous conditioning, but also of the present state of deprivation (or satiation) of the organism. A person who has been deprived of food prior to time t_1 is more likely to hum the tune at t_1 than he would be if he has been eating continuously just prior to t_1.

Instead of reinforcing a person whenever a given response is emitted (or a certain proportion of the times that the response is emitted), one can instead reinforce a person only when the response is emitted in the context of certain stimuli. Instead of presenting food whenever the tune is hummed, for example, we may present food to the subject only when his humming is accompanied by a certain light being on. This process is called *"operant discrimination."* When a discrimination has been established, the response comes under the control of the stimulus. We may raise the probability of a response instantly by presenting the discriminative stimulus—e. g., by turning on the light we raise the probability of the person's humming the tune.

There are numerous difficulties inherent in Skinner's scheme, especially

---

[35] My summary of Skinner's approach—which mentions only its barest essentials—is based mainly on his exposition in *Science and Human Behavior*, esp. Chapters 5, 6, and 7. The original and more precise exposition of his system is found in *The Behavior of Organisms* (New York: Appleton-Century-Crofts, 1938).

when applied to human behavior.[36] This is not the place, however, to engage in a critical appraisal of Skinner's approach. For present purposes the question is not whether Skinner's account of behavior is correct or true, but whether, *if true*, it would be compatible with want-and-belief explanations of behavior. Of course, if we could be sure that Skinner's system does not work for explaining human behavior, or works for only a very small fraction of human behavior, then it would not constitute much of a challenge to the want-and-belief model. But there is no quick or easy way of assessing the correctness or fruitfulness of Skinner's approach; and anyway, other people are better equipped to do this than I am. Thus, I shall address myself only to the following question: *if* Skinner's account of human behavior were correct, would it *preclude* or *undermine* purposive explanations of behavior?

On the face of it, Skinner's approach definitely seems to preclude the want-and-belief model. First of all, Skinner seeks to explain behavior exclusively in terms of such factors as histories of reinforcement, periods of deprivation, and stimuli presented to the subject. All of these factors are intended to be external physical events; none of them contains a hint of purpose, teleology, or intention. Secondly, as we saw in Section 1, Skinner often denounces explanations in terms of inner events as spurious or unenlightening. How, then, could one possibly imagine that Skinner's system is compatible with the want-and-belief model of behavior?

To reply to the second point first, I wish to insist upon distinguishing between Skinner's substantive system of behavior and his assessment of the implications of his system. It is certainly conceivable that Skinner's system of behavior is quite correct though his assessment of the implications of this system are completely unjustified; the system may be correct though some of the methodological presuppositions that led him to the system are unfounded. Skinner's system may be useful for predicting, controlling, and explaining behavior. Yet he may be wrong in implying that it is in conflict with traditional forms of explaining behavior.[37] His own system of behavior may do without mental events or purposive concepts of any sort. But his methodological presupposition that it is *illegitimate* to employ mentalistic concepts in a science of behavior may be proved wrong by a more enlightened methodology of science. Thus, Skinner's own comments on the implications of his system are not necessarily authoritative.

---

[36] For a general critical discussion of Skinner's work, see the article on Skinner by William S. Verplanck, in W. K. Estes, *et al.*, eds., *Modern Learning Theory* (New York, 1954). Another critical article, with primary attention to Skinner's treatment of verbal behavior, is Noam Chomsky's "A Review of B. F. Skinner's *Verbal Behavior*," *Language*, XXXV (1959), 26–58, reprinted in Jerry A. Fodor and Jerrold J. Katz, eds., *The Structure of Language* (Englewood Cliffs, N. J.: Prentice-Hall, Inc., 1964), pp. 547–78.

[37] Actually Skinner tends to vacillate on this point. At times he intimates that his approach to behavior is clearly in conflict with traditional approaches. At other times he tries to reinterpret traditional notions, including teleological notions, in his own vocabulary. In one passage, for example, he writes: "Statements which use such words as 'incentive' or

Let me now return to the first point. Suppose that, as Skinner envisages, all human behavior can be accounted for in terms of histories of reinforcement, states of deprivation, and stimuli impinging on the organism. Would this preclude the causal or explanatory relevance of wants and beliefs? Not so, I believe; at least not without further premises. In general, any event *Z* can be the effect of numerous sets of causal factors; there might, for example, be a series of successive events, *U*, *V*, *W*, *X*, and *Y*, *each* of which is a cause of *Z*. Thus, even if all behavior were caused by "Skinnerian" events, it might still be true that behavior is caused by wants and beliefs *too*. For it is at least conceivable that the Skinnerian events and the wants and beliefs are simply successive links in a chain of causes leading to behavior: the reinforcements, deprivations, and stimuli cause the wants and beliefs which in turn cause the behavior.

That this is not an idle or arbitrary supposition is supported by the fact that, as we saw in Section 2 of this chapter, Tolman thought of purposes and cognitions as "intermediate in the causal equation between the initiating causes and the final resultant behavior." The "initiating" causes, for Tolman, are environmental stimuli and physiological states. These are causes of behavior, according to Tolman, but only *via* the intermediate causes—viz., purposes and cognitions. Moreover, Skinner himself in one passage seems to allow just such a possibility!

> The physiologist may point out that several ways of raising the probability of drinking have a common effect: they increase the concentration of solutions in the body. Through some mechanism not yet well understood, this may bring about a corresponding change in the nervous system which in turn makes drinking more probable. In the same way, it may be argued that all these operations make the organism "feel thirsty" or "want a drink" and that such a psychic state also acts upon the nervous system in some unexplained way to induce drinking. In each case we have a causal chain consisting of three links: (1) an operation performed upon the organism from without—for example, water deprivation; (2) an inner condition—for example, physiological or psychic thirst; and (3) a kind of behavior—for example, drinking. Independent information about the second link would obviously permit us to predict the

'purpose' are usually reducible to statements about operant conditioning, and only a slight change is required to bring them within the framework of natural science. . . . Expressions involving goals and purposes are abbreviations." (*Science and Human Behavior*, pp. 87, 90.)

The latter is an example of how Skinner's meta-systemic remarks may be entirely wrong even if his system is a good one. For even if behavior can be accounted for by operant conditioning, Skinner is surely wrong in saying that statements about goals are simply abbreviations for, or translatable into, statements about operant conditioning. Skinner says that the sentence "I am looking for my glasses" is not a further description of a man's behavior "but of the variables of which his behavior is a function; it is equivalent to 'I have lost my glasses,' 'I shall stop what I am doing when I find my glasses,' or 'When I have done this in the past, I have found my glasses.' " (*Science and Human Behavior*, p. 90.) These are obviously absurd translations.

third without recourse to the first. It would be a preferred type of variable because it would be nonhistoric; the first link may lie in the past history of the organism, but the second is a current condition. Direct information about the second link is, however, seldom, if ever, available. Sometimes we infer the second link from the third: an animal is judged to be thirsty if it drinks. In that case, the explanation is spurious. Sometimes we infer the second link from the first: an animal is said to be thirsty if it has not drunk for a long time. In that case, we obviously cannot dispense with the prior history.

   The second link is useless in the *control* of behavior unless we can manipulate it. At the moment, we have no way of directly altering neural processes at appropriate moments in the life of a behaving organism, nor has any way been discovered to alter a psychic process. We usually set up the second link through the first: we make an animal thirsty, in either the physiological or the psychic sense, by depriving it of water, feeding it salt, and so on. In that case, the second link obviously does not permit us to dispense with the first.[38]

In this passage Skinner admits the possibility of psychic causes of behavior and fits them into a chain of causes of the sort suggested above. His only reasons in this passage for minimizing the importance of psychic states is that we cannot *directly* know about psychic states and that we cannot *directly* control psychic states. Such considerations, however, are not reasons for denying the *existence* of psychic states or for denying their *causal* relevance to behavior.

   I have said that both Skinnerian events and wants and beliefs could be causes of behavior if the Skinnerian events caused the wants and beliefs which in turn caused the behavior. In order for this to transpire, however, it is not necessary that the Skinnerian events all occur simultaneously at t_1, thereby causing the wants and beliefs to occur at t_2, thereby causing behavior to occur at t_3. In particular, it is not necessary that the Skinnerian events occur simultaneously. A more realistic illustration of what might happen is this. Between times t_1 and t_5 the agent undergoes reinforcement whenever he hums the tune while the light is on. If he hums the tune while the light is on he receives a piece of cake; if he hums when the light is off, he does not receive a piece of cake. This process of reinforcement causes him to have the standing belief that he will receive a piece of cake whenever he hums the tune while the light is on. During a subsequent time period, say from t_6 to t_{10}, the light is kept off and the agent does not receive any cake. This period of cake-deprivation causes him to want a piece of cake, a want which begins at t_{10} and persists until t_{11}. Meanwhile, at t_{10}, the light goes on, and this causes the agent to have a belief that the light is on. This (occurrent) belief combines with the standing belief indicated above to bring about another (occurrent) belief, at t_{11}—viz., that if he hums the tune *now* he will receive a piece of cake. This occurrent belief and the occurrent desire for a piece of cake jointly cause him to emit the behavior (perform the act) of humming the tune at t_{12}.

---

[38] *Science and Human Behavior*, pp. 33–34.

This entire causal sequence is diagramed in Figure 11. Skinnerian events (the history of reinforcement, the deprivation, and the stimulus) are presented by darkened circles. Wants and beliefs are represented by empty circles; and behavior is represented by a circle with an "*X*". Arrows indicate causal connections.

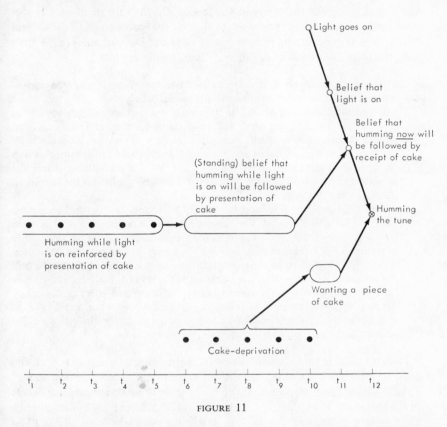

FIGURE 11

The foregoing example suggests the following relationships between Skinnerian events, on the one hand, and wants and beliefs, on the other: (A) states of deprivation are the causes of wants, and (B) present stimuli together with past reinforcements are the causes of beliefs. Of course, this schema is far too simple. And in fact Skinner's system contains other devices—e.g., "stimulus generalization," "conditioned reinforcers," "generalized reinforcers," etc.—which help account for the formation of beliefs and desires. As an initial indication of the possible relationships between Skinnerian events and purposive factors, however, these suggestions are helpful. Moreover, these relationships are corroborated by discussions of other behaviorists. Consider a case analyzed by Neal Miller and John Dollard.

Miller and Dollard describe an experiment in which a little girl, who is known to be hungry and want candy, is brought into a room where some candy is hidden under a book on a certain bookcase. She is told that a candy is hidden under one of the books and that she may eat the candy if she finds it. The girl begins searching. On the first trial it takes her 210 seconds to find the candy. On the next trial, however, when candy is again hidden under the same book, she finds the candy in 86 seconds. On the third trial only 11 seconds are required to find the candy. In the end she learns to go to the correct book at the very beginning of each trial. Miller and Dollard analyze the girl's behavior with the concepts of "drive," "cue," and "reward."

> The first factor involved in learning is *drive*. Before beginning, the experimenters had to be sure that the little girl wanted candy. . . .
>
> Responses are elicited by *cues*. In this case, the drive for candy, the directions given to the girl, and the whole setting of the room are parts of the general pattern of cues. Possible specific cues to the response of picking up a given book are the sight of the color, size, and marking of the book and the position of that book in relation to the rest of the bookcase. Were there nothing distinctive about the correct book to serve as a cue, it would be impossible for the girl to learn to solve this problem. . . .
>
> Finally, one of the responses is followed by seeing, seizing, and eating the candy. This is the *reward*. On subsequent trials a response that has been followed by reward will be more likely to recur. This increase in the probability of recurrence of a rewarded response may be expressed in shorthand fashion by saying that the reward has strengthened the connection between the cues and the rewarded response. Without some sort of a reward, the girl would never learn to go regularly to the correct book. The rewarding effect of the candy depends upon the presence of the drive and tends to produce a reduction in strength of this drive. After eating a large amount of candy, the girl would be satiated and stop looking for it.[39]

It seems clear in this example that *drive* is the cause of a *desire*. In fact, the passage sometimes seems to suggest that drive simply *is* a desire or a want.[40] Similarly, it is fairly obvious that the function of the *cues* is to induce *beliefs* in the little girl. The color, size, and markings of different books cause her to have beliefs concerning the various particular books in front of her. The

---

[39] Miller and Dollard, *Social Learning and Imitation*, pp. 16–17.

[40] Chomsky contends that Skinner too sometimes uses "deprivation" as a mere synonym for "wanting." In his review of Skinner's *Verbal Behavior* (in Fodor and Katz, eds., *op. cit.*, p. 566), Chomsky writes:

"Suppose however that the speaker says *Give me the book*, *Take me for a ride*, or *Let me fix it*. What kinds of deprivation can be associated with these mands? How do we determine or measure the relevant deprivation? I think we must conclude in this case, as before, either that the notion *deprivation* is relevant at most to a minute fragment of verbal behavior, or else that the statement '*X* is under *Y*-deprivation' is just an odd paraphrase for '*X* wants *Y*' . . . "

function of the *cue-response-reward* sequences is also, I think, to cause *beliefs*. These sequences cause her to have beliefs about the sorts of cues which must be present in order for a certain response to bring a certain reward. Each time she emits the response of seizing a book with specific cue-properties, she is rewarded by finding and eating a candy. Hence, by a simple inductive process she comes to believe that that sort of response in that sort of cue-situation will result in the reward of a candy.

Now a defender of stimulus-response psychology who *opposes* use of the want-and-belief model might argue as follows: "Granted that many histories of deprivation are causes of wants, and that stimuli are causes of beliefs. Etc. Still it does not follow from this that wants and beliefs are necessary factors in the causation of behavior. Goldman claims that Skinnerian events cause behavior only by first causing wants and beliefs which in turn cause the behavior; in other words, that Skinnerian events operate on behavior *only via* wants and beliefs. But this is far from evident. Even if we grant that Skinnerian events cause wants and beliefs, there are two possible remaining pictures of the causation of behavior. First, as Goldman suggests, Skinnerian events may cause wants and beliefs which in turn cause behavior. But secondly, Skinnerian events may *directly* cause behavior and at the same time *incidentally* cause wants and beliefs. (See Figure 12.) In the right-hand picture,

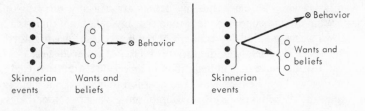

FIGURE 12

it would not be correct to say that the behavior is caused by the wants and beliefs, for in this situation the Skinnerian events would cause the behavior *whether or not* the wants and beliefs occurred. The wants and beliefs do occur, but they are causally irrelevant to the behavior since the behavior would be emitted even if the wants and beliefs had not occurred."

There are two points to notice about this proposal. First, if it were true that wants and beliefs were causally irrelevant to behavior, then the Skinnerian events would be causing *mere* movement or *mere* behavior as opposed to *action*. According to my definition of "action," no event is an "*act*" unless it is caused by wants and beliefs (at least by wants). Hence, if wants and beliefs did not cause the behavior, the behavior would not be genuine action. Secondly, since it is part of the very notion of wanting that wants tend to cause acts, it would be very surprising should there be large numbers of wants none of which cause any acts. Yet this is what the objector apparently envisages: he seems to suppose that Skinnerian events regularly cause there to *be* wants and beliefs but that these wants and beliefs do not *cause* behavior.

These two points, however, depend very heavily on the specific explications I have given of the terms "act" and "want." It should be expected that a proponent of the view that Skinnerian events directly cause behavior would challenge or deny these explications.[41] Let us, therefore, for the sake of argument, waive these two points. Let us consider it a purely empirical matter, not to be decided by our definition of "act" or of "want," whether wants and beliefs are causally relevant to behavior. Let us assume that there are items of behavior such as taking a book, humming a tune, uttering a sentence, such that it is logically possible that they are not caused by wants and beliefs. Then let us ask whether, *as a matter of fact*, they are causally dependent on wants and beliefs or whether they are dependent on Skinnerian events alone, while the occurrence of wants and beliefs is quite incidental. As soon as the question is posed, however, the answer seems to me clear. Who can seriously deny that a person would act one way if he had certain wants and another way if he had other wants? Who can deny that my wanting to hum "Three Blind Mice" is causally relevant to my humming "Three Blind Mice," that if I had *wanted* to hum a different tune then I *would* have hummed a different tune? Similarly, who can deny that my beliefs are causally relevant to my behavior? What could be more evident than that my belief that there is a lake north of town was a genuine determinant of my behavior of driving north on this hot day? Isn't it perfectly evident that if I had not believed there is a lake to the north, I would have driven in a different direction? Admittedly, almost all the evidence we have in support of the position that wants and beliefs are causally relevant to behavior is of a commonsense variety. Nonetheless, it seems to me to be very strong evidence indeed. Given all this evidence, if we could be persuaded that behavior is (also) determined by operant conditioning, the most plausible position to adopt is not that operant conditioning "directly" causes behavior, but that it first causes wants and beliefs which in turn cause behavior.

Despite the fact that our commonsense evidence is, in my opinion, extremely strong, we will do well to take a look at some cases studied under experimental conditions. I shall mention two such cases. In one of them, the behavioral scientists themselves analyze their case in a way which points to the relevance of purposive factors. In the other case, it appears at first glance that operant conditioning is "directly" affecting behavior; but I shall contend that this is not really so.

---

[41] Alternatively, a proponent of this view might concede the definition of "act" which implies that an act must be caused by wants (and beliefs). He could then deny that there *are* any acts, so defined.

The first case I wish to examine is the Miller-Dollard example discussed briefly above. In their experiment, the little girl takes 210 seconds to find the candy on the first trial, 86 seconds on the second trial, and only 11 seconds on the third trial. On the fourth trial, however, the girl inexplicably does significantly worse than on the third one: it takes her 86 seconds to find the candy. Now this is quite an unexpected result, since her history of conditioning during the experiment would have led one to predict that her time on the fourth trial would improve over that of the third trial. Miller and Dollard try to account for this anomaly by hypothesizing that "some uncontrolled factor has intervened." "For example, the little girl might say to herself as a result of previous experience with hiding games, 'He'll probably change the place now that I know it.' "[42] In other words, Miller and Dollard go on the assumption that the reason why the girl did badly on the fourth trial is that her *beliefs* about the hiding place were different than would have been expected. Normally the experimental situation would have so affected her beliefs as to produce a continual improvement in her time. When her time gets worse, they conjecture that her beliefs must have been affected by other factors. And this conjecture has obvious plausibility to it.

I do not adduce this case as a counter-example to S-R theory, as an attempt to show that the girl's behavior cannot be accounted for in S-R terms. It is quite possible, as Miller and Dollard conjecture, that the girl's expectation of a change in hiding place can adequately be explained by reference to earlier conditioning, prior to the controlled experiment. The important point is that the girl's behavior—as Miller and Dollard recognize—does depend on the girl's beliefs. Whether her beliefs are caused exclusively by events that occurred during the experiment or whether they are partly caused by events that occurred during previous hiding games, in any case her beliefs *matter* in determining her behavior. It does not appear to be true that the girl's beliefs are *irrelevant* to her behavior, that she would have behaved the same way even if she had *not* thought to herself that the hiding place would be changed. The very fact that this belief or thought is hypothesized in order to account for her otherwise anomalous behavior indicates that it would be a critical factor in determining her behavior. If such a belief would not have had any effect on her behavior, why should the hypothesis of such a belief explain the behavior which was not otherwise expected?

Let me next mention experimental evidence which apparently supports the view that operant conditioning can cause behavior without the mediation of wants or beliefs. Many experiments on verbal behavior have been performed in which subjects are caused by operant conditioning to exhibit certain patterns of utterance.[43] For example, an investigator asks the subject to utter

---

[42] Miller and Dollard, *op. cit.,* p. 16.

[43] Cf. L. Krasner, "Studies in the Conditioning of Verbal Behavior," *Psychological Bulletin*, LV (1958), 148–70, which contains a survey of such experiments.

a sequence of single words, whichever words come to mind. As the subject proceeds the investigator "reinforces" any utterance of a plural noun by saying "mmm-hmm" approvingly. Soon the proportion of plural nouns uttered by the subject substantially increases. Of interest here is the fact that the subject normally does not realize—i.e., does not believe—that his frequency of uttering plural nouns has increased. Nor is he aware of the fact that this increase results from the "approval sounds" of the investigator. This may suggest that the behavior is emitted without being caused by beliefs or wants. That conclusion is unwarranted, however.

What is true is that the subject does not have a conscious want to get the experimenter to say "mmm-hmm" approvingly. Nor does he have a (conscious) belief that the way to get the experimenter to reinforce him with approval is by uttering a plural noun. Nevertheless, the subject does have some wants and beliefs; and these wants and beliefs are relevant to his behavior. The subject has an over-all want to utter whatever words come to mind. And, as each word comes to mind successively, he believes (knows) that it has come to mind. He believes that "cats" has come to mind, that "teeth" has come to mind, etc. He also forms (extrinsic) wants to utter each of the words as they pop into his mind. He has an (extrinsic) want to utter "cats," he has a want to utter "teeth," etc. It is false to say, therefore, that his behavior is not causally dependent on any wants. If he did not have a want to utter whatever words come to mind, he would probably not utter anything at all. And if, just prior to uttering "cats," he did not have a want to utter "cats," then he would not utter "cats." Etc.

What is interesting about the case is that the subject does not have a conscious desire to be reinforced in the way that the experimenter has been reinforcing him. Nor does he have a conscious belief about the acts he should perform in order to be reinforced. Nevertheless, the past reinforcements do have an obvious effect on his behavior. It should not be inferred from this, however, that the subject's behavior is affected "directly" by the operant conditioning, without the operant conditioning working *via* wants or beliefs. In fact, the words which come to the subject's mind, and hence the various wants he has to utter each of these words, are obviously affected by the reinforcements. If the subject were not reinforced when he utters plural nouns, fewer plural nouns would pop into his mind and he would form fewer wants to utter words which happen to be plural nouns. Thus, the operant conditioning does affect the subject's wants and thereby affects his behavior; it does not affect the behavior "directly." The interesting fact, of course, is that the conditioning affects his wants by a largely unconscious (or not fully conscious) process. There is no explicit conscious recognition that plural nouns are being reinforced by the experimenter or that a large proportion of the words being uttered are plural nouns. While this is an interesting finding, it does not prove that operant conditioning affects behavior quite independently of the agent's wants (or beliefs).

I do not wish to deny the possibility that there are *some* occurrences that are caused by operant conditioning though not by wants and beliefs. There may be bodily changes such as sweating or salivating, for example, which can be controlled by operant conditioning[44] but which are not causally dependent on wants and beliefs. It is quite possible, in other words, that the range of phenomena which can be controlled by operant conditioning is broader than the class of events which we normally call "behavior" or "action." But even if involuntary bodily changes like sweating or salivating are controllable by operant conditioning, that is not of much interest here. The issue I have been raising concerns those changes or events which seem *pre-analytically* to be caused by wants and beliefs: events like raising one's hand, uttering a certain word, taking a book from a shelf, etc. It is about *these* events that the question has been raised: Would a Skinnerian explanation of such events rule out a want-and-belief explanation? It is to *this* question that I have ventured a negative answer.

To conclude this section, I wish merely to register my personal doubt that a system such as Skinner's, as it stands at present, will actually succeed in accounting for all or even a significant portion of human behavior. While the evidence continues to come in, however, we can ask ourselves what would follow *if* such a system were successful. In particular we can ask whether its success would be incompatible with the validity of our commonsense explanations of behavior in terms of wants and beliefs. This has been the issue to which I have addressed myself in this section.

5. Neurophysiology and the Purposive Model

I turn now to the relationship between neurophysiological investigation of behavior and the want-and-belief model of behavior. As with the case of stimulus-response theories, it may appear at first blush that neurophysiology is trying to uncover *rival* causes or *rival* explanations. It may appear that the discovery of specific neurophysiological causes of all behavior would undermine the validity of the want-and-belief model. But I shall argue that this is not so, that explanations of action in terms of wants and beliefs may be perfectly compatible with explanations of action in terms of neurophysiological processes.

The most explicit recent statement of the view that neurophysiological explanations of behavior would be incompatible with explanations in terms

---

[44] Recent experiments do indeed suggest that processes controlled by the autonomic nervous system, such as the heart rate and intestinal contractions, can be influenced by operant conditioning in the absence of conscious, voluntary control. See Leo V. DiCara, "Learning in the Automic Nervous System," *Scientific American*, Vol. 222, No. 1 (January, 1970), 31–39.

of wants or intentions is found in Norman Malcolm's article, "The Conceivability of Mechanism."[45] Malcolm imagines a neurophysiological theory that provides "sufficient causal explanations" of human behavior. Given such a theory, he says, a man's behavior would not be explainable in terms of his desires or intentions. If, for example, the movements of a man up a ladder were explainable by reference to neurophysiological states, reference to the man's desires or intentions would be irrelevant:

> ... the movements of the man on the ladder would be *completely* accounted for in terms of electrical, chemical, and mechanical processes in his body. This would surely imply that his desire or intention to retrieve his hat had nothing to do with his movement up the ladder. It would imply that on this same occasion he would have moved up the ladder in exactly this way even if he had had no intention to retrieve his hat, or even no intention to climb the ladder. To mention his intention or purpose would be no explanation, nor even part of an explanation, of his movements on the ladder. Given the antecedent neurological states of his bodily system together with general laws correlating those states with the contractions of muscles and movements of limbs, he would have moved as he did regardless of his desire or intention. If every movement of his was completely accounted for by his antecedent neurophysiological states (his "programming"), then it was not true that those movements occurred *because* he wanted or intended to get his hat.[46]

Malcolm claims that the man's intentions or desires would not be *causes* of his movement. This is defended by an examination of the implications of causal attributions.

> It has often been noted that to say *B causes C* does not mean merely that whenever *B* occurs, *C* occurs. Causation also has subjunctive and counterfactual implications: if *B were* to occur, *C would* occur; and if *B* had *not* occurred, *C would not* have occurred. But the neurophysiological theory would provide sufficient causal conditions for every human movement, and so there would be no cases at all in which a certain movement would not have occurred if the person had not had this desire or intention. Since the counterfactual would be false in all cases, desires and intentions would not be causes of human movements. They would not ever be sufficient causal conditions nor would they ever be necessary causal conditions.[47]

Let us look at the last sentence of this passage. It makes two claims: first, that desires and intentions would never be *sufficient* conditions for human movements, and secondly, that desires and intentions would never be *necessary* conditions of human movements. The first claim seems to me unfounded and unargued for. Malcolm himself admits that "generally speaking,

---

[45] *The Philosophical Review*, LXXVII (1968), 45–72. My criticism of Malcolm's position in the following pages originally appeared in "The Compatibility of Mechanism and Purpose," *The Philosophical Review*, LXXVIII (1969), 468–82.

[46] *Ibid.*, p. 53.

[47] *Ibid.*, pp. 56–57.

it is possible for there to be a plurality of simultaneous sufficient causal conditions of an event."[48] Thus, from the fact that there are neurophysiological states which are causally sufficient for a given movement, it does not follow that desires or intentions (together with beliefs and other relevant events) are not (also) causally sufficient for the same movement. It is at least conceivable that all human movements have two sets of sufficient conditions, one involving neurophysiological states and one involving desires or intentions. An argument is needed to prove that this is not, or could not be, the case.

Malcolm's second thesis, however, seems to be completely justified, and perhaps this is all he needs for his central contention. This claim seems to flow naturally from the definitions of "sufficient" and "necessary." To say that X is sufficient for Y seems to mean that nothing over and above X is needed for the occurrence of Y, in other words, that nothing over and above X is *necessary* for the occurrence of Y. Thus, if neurophysiological states are sufficient for the occurrence of certain movements, it would seem to follow that intentions or desires are not necessary for the occurrence of these movements. If, moreover, desires or intentions could not be causes or explanatory factors of movements unless they were necessary for the movements,[49] then the fact that neurophysiological states are sufficient for the movements would imply that desires or intentions are not causes of the movements and cannot be used to explain the movements.

I wish to challenge this alleged connection between necessary and sufficient conditions. I admit that intentions of desires can be causes of behavior only if they are necessary for behavior. What I wish to deny is the contention that *if* neurophysiological states are *sufficient* for behavior, then desires or intentions are *not necessary* for behavior. This latter contention seems to me the crux of Malcolm's argument for the incompatibility of neurophysiological explanations and purposive explanations; but this contention is mistaken.

The principle Malcolm seems to presuppose can be formulated as follows.

(I)　　*If events $C_1, \ldots, C_n$ are jointly sufficient for the occurrence of event E, then no events other than $C_1, \ldots, C_n$ are necessary for the occurrence of E.*

To say that $C_1, \ldots, C_n$ are jointly "sufficient" for E is to say that there are

---

[48] *Ibid.*, p. 56.

[49] Actually, in cases of "overdetermination" a cause of Y is not a necessary condition for the occurrence of Y. If George's shooting his gun (at t_1) and Oscar's shooting his gun (at t_1) are individually sufficient for John's dying (at t_2), then each shooting is a cause of John's dying. But neither of the shootings is a necessary condition of John's dying, for if one of the shootings had not occurred the other would have sufficed to cause John's death. Thus, it is not quite accurate to say that being a cause of Y entails being a necessary condition of Y. However, I shall henceforth waive this point, since I do not wish to suggest that behavior is overdetermined in the way that John's death is overdetermined. I shall admit that in order for intentions or desires to be causes of behavior, they must be necessary for behavior.

laws or regularities which, given the occurrence of $C_1, \ldots, C_n$, ensure the occurrence of E. To say that some event is "necessary" for the occurrence of E is to say that laws and regularities ensure that, if this event had not occurred, then E would not have occurred.

Despite the initial plausibility of principle (I), it can be shown to be false. Reflection on (I) reveals that it has the effect of precluding the possibility of a chain of events (or sets of simultaneous events) each link of which is a cause of a succeeding link, and each of which can be considered a cause of the final link of the chain. That there are such chains seems obvious: if W causes X which causes Y which causes Z, then *each* of the links, W, X, and Y, can be considered a cause of Z. But principle (I) precludes such a chain. (It thereby would preclude the possibility that behavior is caused both by Skinnerian events and by wants-and-beliefs in the manner I suggested in the previous section.)

To show that principle (I) precludes chains of causes, let us suppose that there are events $C_1, \ldots, C_n$ which occur simultaneously at t_2 and which, together with laws of nature, are sufficient for the occurrence of E at t_4. Further suppose that $C_1, \ldots, C_n$ are simply one group of events in a sequence of causes of E; i.e., suppose that there are events at t_1 which are sufficient for the occurrence of $C_1, \ldots, C_n$ at t_2, that $C_1, \ldots, C_n$ are sufficient for certain events at t_3, and that these events at t_3 are sufficient for E at t_4. Now since $C_1, \ldots, C_n$ are sufficient for the occurrence of E, principle (I) implies that no events other than $C_1, \ldots, C_n$ are necessary for the occurrence of E. From this it follows that no events either before or after t_2 are necessary for the occurrence of E. This means that the indicated events at t_1 or t_3 are not necessary for the occurrence of E. But if they are not necessary for the occurrence of E, then they are not a *cause* of E. This, however, contradicts our original assumption—viz., that each of these groups of events is a cause of E.

A slightly different way of seeing how chains of causes prove the unacceptability of (I) is this. *Ex hypothesi*, $C_1, \ldots, C_n$ are a cause of E, and hence necessary for the occurrence of E. But precisely the reason we would have for saying that $C_1, \ldots, C_n$ are necessary for E is equally a reason for saying that, for example, the indicated events at t_3 are necessary for E. We say that $C_1, \ldots, C_n$ are necessary for E because if they had not occurred (at t_2), then the relevant events at t_3 would not have occurred; and if the events at t_3 had not occurred, then E would not have occurred. But this very argument shows that the events at t_3 are necessary for E, since it was explicitly stated in the argument that if these events at t_3 had not occurred, then E would not have occurred. It must be admitted, therefore, that if $C_1, \ldots, C_n$ are causes of E, then the events at t_3 are necessary for E. Yet this contradicts principle (I).

It is tempting to reply to the last argument as follows: "The events at t_3 are not really necessary for the occurrence of E. As long as $C_1, \ldots, C_n$ occur at t_2, the occurrence of the relevant events at t_3 is ensured. Hence, the occurrence of E does not *really* depend on the events at t_3, but only on $C_1, \ldots, C_n$."

if and only if a certain neural state obtains. For example, suppose that John has neural pattern P, and this fact, together with certain general laws, entails that John will want to retrieve his hat if and only if he is in neural state N. Then John's wanting to retrieve his hat (at t_1) is nomically related to John's being in neural state N (at t_1) in the sense that, given the general neural laws, and given the fact that John has neural pattern P, it follows that John's wanting to retrieve his hat (at t_1) is necessary and sufficient for John's being in neural state N (at t_1). Since these events are nomically related in this way, one of them will have the same causal status as the other *vis-à-vis* any behavior of John's. Hence, even in this case a given act of John's may be caused *both* by his having a certain want and by his being in a certain neural state.

A fourth possible way of defending the compatibility of purposive causation of behavior and neural causation of behavior is, of course, the familiar identity thesis. Clearly if John's wanting to retrieve his hat is *identical* with John's being in a certain neural state, then any behavior of his that is caused by his being in that neural state is also caused by his having that want. How is my position related to the identity thesis?

If we employ the property criterion for individuating events generally, and not simply human acts, then the identity thesis can be accepted only if the *properties* of being in neural state N and wanting to retrieve one's hat are the same. But if we employ a criterion for individuating events of the sort proposed by Anscombe and Davidson, we might contend that John's being in neural state N at t_1 is identical with John's wanting to retrieve his hat at t_1, while admitting that being in neural state N is a different property from wanting to retrieve one's hat. Since I am favorably disposed toward the property criterion, let us pursue the question of the identity of these properties in greater detail.

The question of whether wanting to retrieve one's hat might conceivably be the same property as being in neural state N is not an easy one. In Chapter One, of course, a synonymy criterion was proposed for property-individuation. But it might be argued that this criterion is too strong. After all, one might contend, "having temperature T" and "having the mean kinetic energy of one's molecules equal K" were not originally synonymous, and yet it turns out that they express (and perhaps always expressed) the same property.

Even if we choose to revise our criteria for property-individuation, however, it is not evident that the relation between wanting and being in certain neural states is like the relation between having a certain temperature and having a certain mean kinetic energy. In the case of temperature and mean kinetic energy, there is a *universal* correlation between specific temperatures and specific values of mean kinetic energy. This correlation holds for *all* gases. We have seen, however, that there may be no *universal* correlation between specific wants and specific neural states. Rather, there is more likely to be a species-wide correlation or a separate correlation for each separate human organism.

This mode of argument is clearly unacceptable. If we accept it, it will follow that the "real" cause of an event is only an "originating" cause, never an "intermediary" cause. If so, most if not all of the things we ordinarily call "causes" will turn out not to be causes at all. Moreover, $C_1, \ldots, C_n$ will turn out not to be causes of E. For we can argue, as above, that since $C_1, \ldots, C_n$ must occur as long as the relevant events at t_1 occur, then the occurrence of E does not "really" depend on $C_1, \ldots, C_n$, but only on the events at t_1.

My objection to principle (I) has rested on the fact that some events occurring at a different time from $C_1, \ldots, C_n$ may be necessary for the occurrence of E even though $C_1, \ldots, C_n$ are sufficient for the occurrence of E. But this may be considered irrelevant to Malcolm's purposes. The neurophysiological theory envisaged by Malcolm is one which presumably describes continuous neurophysiological activity leading to the overt behavior. Thus, if desires or intentions were to cause behavior, they would not be *subsequent* to all relevant neurophysiological states, nor would they be *prior* to all relevant neurophysiological states. Rather, they would have to be *simultaneous* with some set of neurophysiological states that are causally sufficient for the behavior. Thus, if I am to maintain that desires or intentions would be causally necessary for the behavior, a principle weaker than (I) must be disproved. Instead of principle (I) it would adequately serve Malcolm's purposes to employ the weaker principle (II):

(II)   *If events C^* occurring at t_1 are sufficient for the occurrence of E at t_2, then no other events at t_1 are necessary for the occurrence of E at t_2.*

I believe that principle (II), like principle (I), can be proved unacceptable. Suppose there is a law saying that for any object o and any time t, the object has property ϕ at t if and only if it has property ψ at t.[50] Then if a particular object o has properties ϕ and ψ at a particular time t_1, I shall say that o's having ϕ at t_1 is a "*simultaneous nomic equivalent*" of o's having ψ at t_1. Now suppose that particular events (or sets of events) C^* and C^{**} are simultaneous nomic equivalents. This means that C^* is sufficient for C^{**} and that C^{**} is sufficient for C^*; equivalently, it means that C^* is necessary for C^{**} and that C^{**} is necessary for C^*.[51] Further, suppose that C^* is *sufficient* for the occurrence of a subsequent E (at t_2) and *necessary* for the occurrence of E. Then there is another event (or set of events)—viz., C^{**}—that is simultaneous with C^* and is also necessary for the occurrence of E. This follows directly

---

[50] This point is suggested by Richard Brandt and Jaegwon Kim's principle of "simultaneous isomorphism," in "The Logic of the Identity Theory," *The Journal of Philosophy*, LXIV (1967), 515–37.

[51] Each event is sufficient for the other, but perhaps neither is *causally* sufficient for the other. It may be inappropriate to speak of a *causal* relationship holding between such a pair of events, first, because they are simultaneous, and secondly, because causal relationships must be unidirectional, and there may be no grounds for deciding the directionality of the causation in such cases.

from the transitivity of the relation, "*A* is necessary for *B*." Since C^* and C^{**} are simultaneous nomic equivalents, C^{**} is necessary for C^*. But *ex hypothesi*, C^* is necessary for the occurrence of *E*. Hence, C^{**} is also necessary for the occurrence of *E*. If C^* had not occurred (at t_1), then *E* would not have occurred (at t_2); but similarly, if C^{**} had not occurred (at t_1), then *E* would not have occurred (at t_2). (By a similar argument, C^{**} is seen to be sufficient for *E* as well.) We have a case, then, in which principle (II) is violated, for here is an event (causally) sufficient for *E* that is accompanied by a different but simultaneous event that is necessary for *E*.

Notice that the grounds for saying that C^{**} is necessary for *E* are precisely those presupposed in saying that C^* is necessary for *E*. C^* is said to be necessary for *E* because, given the laws of nature, the omission of C^* (at t_1) would have meant that the events at t_1 would not be sufficient for the occurrence of *E*. Similarly, given the laws of nature, the omission of C^{**} (at t_1) would have meant that the events at t_1 would not be sufficient for the occurrence of *E*. Given the laws of nature, the omission of C^{**} (at t_1) would have necessitated the omission of C^* (at t_1). And the omission of C^*, we have seen, would have resulted in the non-occurrence of *E*.

The possibility of simultaneous nomic equivalents shows the unacceptability of principle (II), and this possibility is directly applicable to the relation between wants or intentions and neurophysiological states. It is certainly possible—at least theoretically possible—that there should turn out to be laws saying that any entity has a certain specific want at a given time if and only if it is in a certain specific neural state at that time. For example, it is possible that there should be a law saying that an entity will have a desire to retrieve its hat at a given time if and only if it is in neural state *N* at that time. If so, then John's wanting to retrieve his hat at t_1 will be a simultaneous nomic equivalent of John's being in neural state *N* at t_1. Then any movement or behavior for which John's being in state *N* (at t_1) is a necessary condition is also a movement or bit of behavior for which John's wanting to retrieve his hat (at t_1) is a necessary condition. And any movement or behavior for which John's being in state *N* is a sufficient condition is also a movement or behavior for which John's wanting to retrieve his hat is a sufficient condition. Thus, John's wanting to retrieve his hat might have the same causal status as John's being in state *N vis-à-vis* any movement of his, including, for example, his movement up the ladder. John's movement up the ladder could be caused *both* by his want to retrieve his hat *and* by his being in neural state *N*.

That wants are simultaneous nomic equivalents of certain neural states is certainly a theoretical possibility. But there are two other ways in which wants might be related to neural states, both of which are a good deal more likely to be true and both of which would preserve the causal relationship between wants and behavior that is ensured by the simultaneous nomic equivalents relationship.

According to my definition of "simultaneous nomic equivalents," *o*'s

having ϕ at t_1 is a simultaneous nomic equivalent of *o*'s having ψ at t_1 only if there is a universal law, covering all entities whatsoever, to the effect that an entity has ϕ at *t* if and only if it has ψ at *t*. Now such a law, in the case of wants and neural states, would be extremely strong. Consider, for example, the property of wanting to retrieve a ball. If instances of this property were to be simultaneous nomic equivalents of instances of some neural property *N*, there would have to be a law saying that *any* organism—including not just a human being, but also a dog, a cat, or even a dolphin—will have this want-property if and only if it has the specific neural property *N* (at the same time). I think it is quite unlikely that there are such laws. Dogs, cats, and perhaps even dolphins, as well as human beings, of course, can have the property of wanting to retrieve a ball. But since the brain structures of these species are significantly different, it is most unlikely that their having this want would be correlated with their being in the same neural state.

It is more likely, therefore, that there are laws correlating wants with neural states with respect to each particular species. Thus, there might be a law saying that any organism of the species *homo sapiens* has the property of wanting to retrieve a ball at *t* if and only if it has the property of being in neural state *N* at *t*. Similarly, there might be a different law saying that any organism of the species *canis familiaris* has the property of wanting to retrieve a ball at *t* if and only if it has the property of being in neural state *N'* at *t*. And so on. If there were laws of this sort, it would still be true that any human agent, say John, would want to retrieve a ball at t_1 if and only if he is in neural state *N* at t_1. And it would still be true that John's wanting to retrieve a ball at t_1 would have the same causal status as John's being in neural state *N* at t_1 *vis-à-vis* an action of his—e.g., running toward the ball. Even with less inclusive laws, then, the compatibility of purposive causation and neurophysiological causation would be preserved.

A third possibility—which I would regard as the most probable—is that there are no laws even of a species-wide sort. The neural state corresponding to wanting to retrieve a ball may be different for each distinct human being, though each individual human being may have his own correlation holding for the various occasions when he wants to retrieve a ball. Even in this situation, however, there may still be a form of nomic interdependence between wants and neural states. Although there are no laws which stipulate a single neural state to be correlated with a specific want for all members of the species, there may be laws which ensure that certain patterns of neural connections imply certain correlations of brain state and desire. For example, these laws may ensure that if one has neural pattern *P*, then one will want to retrieve a ball if and only if one is in neural state *N*; that if one has neural pattern *P'*, then one will want to retrieve a ball if and only if one is in neural state *N'*; and so on. Since different people have different neural patterns, their having a given want will be correlated with different neural states. Nevertheless, in each individual case it can be said that a certain want occurs

Now the case of species-wide but non-universal correlations would make the relationship between wants and neural states analogous to the relationship between temperature and vapor pressure point. (A vapor pressure point is the amount of pressure just sufficient to cause condensation of a gas.) Every real gas has a schedule which associates a specific temperature with a specific vapor pressure point. But since each different kind of gas has a different schedule, one could not pick out any single temperature and say that the property of having vapor pressure point V is the same as the property of having temperature T. There may indeed be a correlation between having vapor pressure point V and having temperature T for a *particular* kind of gas, but vapor pressure point V will be correlated with other temperatures for other kinds of gases.

As an analogue to the case in which there are different correlations for different individual human beings we might take the relationship between the functional states of a computer and its corresponding electrical states.[52] A functional state of a computer is definable in terms of the output it gives rise to and the input which gives rise to it. Two different computers can be in the same functional state without being in the same electrical state at all, for their respective wiring systems may be very different. In this situation we obviously cannot say that a particular functional-state property is identical with any particular electrical-state property, for a particular functional-state property will correlate with as many different electrical-state properties as there are different wiring systems of the appropriate complexity. However, given that a certain computer has a particular wiring system, it may follow that that computer will be in a specific functional state at a given time if and only if it is in a specific electrical state at that time. In other words, *given* a particular wiring system, there is a one-one correspondence between functional states and electrical states.

Since I think that the third sort of situation is the one which probably obtains in actuality, I do not think that we should expect to find that we can identify a particular want-property with any particular neural-property. Moreover, if we are to adopt the sort of property criterion of event-individuation that I have proposed, it will follow that John's wanting to retrieve his hat (at t_1) will not be identical with John's being in neural state N (at t_1), for any state N. Nonetheless, as we have seen, John's wanting to retrieve his hat (at t_1) and John's being in neural state N (at t_1) may both be causes of John's moving up a ladder.

Let me turn now from the question of the *compatibility* of neural explanations and purposive explanations of action to the question of whether neural information can throw additional light on the nature of action and its rela-

---

[52] This analogy is due to Hilary Putnam, "Psychological Predicates," in W. H. Capitan and D. D. Merrill, eds., *Art, Mind, and Religion* (Pittsburgh: University of Pittsburgh Press, 1967), and J. A. Fodor, "Explanation in Psychology," in Max Black, ed., *Philosophy in America* (London: George Allen and Unwin Ltd, 1965).

tion to wants and beliefs. The reader will recall that the analysis of intentional action given in Chapter Three specified that basic acts be caused "in
a certain characteristic way" by wants and beliefs. I confessed at that time
that I could not say precisely what this "characteristic" way is, and I argued
that this would be primarily a matter for neurophysiological investigation.
Let us now ask whether neurophysiological information can really be of help
in clarifying this "characteristic" manner in which wants and beliefs cause
acts. At the same time, let us see whether neurophysiology can tell us why
our three examples of grimacing, salivating, and fidgeting[53] are not caused in
the "characteristic" manner.

In the case where the agent grimaces in response to foul-tasting soup, we
have an instance of a reflexive response. This response can ultimately be
traced to wants and beliefs of the agent, since these wants and beliefs led a
practical joker to put the foul-tasting stuff in the soup. But, despite the fact
that the grimacing is caused (in part) by these wants and beliefs, it is not a
voluntary or intentional act. Why not? If D. O. Hebb is right,[54] reflex movements can be distinguished from voluntary movements in terms of different
paths from receptors to effectors. Hebb thinks that reflexive behavior, or
"sense-dominated" behavior, results from "straight-through" connections
between receptors and effectors, while higher, purposive behavior depends on
complex "closed loop" connections, or "cell assemblies," located in the
cortex. If this is correct, then any movement which is caused by a "straight-
through" connection independent of the operation of cell assemblies (with
which wants and beliefs might be correlated) would be reflex movement
rather than purposive or intentional action. Now this is precisely what would
be expected in the grimacing example. The foul taste of the soup leads directly, via "straight-through" connections, to contraction of the face muscles;
there is no causal role to be attributed to closed loop systems which are correlated with wants and beliefs. Admittedly, since the foul taste of the soup is
ultimately traceable to earlier wants and beliefs of the agent, it is also traceable
to the operation of certain closed loop systems at that earlier time. Nevertheless, the fact that the *proximate* cause of the grimacing includes "straight-
through" afferent-efferent paths, and is independent of closed loop system
activity, indicates that the grimacing is not purposive action.

We might hope to account for Richard Taylor's examples of salivating and
fidgeting by noticing the crucial causal role that would be played in these
cases by the autonomic nervous system and the sympathetic nervous system,
respectively. Purposive behavior, it may be expected, is a function of events
occurring in the central nervous system alone, independent of the autonomic
nervous system and the sympathetic nervous system. But in the salivating
case the agent's autonomic nervous system plays a crucial causal role, while

---

[53] Cf. Chapter Three, Section 3.
[54] Cf. *A Textbook of Psychology* (Philadelphia: W. B. Saunders Company, 1967), pp. 82 ff.

in the fidgeting case the sympathetic nervous system has a crucial causal role.

The autonomic nervous system controls a variety of bodily states that are not under voluntary control.[55] The heart rate, the flow of blood to the muscles, sweating, pupil dilation, movement of the stomach and gut, goose pimples, and salivating are all caused by, or controlled by, the autonomic nervous system. Now it is possible that cortical events associated with desires could contribute to the operation of the autonomic nervous system, and this is presumably what happens when a desire to eat results in salivation. The cortical events cause the activation of the autonomic nervous system which causes salivation. But although salivation is here caused by a desire, the causal chain leading to the salivation does not lie exclusively within the central nervous system. Hence the salivating is not caused by the desire "in the characteristic way."

The case of fidgeting, I think, can be accounted for by appeal to the function of the sympathetic nervous system. It is obvious from Taylor's description of this case that the agent's desire to attract the speaker's attention has caused him (the agent) to be nervous, tense, and fearful. It is likely that this nervousness, tension, or fear is associated with an excitation of the sympathetic nervous system, which causes an increase in the secretion of adrenalin into the bloodstream. An increase of adrenalin has the consequence of heightening the susceptibility of the synapses to firing: much smaller amounts of charge will now result in the firing of the synapses. Because of this, muscle movements begin to occur with great frequency throughout the agent's body, and this collection of muscle movements constitutes his fidgeting. The agent's fidgeting has indeed resulted, then, from his desire to attract the speaker's attention. But the route of the causation has involved the sympathetic nervous system in an essential way; it has not been oriented exclusively within the central nervous system. For this reason we can say that the causation of the fidgeting by the desire does not exemplify the "characteristic" way in which desires cause purposive action.

Needless to say, the suggestions made here are rather conjectural. They provide some indication, however, of the manner in which neurophysiological information might enable us to identify the specific "characteristic way" in which purposive or intentional behavior is caused.

In the last few paragraphs I have argued that neurophysiological information can help explain how it is that wants and beliefs cause action. But there appears to be a general logical objection to this idea. I have maintained that the connection between wants and action is a logical one—i.e., that the proposition that wants tend to cause acts is logically true rather than con-

---

[55] Recent experiments have apparently shown that some of these bodily states, i.e., the heart rate and blood pressure, can be brought under voluntary control with the help of certain stimuli. This finding seems to conflict with the suggestion made here about the unique role of the central nervous system in purposive behavior. But this suggestion is, in any case, just intended as an *illustration* of how neurophysiological information would relate to the analysis of purposive behavior.

tingently true. But logical truths, it may be argued, do not *depend on* any contingent truths; hence logical truths must not be *explainable by* contingent truths. Yet this is what one seems to be doing when one tries to explain how wants cause acts by appealing to contingent truths about the neurophysiology of the human organism. This point has been made by Charles Taylor:

> Because explanation by intentions or purposes is like explanation by an "antecedent" which is non-contingently linked with its consequent, i.e. because the fact that behavior follows from the intention other things being equal is not a contingent fact, we cannot account for this fact by more basic laws. For to explain a fact by more basic laws is to give the regularities on which this fact causally depends. But not being contingent, the dependence of behavior on intention is not contingent on anything, and hence not on any such regularities.[55]

Suppose a child asks: "Why is grass green?" Shall we answer: "It is a logical truth that grass is green. Hence, you can't ask *why* grass is green. If it weren't green it wouldn't be grass." Not at all. The child has a perfectly good question to which there is a perfectly good answer—an answer which makes reference to chlorophyll, photosynthesis, etc. The question the child wants to ask might be spelled out as follows. "Granted it is a logical truth that if X is grass then X is green (at least when it is healthy). But what is it about grass that enables it to be green? What is it about those things which happen to be grass that enables them to satisfy this logically necessary condition of being grass?" This is a legitimate question to which there is an informative answer.

Similarly, suppose it is a matter of definition (as it once was) that an acid turns litmus paper red. In other words, "X is an acid" logically entails "X turns litmus paper red." This does not imply that the question, "Why do acids turn litmus paper red?" is a bad or illegitimate question. The question can be paraphrased as follows: "What is it about those things which happen to be acids that enables them to turn litmus paper red? What is it about those things which in fact have the ability to turn litmus paper red that *enables* them to turn litmus paper red?" This question can be answered by referring to the molecular structure of acids and indicating its relationship to the molecular structure of litmus.

The question "Why do wants tend to cause acts?" is similar to the questions, "Why is grass green?" and "Why do acids turn litmus paper red?" It can be paraphrased as follows: "What is it about those mental events which are wants that enables them to cause acts? What is it about those mental events which in fact have the ability to cause acts that *enables* them to cause acts?" This is a perfectly legitimate question. And perhaps the answer is that wants are correlated with closed loop systems in the cortex, the firing of which causes efferent neuron firings which in turn cause muscle movements and limb movements.

CHAPTER SIX

Determinism[1] and Predictability

1. The Issue and Some Definitions

I have maintained that acts are *caused*, but I have not maintained, at least not until now, that acts are *determined*. To say that an event is determined is to say something that implies the existence of universal laws pertaining to that event. Pending an adequate analysis of causality, however, it is not obvious that it must be analyzed in terms of laws. Moreover, even if causality must be analyzed in terms of laws of some sort, it is not evident that *universal* laws are required. It is possible that although acts are caused, the laws pertaining to them are statistical rather than universal. We must distinguish, therefore, between the claim that acts are caused and the claim that acts are determined. Until now I have talked about the question of whether acts are caused; in this chapter I want to talk about the question of whether acts are determined. I shall not myself assert categorically that acts are determined. Instead, I shall defend the *tenability* of this position against certain attacks.

Since it is difficult to tell "directly" whether or not acts are governed by universal laws, some philosophers resort to the following "indirect" argument:

> If acts are determined, then it is possible in principle to predict them (with certainty).
>
> It is not possible in principle for acts to be predicted (with certainty).
>
> Therefore, acts are not determined.

A defender of this argument I shall call an "anti-predictionist"; his position

---

[1] This chapter is a somewhat revised version of a paper originally published under the title "Actions, Predictions, and Books of Life," in the *American Philosophical Quarterly*, V (1968), 135-51.

will be called "anti-predictionism." The main purpose of this chapter is to rebut anti-predictionism.

Both premises of the anti-predictionist argument will come under attack here. The first premise, affirming that determinism entails predictability, is often accepted without adequate scrutiny. Some writers not only assume that determinism entails predictability but even define determinism as the thesis that every event is predictable in principle.[2] I believe, however, that it is essential to distinguish between determinism and predictability. We must first notice that there are various kinds or senses of "possibility" which may be involved in the "possibility of prediction." Moreover, it can be shown that in many of these senses, determinism does *not* entail the possibility of prediction. Many anti-predictionists have failed to notice this, however. Therefore, upon discovering some unpredictability in the arena of human action, they have wrongly concluded that acts must be undetermined. This error will be avoided only if we carefully distinguish between determinism and predictability. Hence, an important aim of this chapter will be to differentiate various senses of "possibility of prediction" and to ascertain how they are related to determinism.

Let us assume now that we can find some suitable sense of "possibility of prediction" which is closely related to, if not entailed by, determinism. The second premise of the anti-predictionist argument asserts that, in such a sense, it is impossible for acts to be predicted. Various arguments have been offered in support of this premise. One that I shall consider concerns the possibility of writing a complete description of an agent's life—including his voluntary acts—even before he is born. According to anti-predictionism, if acts were determined, it would be possible to write such books. Indeed, it would be possible for such a "book of life" to be written even if the agent were to read its prediction of a given act before he is to perform that act. It seems clear to the anti-predictionist, however, that such books of life are impossible. Predictions of my acts cannot be made with certainty; for when I read these predictions, I can easily choose to falsify them. So argues the anti-predictionist. But it is far from clear that he is right. I think, on the contrary, that it may well be possible (in a suitable sense) for books of life to be written. And thus it seems to me that the anti-predictionist is unable to establish the truth of his second premise.

In general, anti-predictionists support their second premise by contrasting the predictability of human behavior with that of physical events. It is alleged that special difficulties of a purely conceptual sort arise for the prediction of action and that these difficulties are unparalleled in the realm of merely physical phenomena. I shall claim, however, that there are no essential dif-

---

[2] Karl Popper, for example, defines "determined" as "predictable in accordance with the methods of science," in "Indeterminism in Quantum Mechanics and in Classical Physics," *The British Journal for the Philosophy of Science*, I (1950–51), 120.

ferences between acts and physical events with respect to the problem of prediction. More precisely, I shall claim that *conceptual* reflection on the nature of human behavior (as opposed to investigation by the special sciences) does not reveal any peculiar immunity to prediction.

It must be emphasized that I offer no proof of the thesis that acts are determined; I merely wish to show that the anti-predictionist's arguments fail to prove that they are *not* determined. It is conceivable, of course, that acts are not determined. And if acts are not determined, then I would admit that they are not perfectly predictable (in any sense at all). What I contend, however, is that the arguments of philosophers, based on familiar, commonsense features of human action and human choice, do not prove that acts are undetermined or unpredictable. The basic features of human action are quite compatible with the contention that acts are determined and susceptible of prediction. In other words, my aim here is not to establish the *truth*, but merely the *tenability*, of the thesis that acts are determined.

In this chapter I shall employ a "property" criterion not only for individuating acts, but also for individuating events, states of affairs, and processes of all kinds. For brevity I shall use the term "events" to cover states of affairs and processes as well as what we would ordinarily call "events." Negative events, like a ball's *not* moving at 10 m.p.h. (at *t*) are also included.

I shall define *determinism* as the view that *every event is determined*. The notion of "determined" is defined as follows.

> Event e *is determined if and only if a proposition asserting that* e *occurs* (*at* t) *is deducible from some conjunction of* (*true*) *propositions describing laws of nature and events prior to* t (*but not deducible from propositions describing prior events alone*).[3]

Notice that my definition of "determined," and *ipso facto* the definition of "determinism," is in terms of a formal relationship—i.e., the relationship of deducibility holding between various true propositions. In particular, this definition makes no explicit reference to the ability of anyone to predict any event, and thereby leaves open the question of the connection between determinism and predictability.

---

[3] It should be noted that the definition given here is rather stringent. For example, suppose we have a conjunction of sentences describing laws and prior events which entails a sentence asserting that *S* extends his arm out the window (at *t*). But this conjunction does not entail a sentence asserting that *S* signals for a turn (at *t*). For this latter sentence also to be entailed, further premises must be added. It won't do, however, to add the premise that there is a traffic convention (at *t*) saying that extending one's arm out the car window counts as signaling; because this sentence describes a *present* event, not a *prior* one. In order for *S*'s signaling for a turn (at *t*) to be determined, it will probably be necessary that the existence of the convention (at *t*) is also determined. If this generational condition is determined and if *S*'s extending his arm out the car window (at *t*) is determined, then *S*'s signaling for a turn (at *t*) will also be determined.

We could substitute for the given definition one which does not require generational conditions to be determined. But the given definition is adequate for present purposes.

If determinism is true, then all human acts are determined. But determinism alone does not tell us what laws or kinds of laws take human acts as their dependent variables.[4] I shall assume, however, that these laws would either include psychological states like desires and beliefs as their independent variables, or would include factors that correlate somehow with wants and beliefs. The second alternative is more likely, I think. The most precise laws of behavior are probably going to be laws which involve neural and physiological properties, because these phenomena can be studied with sufficient precision and subtlety. Nevertheless, even if the laws are formulated in terms of neural event properties, this does not imply that wants and beliefs are not causes of action. Wants and beliefs may correlate with neural events in a way that ensures that relevant acts will not occur unless relevant wants and beliefs occur.[5] Moreover, if proper correlations obtain between neural events and wants and beliefs (either species-wide correlations or correlations based on the particular neural structure of each separate individual), it may be possible for propositions describing wants and beliefs to be among the propositions which, together with propositions expressing laws of nature, entail propositions asserting that certain (subsequent) acts are performed. Let us assume that this is the case. Then the relationship between wants, beliefs, and acts can be formulated with the help of the term, *"causally necessitate."* If a proposition describing event e is deducible from propositions expressing laws of nature and prior events $c_1, c_2, \ldots, c_k$, the events $c_1, c_2, \ldots, c_k$ will be said to *causally necessitate* event e. What I am assuming, then, is that if acts are determined, wants and beliefs are among the factors which causally necessitate them.

In our discussion of predictability we need a sense of "prediction" distinct from mere lucky guessing or precognition. We must be concerned with predictions made on the basis of laws and antecedent conditions. I shall call a prediction a *"scientific prediction"* if and only if the predictor makes the prediction by *deducing* a proposition describing the predicted event from propositions describing prior events and laws of nature which he knows to be true. A scientific predictor may learn of the laws and prior events in any number of ways. (On my definition, most predictions made by actual scientists are not "scientific" predictions, for real scientists seldom if ever *deduce* what will occur from laws and prior events. Nevertheless, scientific prediction

---

[4] Remember that an act-token, to be determined, need not be an instance of a property that appears as a dependent variable in some law. The act-token of Drysdale's pitching his sixth straight shutout (at t) can be determined even if there is no law which has the property of pitching one's sixth straight shutout as a dependent variable. (Cf. Chapter Three, Section 5.) It can be expected, however, that on every act-tree there is some act—probably a basic act—which is an instance of a property which appears in a law. The property of signaling for a turn, for example, may not appear in any law of nature; but perhaps the property of extending one's arm does appear in some law of nature.

[5] Cf. Chapter Five, Section 5.

as defined here may be regarded as an ideal of prediction to which scientists can aspire.)

As indicated above, it is important to identify different senses of the phrase "possibility of prediction." I shall now distinguish four relevant species of possibility, though further distinctions will be made later within some of these categories. The four species are: (1) *logical possibility*, (2) *logical compossibility*, (3) *physical possibility*, and (4) *causal compossibility*.

An event is *logically possible* if and only if any proposition expressing it is not self-contradictory. An event is logically impossible if there is a proposition expressing it which is self-contradictory. *S*'s jumping 90 feet (at *t*) is a logically possible event; but *S*'s drawing a square circle (at *t*) is a logically impossible event, because the proposition "*S* draws a square circle (at *t*)" is self-contradictory (or inconsistent).[6]

Logical *compossibility* is defined for two or more events. A set of two or more events is logically compossible if and only if the conjunction of any set of propositions which express all the members of the set is logically consistent. A set of events is *logically incompossible* (i.e., not logically compossible) if and only if each of the events is logically possible but the conjunction of some set of propositions expressing all the members of the set is logically inconsistent. Thus, the pair of events (a) *x*'s being a pumpkin from 11 o'clock to 12 o'clock, and (b) *x*'s turning into a pumpkin at 12 o'clock, is a logically incompossible pair. I shall say either that a *set* is logically incompossible, or that a *member* of a set is logically incompossible *with*, or *relative to*, other members of the set.

An event is *physically possible* if and only if no proposition expressing it is inconsistent with any proposition or propositions expressing laws of nature. An event is physically impossible just in case there is a proposition expressing it which is inconsistent with some proposition or propositions expressing laws of nature. *S*'s traveling faster than the speed of light, for example, is physically impossible. Similarly, since laws of nature make it impossible for a (normal) human being to lift a ten-ton weight, the lifting of a ten-ton weight by such a being is physically impossible.

Causal compossibility differs from physical possibility in attending to groups of events rather than events taken singly. Roughly, a set of events is causally compossible just in case laws of nature allow each of them to occur singly and allow them to occur as a group.[7] More precisely, consider a set of

---

[6] As I am using the term "event," *S*'s drawing a square circle (at *t*) is called an "event," even though it is logically impossible. The term is not restricted to *possible* events, nor, of course, to *actual* events. On the other hand, the term "law" will be used only to designate actual laws—i.e., laws that obtain in the real world, and not merely possible laws.

[7] Events to be considered will all have built-in time references, as usual. Sam's jumping rope at 10:35 is to be treated as a distinct event from Sam's jumping rope at 10:45. Thus, when we ask whether a set of events is a causally compossible set, we may be interested in events at a variety of times. But it must be clear, for each event considered, what its temporal position is.

events $\{e_1, \ldots, e_n\}$ each of which is logically possible and physically possible, and which jointly constitute a logically compossible set. Then the set $\{e_1, \ldots, e_n\}$ is a causally compossible set if and only if there are no propositions expressing laws of nature such that the conjunction of these propositions with propositions expressing events $e_1, \ldots, e_n$ is logically inconsistent. I shall say that the *set* is causally compossible or that each *member* of the set is causally compossible *with*, or *relative to*, the other members.

A set of events $\{e_1, \ldots, e_n\}$ is causally *in*compossible (i.e., not causally compossible) if and only if there are some laws of nature $L_1, \ldots, L_k$ such that the conjunction of propositions expressing $L_1, \ldots, L_k$ with propositions expressing $e_1, \ldots, e_n$ is logically inconsistent. Assuming, as we do, that $e_1, \ldots, e_n$ satisfy the other three species of possibility, the set $\{e_1, \ldots, e_n\}$ will be causally incompossible if and only a proposition expressing the *negation* of (at least) one member of the set is entailed by the conjunction of some propositions expressing the other members of the set together with propositions expressing $L_1, \ldots, L_k$. Thus, if the negation of a given member of the set is causally necessitated by the other members of the set, then the set is causally incompossible.

2. Logical Compossibility and Physical Possibility

The most interesting questions concerning the prediction of action are best handled in terms of the notion of causal compossibility. The reflexivity of predictions—the fact that a prediction often has an effect which bears on its own truth—can be understood properly with the use of this notion. But the question of the causal compossibility of predictions of action cannot arise unless the other three species of possibility are satisfied. Our definition of causal compossibility makes a set causally compossible only if its members are logically possible, physically possible, and (jointly) logically compossible. For example, if it is physically impossible to make scientific predictions of acts, the question of causal compossibility does not even arise. Therefore, before turning to the questions of reflexivity, including the question of whether "books of life" can be written, we must focus on certain problems connected with the logical compossibility and the physical possibility of predicting acts.

The logical possibility and compossibility of predictions can be discussed together, since the distinction between them is somewhat blurred. This is because a correct prediction is not really a single event, but a pair of events— a prediction and an event predicted. Two different examples of logical incompossibility have been uncovered in connection with the prediction of behavior. I shall discuss these examples and argue that, contrary to what their authors suppose, they do not prove that acts are undetermined and they do not prove that acts have a peculiar immunity to prediction unparalleled by physical phenomena.

The first logical incompossibility, as discussed by Maurice Cranston,[8] can be summarized as follows. Suppose that Sam invents the corkscrew at *t*. In the intended sense of "invent," this means (a) that Sam thinks of the corkscrew at *t*, and (b) that no one ever thought of the corkscrew before *t*. Cranston argues that no one could have predicted Sam's inventing the corkscrew. In order for him to make this prediction, he would himself have to think of the corkscrew. And had he thought of the corkscrew, it would be false to say that Sam "invented" the corkscrew. Yet, *ex hypothesi*, Sam *did* invent the corkscrew. Using the terminology of "logical incompossibility," we can formulate Cranston's problem by saying that the three events, (a) Sam thinks of the corkscrew at *t*, (b) no one ever thought of the corkscrew before *t*, and (c) someone predicted Sam's inventing the corkscrew, are logically incompossible.

The second example poses a problem for predicting decisions rather than acts. However, since the concept of voluntary action is so closely tied to that of a decision, an unpredictability connected with decisions is very important for us to discuss. Carl Ginet claims that it is impossible ("conceptually" impossible) for anyone to predict his own decision.[9] The argument begins by defining "deciding to do *A*" as *passing into* a state of knowledge (of a certain kind) that one will do *A*, or try to do *A*. Suppose now that Sam, at *t*, decides to do *A*. Had Sam predicted that he would make this decision—and had this prediction involved *knowledge*—he could not have decided later to do *A*. For if, before *t*, he had known that he would decide to do *A*, he would have known then that he would do *A*, or try to do *A*. But if, before *t*, he had known that he would do *A* (or try to do *A*), then he could not, at *t*, have *passed into* a state of knowing that he would do *A*. Thus, according to Ginet, Sam could not have predicted that he would make this decision.

Of course, Sam might make his prediction and then forget it. If so, he can still decide, at *t*, to do *A*. However, if Sam not only knows, before *t*, that he will decide to do *A*, but also *continues* to know this up until *t*, then Sam cannot, at *t*, decide to do *A*. In other words, the following three events are logically incompossible: (a') Sam decides, at *t*, to do *A*, (b') Sam predicts (i.e. knows) that he will decide to do *A*, and (c') Sam continues to know this until *t*.

One thing wrong with Ginet's argument is the definition of "deciding" which he presupposes. Deciding to do *A* does not consist, as Ginet implies, in passing into a state of *knowing* that one will do (or try to do) *A*. Rather, it consists in passing into a state of *wanting*, or *intending*, to do *A*. Deciding consists in coming to assent to an *optative* proposition, "Let it be the case

[8] Maurice Cranston, *Freedom: A New Analysis* (London: Longmans, Green, 1953), p. 169.
[9] "Can the Will be Caused?" *Philosophical Review*, LXXI (1962), 49–55.

that I do *A*," not in coming to assent to a *declarative* proposition, "I will do *A*." Even if one knows prior to *t* and continuously up until *t* that one *will* do *A*, it is still possible, at *t*, to pass into a state of *wanting*, or *intending*, to do *A*. It is possible (as I shall argue in Section 6) to know that one will perform an act without yet wanting or intending to do it.

Let us waive this criticism, however, for the sake of argument. Let us suppose that there *is* a logical incompossibility in the set of events (a′), (b′), and (c′), just as there is a logical incompossibility in the set of events (a), (b), and (c). What do these two logical incompossibilities prove? Do they prove that decisions and inventions are undetermined? Do they prove that voluntary acts, including the decisions which lead to them, have a special immunity to prediction? The answer is "No," I believe, to both questions.

Our examples of logical incompossibilities do not establish any special status for human behavior, since precisely analogous incompossibilities can be produced for physical phenomena. Let the expression "a tornado strikes *x by surprise*" mean: (1) a tornado strikes *x* at a certain time, and (2) before that time nobody ever thought of a tornado striking *x*. Now suppose that, as a matter of fact, a tornado strikes Timbuktu by surprise (at *t*). Then the set consisting of the tornado striking Timbuktu by surprise (at *t*) and a prediction of the tornado striking Timbuktu by surprise (made at some time prior to *t*) is a logically incompossible set. In order for there to be an event of the tornado striking Timbuktu by surprise (at *t*), it would have to be level-generated by an event of the tornado striking Timbuktu (at *t*). In order for the tornado striking Timbuktu (at *t*) to level-generate the tornado striking Timbuktu by surprise (at *t*), there must obtain the generational condition that no one ever thought of a tornado striking Timbuktu before *t*. But the existence of this generational condition is logically incompatible with there ever having been a prediction that a tornado would strike Timbuktu by surprise (at *t*).

This case is precisely analogous to the invention and decision cases. In the invention case there is an act-type—viz., inventing the corkscrew—which can be exemplified only if there has been no prediction that it would be exemplified. Again, in the decision case, there is a property—viz., deciding to do *A*—which can be exemplified by a person only if he does not have (continued) foreknowledge that he would exemplify it. Similarly, in the tornado case, there is an event property—viz., striking Timbuktu by surprise—which can be exemplified by a tornado only if there has been no prediction that a tornado would exemplify it. In each case it is possible, both logically and physically, for the property to be exemplified.[10] It is just not logically *com*possible for

---

[10] If the property of striking Timbuktu by surprise is exemplified by a tornado, this would be a *physical event*, I think, since it would be level-generated by the tornado's striking Timbuktu, which is clearly a physical event. Thus, the tornado case is one in which there is a logical incompossibility for a *physical* event to be predicted.

these properties to be exemplified *and* for their exemplifications to have been predicted.

I wish next to argue that the issue of whether it is logically incompossible for an event to be predicted is *unrelated* to the issue of whether the event is determined. In particular, an event might well be determined even though it is logically incompossible for that event to be predicted.

Suppose that a tornado strikes Timbuktu at *t*, and further suppose that this event is determined. (That this event is determined is surely possible.) Now make the further assumption that, before *t*, no one ever thought of a tornado striking Timbuktu. Then there exists another event consisting of *the tornado's striking Timbuktu by surprise* (at *t*). Moreover, since the tornado's striking Timbuktu (at *t*) is determined, the tornado's striking Timbuktu *by surprise* (at *t*) is also determined. Given that there are propositions describing laws and antecedent conditions which entail a proposition asserting that a tornado strikes Timbuktu (at *t*), we may simply add to the original list of entailing propositions the further proposition describing the (antecedent) condition that no one, before *t*, ever thought of a tornado striking Timbuktu. This new list of propositions describing laws and antecedent conditions entails the proposition asserting that a tornado strikes Timbuktu *by surprise* (at *t*). Hence, the tornado's striking Timbuktu by surprise (at *t*) is a determined event, despite the fact that it is logically incompossible for that event to have been predicted.

The lesson to be learned is that the fact that an event is logically incompossible relative to a prediction of it does not entail that such an event is undetermined. Thus, the fact that an invention is logically incompossible relative to a prediction of it does not entail that inventions are undetermined, and the fact that a decision is logically incompossible relative to a prediction of it by the decider does not entail that decisions are undetermined. What is to be learned is simply that the alleged entailment between determinism and the possibility of prediction is not an entailment at all. It is an error to assume that if an event is determined, it must be *possible* to predict it. At any rate, it is an error to assume that if an event is determined, it is *logically compossible* for it to have been predicted.[11]

Let us turn now to the question of whether it is *physically* possible to make

---

[11] It is also an error—committed at least as frequently—to think that determinism entails the possibility of retrodicting (or explaining) every event. Suppose that Sam thinks of the corkscrew at *t* and that no one ever thinks of the corkscrew *after t*. Suppose, moreover, that these events are causally necessitated by events prior to *t*. Now let us introduce the expression "postventing *x*" to mean "thinking of *x* for the *last* time" (just as "inventing *x*" means "thinking of *x* for the *first* time"). Clearly, we may say of Sam that he postvented the corkscrew, and this act of his is determined. However, it is logically incompossible for anyone to *retrodict* Sam's postventing the corkscrew. To do so, the retrodicter would himself have to think of the corkscrew; but, *ex hypothesi*, Sam thought of the corkscrew for the *last* time at *t*.

scientific predictions of human acts. Here the emphasis should be placed on the qualifier "scientific." Although it may well be physically possible to make "lucky guess" predictions, or perhaps even predictions based on "intuition," it is not obvious that predictions can be made by *deducing* an act from laws and prior events.[12] And this is the only kind of prediction which bears on the issue of determinism.

Anti-predictionists might claim that it is physically impossible for human beings to make scientific predictions of acts, because human beings cannot learn enough antecedent events to *deduce* what will be done in the future. But it is inessential to the predictionist's position to restrict the range of predictors to human beings. In order to avoid theological or supernatural issues, we may require that any predictor be a finite entity operating within the causal order of the universe. But apart from this, no arbitrary limits should be placed on admissible predictors.

Karl Popper[13] has tried to show that there are certain limitations of the predictions which can be made by "classical mechanical calculating" machines. But to restrict the range of predictors to calculating machines is an important restriction; even if Popper is right about the prediction limitations of machines of the sort he discusses, there may be other beings that can make predictions his machines cannot. Another limitation on Popper's discussion is that much of it is aimed at establishing the physical impossibility of a *single* being, like Laplace's demon, making scientific predictions of *all* events or of a very large number of events. But the fact that all events cannot be predicted by a single being is compatible with the proposition that every event can be predicted by some being or other.

Anti-predictionists might proffer the following argument for saying that it is physically impossible for *any* finite being, not just human beings, to make scientific predictions of human behavior. Scientific predictions, they might claim, require knowledge of infinitely many facts, but it is physically impossible for a finite being to know infinitely many facts. The infinity requirement seems necessary because in order to *deduce* that even a certain finite system will yield a given result, one must know that no interfering factors will intrude from outside the system. And knowing this may involve knowing *all* states of the world at least at one time.

This argument is of questionable force. It is far from clear that the deduction of acts from antecedent conditions and laws requires knowledge of infinitely many facts. Nor is it clear that no finite being could know infinitely many facts. Even if the argument is correct, however, it would seem to prove *too much*. For if the knowledge of infinitely many facts is required in order to

---

[12] Strictly speaking, I should talk of deducing a *proposition* describing an act from *propositions* describing laws and prior events. For brevity, however, I shall often omit the term "propositions," and speak of deducing acts, events, etc., from other events and laws.

[13] "Indeterminism in Quantum Mechanics and in Classical Physics," *op. cit.*

make scientific predictions of acts, the same would be true for scientific predictions of physical events. Thus, the above argument would fail to establish any special immunity of human action to prediction. Finally, even if it is physically impossible for any finite being to make scientific predictions of acts, this would not prove that acts are undetermined. Here too, as above, we have a sense of "possibility" in which determinism does *not* entail the possibility of prediction. The proposition that an event is (formally) deducible from laws and antecedent conditions does not entail that it is physically possible for any being to perform this deduction. Hence, even if the anti-predictionist could establish that it is physically impossible to predict acts scientifically, he would not thereby establish that acts are undetermined.

We have not conclusively shown either that it is physically possible for some beings to predict acts scientifically or that it is not. But unless we assume that this is physically possible, we cannot turn to the other interesting issues that surround the problem of the prediction of human behavior. Unless we assume this, the question of the causal compossibility of predicting acts cannot even arise. In order to explore these important issues, therefore, I shall henceforth assume that scientific predictions of acts (like scientific predictions generally) are physically possible.

3. Causal Compossibility

Perhaps the anti-predictionist would think it obvious that it is causally incompossible to predict acts scientifically. He might argue as follows: "Let us grant, as is likely, that there have never been any genuine scientific predictions of voluntary human acts. If, as my opponent claims, determinism is true, then it is causally incompossible for any predictions to have been made of these acts. For every actual act A, there is an actual event $\overline{P_A}$, the *absence* of a prediction of A. Since each of these events $\overline{P_A}$ is actual, and since determinism is true, each of these events $\overline{P_A}$ must be causally necessitated by some set of actual events prior to it. But if each of these events $\overline{P_A}$ is causally necessitated by actual prior events, then each event P_A—the prediction of A—is causally incompossible relative to some actual events. In other words, for each actual act A, it is causally incompossible for A to have been predicted."

This argument, like a previous one, proves too much. The anti-predictionist is right in saying that non-actual predictions of acts are causally incompossible with the actual prior events in the world. But this is true simply because, assuming determinism, every non-actual event whatever is causally incompossible with some set of actual prior events. Thus, using the notion of "causal-compossibility-relative-to-all-actual-events," we can establish the impossibility of predicting physical phenomena as well as human behavior. We can point to an act that was never predicted and say that, in this sense, it "could not" have been predicted, since its nonprediction was causally necessitated by other actual events. But by the same token, we can point to a physical event which was never predicted and say that it "could not" have been predicted, since its nonprediction was also causally necessitated by other actual events. Using this notion of "possibility of prediction," the antipredictionist again fails to establish any special immunity of action to prediction.

Apart from this point, however, the notion of "causal-compossibility-relative-to-all-actual-events" does not seem to be a pertinent kind of possibility for our discussion. We have seen that determinism does not entail the possibility of predicting acts in *every* sense of "possible." And here, I believe, we have still another sense of "possible" in which determinism does not entail that it is possible for every act to be predicted. Determinism does not say that, relative to all actual prior events, it is causally compossible for a prediction of an act to be made *even if* those actual prior events causally necessitate that no prediction occur. Thus, the fact that it is impossible, in this sense, for acts to be predicted does not conflict with the thesis that acts are determined. Nor is it surprising that the sense of "possible" here under discussion is not important. Using the notion of "causally-compossible-relative-to-all-actual-prior-events," it turns out, assuming determinism, that only actual events are possible. But it is a strange and unduly restrictive notion of "possible" according to which only actual events are possible!

We need, then, a broader notion of possibility, one which allows for non-actual possibles while also taking into account the notion of causal necessity. We can discover a more relevant notion by examining what is often meant in ordinary contexts when we say, counter-factually, "*e* could have occurred." Suppose we say, counter-factually, "The picnic could have been a success." This sort of statement would normally be made with a suppressed "if"-clause. We might mean, for example, "The picnic could have been a success if it had not rained." Now if the only thing which prevented the picnic from being a success was the rain, we are also likely to say, "The picnic *would* have been a success if it had not rained." In the first case we mean that the substitution of nonrain for rain in the course of events would have *allowed* the picnic to be a success; in the second case we mean that this substitution would have *ensured* the success of the picnic. In both cases we are saying that a certain event could have or would have occurred *if* the prior course of the world had differed from its actual course in specified ways.

Although in ordinary contexts we might not pursue the matter further, in order to be systematic we must inquire further: "*Could* it *not* have rained?" "Could nonrain have occurred instead of rain?" The actual rain was causally necessitated by actual events prior to the rain. If we are to suppose that it did not rain, we must also make changes (in our imagination) of still earlier events. Carrying this argument to its logical conclusion, it is obvious that whenever a determinist says that a non-actual event *e* "could have" occurred, he must be prepared to imagine *an entirely new world.* For the picnic to have been a success, it is required that it not have rained. For it not to have rained, the cloud formation would have had to be different. For the cloud formation to have been different, it is required that the wind velocity (or some other factor) have been different. Etc.

Not only must we change conditions prior to *e*, if we are to suppose *e* occurs, but we probably[14] must change events after *e* as well. Had it not rained, a certain other picnic group near us would not have ended their picnic just then. And had they not ended their picnic just then, they would not have left for home just then. And had they not left for home just then, they would not have had an automobile accident when they did.[15] Etc.

The determinist who says, counter-factually, "*e* could have occurred," must construct a whole world to justify his claim. Nevertheless, this gives him a sense of "possible" that allows non-actual possibles. For a determinist, "*e* could have occurred" may be translated as "a causally compossible world can be imagined in which *e* occurs." Normally the determinist will be able to construct worlds resembling the real one to a large extent. But these worlds will never be exactly like our world except for one event only. Any such imagined world will differ from the real world by at least one event for every moment of time. This will be true, at any rate, if the laws governing these imagined worlds are identical with those of the real world. And I shall assume throughout that these laws (whatever they are, exactly) are held constant.

We can now give what I regard as a reasonable formulation of the question: "Is it possible, in principle, to make scientific predictions of voluntary acts?" The formulation is: "Can one construct causally compossible worlds in which scientific predictions are made of voluntary acts?" In saying that this is a "reasonable" formulation of the question, I do not mean that a negative answer to this question would *entail* that voluntary acts are not determined. I have already pointed out that determinism does not entail that it is physically possible to make scientific predictions of events, including acts. Hence, neither does determinism entail that there are causally compossible worlds in which scientific predictions of acts occur. However, since we are assuming that scientific predictions are physically possible, it would be an important negative result to discover that one cannot construct causally compossible worlds in which scientific predictions are made of voluntary

---

[14] I say "probably" because the definition of determinism does not entail that every event is a determinant of some subsequent event. Thus, if not-*e* actually occurred but had no effect on any subsequent event, then we might substitute *e* for not-*e* without changing any subsequent events. However, though determinism does not require it, it is reasonable to assume that every event will have some differential effect on *some* later event or events.

[15] This is all plausible, at any rate, if we deny fatalism. Fatalism, which is by no means implied by determinism, is the view that certain events will happen at certain times *no matter what* antecedent conditions obtain.

acts. This might not prove that acts are undetermined, but it would suggest a disparity between action and physical phenomena. For, assuming that scientific predictions are physically possible, it does seem to follow that there would be causally compossible worlds in which scientific predictions are made of physical events.

Similar comments are in order on the question, "Can one construct causally compossible worlds in which scientific predictions are made of voluntary acts and in which the agent learns beforehand of the prediction?" Determinism does not entail that there must be such causally compossible worlds. But if no such worlds are constructible—worlds in which "books of life" are found, or things comparable to books of life—one might well claim a disparity between voluntary action and physical phenomena.

Fortunately, I believe that there *are* causally compossible worlds in which scientific predictions are made of voluntary acts and in which, moreover, the agent learns of (some of) these predictions before he performs the predicted acts. I believe that there are causally compossible worlds in which books of life are written before a man's birth. Inscribed in these books are predictions of the agent's acts, predictions based on laws and antecedent conditions. These predictions are correct even though the agent sometimes reads them before he performs the predicted acts. I shall support my claim that there are such causally compossible worlds by giving a sketch of such a world. Before giving my sketch, however, I wish to examine the structure of prediction-making where the prediction itself has a causal effect on the predicted event. This will be essential in understanding how a "book of life" could be written, even though the writer knows that the agent will read it.

Consider the problem of an election predictor. He may know what the precise results of the upcoming election are going to be, if he makes no public prediction of the election. If he publishes a prediction, however, some of the voters, having found out what the results will be, may change their votes and thereby falsify his prediction. How, then, can a pollster make a genuinely scientific and accurate prediction of an election? Can he take into account the effect of the prediction itself? Herbert Simon has shown that, under specifiable conditions, a predictor can do this.[16] Essentially, what the predictor must know is the propensity of the voters in the community to *change* their voting intention in accordance with their expectations of the outcome. If persons are more likely to vote for a candidate when they expect him to win than when they expect him to lose, we have a "bandwagon" effect; if the opposite holds, we have an "underdog" effect. Now let us suppose that a given pollster has ascertained that, two days before the election, 60 percent

---

[16] "Bandwagon and Underdog Effects of Election Predictions," reprinted in *Models of Man* (New York: John Wiley and Sons, Inc., 1957). The requisite condition is that the function relating the actual outcome of the voting to the predicted outcome, given the electorate's original voting intention, be *continuous*.

of the electorate plans to vote for candidate *A* and 40 percent for candidate *B*. He also knows that, unless he publishes a prediction, the percentages will be the same on election day. Further suppose he knows that there is a certain "bandwagon" effect obtaining in the voting community.[17] When the original intention of the electorate is to vote 60 percent for *A*, this bandwagon effect can be expressed by the equation, $V = 60 + .2(P - 50)$, where *P* is the percentage vote for *A* publicly predicted by a pollster, and *V* is the actual resultant vote for *A*. Clearly, if the pollster publicly predicts that *A* will receive 60 percent of the vote, his prediction will be falsified. Putting $P = 60$, the equation tells us that $V = 62$. In other words, the effect of the prediction, combined with the original voting intention of the electorate, would result in a 62 percent vote for *A*. However, the pollster can easily calculate a value for *P* which will make $P = V$. He need only solve the two equations, $P = V$ and $V = 60 + .2(P - 50)$. Such a solution yields $P = 62.5$. Thus, the pollster can publish a prediction saying that 62.5 percent of the electorate will vote for *A*, knowing that his own prediction will bring an additional 2.5 percent of the electorate into the *A* column, and thereby make his prediction come true.

Notice that all the antecedent conditions relevant to the outcome cannot be known until it is known what prediction (if any) the pollster will make. His prediction (or lack of prediction) is itself an important antecedent condition. However, one of the crucial determinants of the outcome—viz., the original voting intention of the electorate—is given independently of the pollster's prediction. Thus, while holding that factor constant, the pollster calculates what the outcome of the election *would* be *if* he were to make certain predictions. By solving the equations given above, he discovers a prediction which, if published, would be confirmed. He thereupon forms an intention to publish that prediction and proceeds to fulfill that intention. Until he forms this intention, he does not know what prediction he will make, and therefore does not know all the requisite antecedent events from which to deduce the election outcome. But at the time he makes the prediction (and perhaps even earlier), he does know all the relevant antecedent conditions and has deduced from these conditions what the results will be. Thus, his prediction of the outcome is a truly scientific prediction.

If someone wishes to predict a single person's behavior and yet let him learn of the prediction, the predictor must employ the same sort of strategy as the pollster. He must take into account what the agent's reaction will be to the prediction. There are several kinds of circumstances in which, having made the appropriate calculations, he will be able to make a correct prediction. (A) The agent learns of the prediction but does not want to falsify it. (B) Upon hearing the prediction, the agent decides to falsify it. But later,

---

[17] That this bandwagon effect holds in the community could be discovered either by studying previous elections or by deducing it from "higher-level" generalizations found to be true of the community.

when the time of the action approaches, he acquires preponderant reasons for doing what was predicted after all. (C) Having decided to refute the prediction, the agent performs the act conforming with it because he doesn't realize that he is conforming with it. (D) At the time of the action the agent is unable to do anything but conform with the prediction, though he may have believed that he would be able to falsify it. In any of these four kinds of case, a predictor would be able to calculate that his prediction, together with numerous other antecedent conditions, would causally necessitate that the agent perform the predicted act. In a case of kind (B), for example, the predictor may be able to foresee that the agent will first read his prediction and decide to falsify it. But other factors will crop up—ones which the agent did not originally count on—which will make him change his mind and perform the predicted act after all. And the predictor also foresees this.

In the first three kinds of cases, (A), (B), and (C), the agent performs the predicted act *voluntarily*—although in (C) he fails to realize that he is also performing an act of *fulfilling the prediction*. In other words, in each of these three kinds of cases, the agent is able to act otherwise. Thus, the possibility of a scientific prediction does not require that the agent be *unable* to act in any way different from the prediction. All that is required is that the agent will not *in fact* act in any way different from the prediction. A predictor might know that an agent will in fact act in a certain way, not because he knows that the agent will be *unable* or *incapable* of doing otherwise, but because he knows that the agent will *choose* or *decide* to act as predicted. This point will be clarified in Chapter Seven where the relevant sense of "able" will be explored and analyzed.

I shall now give a sketch of a causally compossible world in which a large number of correct predictions are made of an agent's behavior. Since I imagine this world to be governed by the same laws as those of the real world, and since I do not know all the laws of the real world, I cannot *prove* that my imagined world is really causally compossible. But as far as I can tell from commonsense knowledge of psychological and physical regularities, it certainly seems to be causally compossible. In this world, predictions of a man's life are made in great detail and inscribed in a "book of life," (parts of) which the agent subsequently reads. Obviously, I cannot describe the whole of this world, but I shall describe some of its most important and problematic features—namely, the interaction between the agent and the book. Unfortunately, I shall have to omit a description of another important part of the world, the part in which the predictor (or predictors) gathers his data and makes his calculations. I am unable to describe this part of the world, first, because I do not know all the laws which the predictor would have at his disposal, and secondly, because I am not able to say just what the structure of this being would be. However, the main features of his *modus operandi* should be clear from our discussion of the pollster, whose technique is at the heart of such predicting.

4. A Book of Life

And now to the description of the world.

While browsing around the library one day, I notice an old dusty tome, quite large, entitled "Alvin I. Goldman." I take it from the shelf and start reading. In great detail, it describes my life as a little boy. It always gibes with my memory and sometimes even revives my memory of forgotten events. I realize that this purports to be a book of my life and I resolve to test it. Turning to the section with today's date on it, I find the following entry for 2:36 p.m. "He discovers me on the shelf. He takes me down and starts reading me . . ." I look at the clock and see that it is 3:03. It is quite plausible, I say to myself, that I found the book about half an hour ago. I turn now to the entry for 3:03. It reads: "He is reading me. He is reading me. He is reading me." I continue looking at the book in this place, meanwhile thinking how remarkable the book is. The entry reads: "He continues to look at me, meanwhile thinking how remarkable I am."

I decide to defeat the book by looking at a future entry. I turn to an entry 18 minutes hence. It says: "He is reading this sentence." Aha, I say to myself, all I need do is refrain from reading that sentence 18 minutes from now. I check the clock. To ensure that I won't read that sentence, I close the book. My mind wanders; the book has revived a buried memory and I reminisce about it. I decide to reread the book there and relive the experience. That's safe, I tell myself, because it is an earlier part of the book. I read that passage and become lost in reverie and rekindled emotion. Time passes. Suddenly I start. Oh yes, I intended to refute the book. But what was the time of the listed action? I ask myself. It was 3:19, wasn't it? But it's 3:21 now, which means I have already refuted the book. Let me check and make sure. I inspect the book at the entry for 3:17. Hmm, that seems to be the wrong place for there it says I'm in a reverie. I skip a couple pages and suddenly my eyes alight on the sentence: "He is reading this sentence." But it's an entry for 3:21, I notice! So I made a mistake. The action I had intended to refute was to occur at 3:21, not 3:19. I look at the clock, and it is still 3:21. I have not refuted the book after all.

I now turn to the entry for 3:28. It reads, "He is leaving the library, on his way to the President's office." Good heavens, I say to myself, I had completely forgotten about my appointment with the President of the University at 3:30. I suppose I could falsify the book by not going, but it is much more important for me not to be late for that appointment. I'll refute the book some other time! Since I do have a few minutes, however, I turn back to the entry for 3:22. Sure enough, it says that my reading the 3:28 entry has reminded me about the appointment. Before putting the book back on the shelf, and leaving, I turn to an entry for tomorrow at 3:30 p.m. "He's still riding the bus bound for Chicago," it reads. Well, I say to myself, *that* prediction will be easy to refute. I have absolutely no intention of going to Chicago tomorrow.

Despite my decision to refute the book, events later induce me to change my mind and to conform to it. For although I want to refute the book on this matter, stronger reasons arise for not refuting it. When I get home that evening I find a note from my wife saying that her father (in Chicago) is ill and that she had to take the car and drive to Chicago. I call her there and she explains what has happened. I tell her about the book. Next morning she calls again with news that her father's condition is deteriorating and that I must come to Chicago immediately. As I hang up I realize that the book may turn out right after all, but that the situation nevertheless demands that I go to Chicago. I might still refute it by going by plane or train. However, I call the airlines and am told that the fog is delaying all flights. The railroad says that there are no trains for Chicago till later in the day. So, acquiescing, I take a bus to Chicago, and find myself on it at 3:30.

5. Objections and Replies

Let me interrupt my narrative here. I have given several cases in which the book is not refuted, and the reader should be convinced that I could easily continue this way. But it is important now to reply to several objections which the anti-predictionist is anxious to make against my procedure.

(1) "*Your story clearly presupposes determinism. But whether or not determinism is true is the central matter of dispute. Hence, you are begging the question.*" Admittedly, my story does presuppose determinism. Unless determinism were true, the imagined predictor could not have figured out what acts the agent would perform and then written them in the book. However, I do not think that this begs the question. For I am not here trying to prove that determinism *is* true. I am merely trying to show that the thesis of determinism is quite compatible with the world as we know it and with human nature as we know it. The world depicted in my story seems to be very much like the real world except that it contains different antecedent conditions. The fact that this imagined world is determined and contains predictions of acts, and yet resembles the real world very closely, suggests to me that the real world may also be determined. At any rate, this supposition seems quite tenable, and its tenability is what I seek to establish here.

(2) "*The story you told was fixed. Events might have been different from the way you described them. For example, the fog might not have curtailed all air traffic.*" No, events could not be different *in the world I am imagining*. That is, in my world all the events I described were causally necessitated by prior antecedent conditions. I did not describe all the antecedent conditions, so perhaps the reader cannot see that each event I did describe was causally

necessitated by them. But, since it is a deterministic world, that is so. No one can imagine *my* world and also substitute the negation of one of the events I described. I'm not "fixing" the story by saying that the fog curtailed air traffic; that just is the way my imagined world goes.

(3) "*But I can imagine a world in which some putative predictions of actions are refuted.*" I have no doubt that you can; that is very easy. You could even imagine a world *somewhat* like the one I have just described, but in which putative predictions are falsified. But this proves nothing at all. I would never deny that one can construct some causally compossible worlds in which putative scientific predictions of acts are not successful. I have only claimed that one can (also) construct *some* causally compossible worlds in which genuine scientific predictions of acts are made and are successful. The situation with predictions of action is no different than the one with predictions of physical events. We can construct causally compossible worlds in which predictions of physical phenomena are correct. But we can also construct worlds in which putative scientific predictions of physical phenomena are incorrect. If our ability to construct worlds in which predictions are unsuccessful proves the inherent unpredictableness of the kind of phenomena unsuccessfully predicted, then we can prove the unpredictableness of physical phenomena as easily as the unpredictableness of human action.

(4) "*The world you have described, though possible, is a highly improbable world. Worlds in which putative predictions of action are falsified are much more probable.*" The notion of one possible world being "more probable" than another seems to me unintelligible. Surely the statistical sense of probability cannot be intended. There is no way of "sampling" from possible worlds to discover what features most of them have. Perhaps the anti-predictionist means that we can *imagine* more worlds in which putative predictions of actions are falsified. But this too is questionable. I can imagine indefinitely many worlds in which successful predictions of acts are made.

Perhaps the anti-predictionist means that it is improbable that any such sequence of events as I described would occur in the *real* world. He may well be right on this point. However, to talk about what is probable (in the evidential sense) in the real world is just to talk about what has happened, is happening, and will happen *as a matter of fact*. But the dispute between predictionists and anti-predictionists is, presumably, not about what *will* happen, but about what *could* happen *in principle*. This "in principle" goes beyond the particular facts of the actual world.

(5) "*The difference between physical phenomena and action is that predictions of acts can defeat themselves; but predictions of physical events cannot.*" This is not so. One can construct worlds in which the causal effect of a putative prediction of a physical event falsifies that prediction. Jones calculates the position of a speck of dust three inches from his nose and the direction and velocity of wind currents in the room. He then announces his prediction that five seconds thence the speck will be in a certain position. He had neglected

to account for the wind expelled from his mouth when he made the prediction, however, and this factor changes the expected position of the speck of dust. Perhaps one can imagine a wider variety of cases in which predictions affect human action than of cases in which they affect physical phenomena. But this is only a difference of *degree*, not of kind.

(6) "*Predictions of physical events can refute themselves because the predictor may fail to account for the effect of his own prediction. But were he to take this effect into account, he would make a correct prediction. On the other hand, there are conditions connected with the prediction of action in which, no matter what prediction the predictor makes, his prediction will be falsified. Here there is no question of inaccurate calculation or insufficient information. Whatever he predicts will be incorrect. Yet this situation arises only in connection with human action, not physical events.*"

This is an important objection and warrants detailed discussion.

Suppose that I wish to predict what act you will perform 30 seconds from now, but that I will not try to change or affect your behavior except by making my prediction. (Thus, I shall not, for example, predict that you will perform no act at all and then make that prediction come true by killing you.) Further suppose that the following conditions obtain. At this moment you want to falsify any prediction that I shall make of your action. Moreover, you will still have this desire 30 seconds from now, and it will be stronger than any conflicting desire you will have at that time. Right now you intend to do act A, but you are prepared to perform $\bar{A}$ (not-A) if I predict that you will perform A. Thirty seconds hence you will have the ability and opportunity to do A and the ability and opportunity to do $\bar{A}$. Finally, conditions are such that, if I make a prediction in English in your presence, you will understand it, will remember it for 30 seconds, and will be able to tell whether any of your acts will conform to it or not. Given all these conditions, whatever I predict—at least, if I make the prediction by saying it aloud, in your presence, in English, etc.—will be falsified. If I predict you will do A, then you will do $\bar{A}$, while if I predict that you will do $\bar{A}$, you will proceed to do A. In other words, in these conditions no prediction of mine is causally compossible with the occurrence of the event I predict. Let $C_1, \ldots, C_n$ be the (actual) conditions just delineated, let P_A be my predicting you will do A (announced in the indicated way), and let $P_{\bar{A}}$ be my predicting you will do $\bar{A}$ (announced in the same way). Then *both* sets $\{C_1, \ldots, C_n, P_A, A\}$ and $\{C_1, \ldots, C_n, P_{\bar{A}}, \bar{A}\}$ are causally *in*compossible sets of events.

Notice that this example does not prove that it is causally incompossible (*simpliciter*) for me to make a scientific prediction of your action. All that it proves is that I cannot make such a prediction *in a certain manner*—viz., by announcing it to you in English. The events P_A and $P_{\bar{A}}$ include this particular manner, and that they do so is important. If I predict your action in some other manner, by thinking it to myself or by saying it aloud in Hindustani, for example, the effect on your action would not be the same as if I say it aloud in English. Assume that, if you do not hear me make any prediction or if you hear me say something you fail to understand, you will proceed to perform act A. Then it is causally compossible for me to predict your act correctly by announcing the prediction in Hindustani. In other words, letting P_A' be my predicting that you will do A by announcing this in Hindustani, then the set of events $\{C_1, \ldots, C_n, P_A', A\}$ is a causally compossible set.

In determining whether or not a certain set of events, including (1) a prediction, (2) the event predicted, and (3) certain other assumed conditions, is a causally compossible set, it is essential to specify the manner of the prediction. This is true *in general*, not just in the case of predictions of action. A prediction which is "embodied" or expressed in one way will not have the same causal effects as the same prediction expressed in another way. We can see this in the case of the speck of dust. Jones predicted the position of the dust by announcing it orally, and this resulted in the falsification of the prediction. But had he made the same prediction in another fashion—say, by moving his toes in a certain conventional pattern—his prediction would not have been falsified, for the position of the dust would not have been affected.

What is the significance of the fact that it is causally incompossible, in some circumstances, for a (correct) prediction of an act to be made in a specified manner? First, this unpredictability does not prove that these acts are undetermined. Indeed, the very construction of the case in which no prediction is possible *presupposed* the existence of laws of nature which, together with a given prediction, would result in a certain act. In short, the case under discussion should, if anything, support rather than defeat the thesis that acts are determined. The only reason one might have for thinking the contrary is the assumption—which should by now appear very dubious—that determinism entails predictability. What our present case shows, I think, is that under some circumstances, even a determined event may not be susceptible of being correctly predicted in a specified manner. This fact can be further supported by adducing a similar case connected with purely physical events. And this brings me to my second point: the case produced above does not reflect a peculiarity of human action, since parallel examples can be found among physical phenomena.

Imagine a certain physical apparatus placed in front of a piano keyboard. A bar extends from the apparatus and is positioned above a certain key. (Only white keys will be considered.) If the apparatus is not disturbed, the bar will strike that key at a certain time. Now let us suppose that the apparatus is sensitive to sound, and, in particular, can discriminate between sounds of varying pitches. If the apparatus picks up a certain sound, the position of the bar will move to the right and proceed to strike the key immediately to the right of the original one (if there is one). Specifically, if the sound has the same pitch as that of the key over which the bar is poised, the bar will move. If the monitored sound has any other pitch, the bar will remain in its position and proceed to strike that key.

Now suppose that someone (or something) wishes to make predictions of the behavior of the apparatus. He wishes to predict what key the bar will strike. But the following restriction is made on the *manner* in which the prediction is to be made. The prediction must be expressed according to a specific set of conventions or symbols. To predict that the bar will strike middle C, for example, the predictor must emit a sound with the pitch of middle C. To predict that the bar will strike D, he must emit a sound with the pitch of that key. Etc. All sound emissions are to be made in the neighborhood of the apparatus. Given this restriction on the manner of prediction, it will be causally incompossible for the predictor to make a correct prediction. For suppose that the bar is poised above middle C. If he predicts that it will strike middle C—that is, if he emits a sound of that pitch—the bar will move and proceed to strike D. But if he predicts any other behavior of the bar, for example, that it will strike D, the bar will remain in its original position and strike middle C.

Admittedly, the manner of prediction I have allowed to the predictor of this physical phenomenon is much more narrowly restricted than the manner of prediction allowed to the predictor of human action. But we could imagine physical apparatuses with a greater degree of complexity, able to "refute" predictions made in any of a wider variety of manners. In any case, the principle of the situation is the same for both physical phenomena and human action, though the manners of prediction which affect one phenomenon may be different from the manners of prediction which affect the other. The latter difference simply reflects that fact that physical objects and human beings do not respond in precisely the same ways to the same causes. But this is equally true of different kinds of physical objects and of different pairs of human beings.

The reader should not suppose that the present discussion in any way vitiates my description of the book of life in Section 4 of this chapter. Our present discussion shows that under *some* conditions it is *not* causally compossible to predict a man's act in a way which allows him to learn of the prediction. But there are *other* conditions, such as the ones described in Section 4, in which such predictions *are* causally compossible. The existence of the latter conditions suffices to establish the possibility (in principle) of scientific predictions of voluntary acts which the agent hears or reads. Admittedly, it is not always possible to make predictions in this manner. But even when it is impossible to let one's prediction become known to the agent, it does not follow that it is impossible to make the prediction "privately." Thus, suppose you are trying to write a book of my life before I am born. Your calculations might show that if you inscribe certain predictions in the book they will be confirmed, for these calculations might reveal that I will not read the book, or that I will perform the acts despite the fact that I will read the book. If so, you may proceed to write the book, having (scientific) knowledge that it will be correct. On the other hand, your calculations might reveal that, no matter what prediction you inscribe in the book, I will refute it. In this case, you will be unable to write a book of my life. But you may nevertheless have scientific knowledge of what I shall do! Your calculations may reveal that I will do a certain sequence of acts, as long as I do not come across any (putative) book of my life. If you decide not to write such a book yourself, and if you know that no one else will, you may conclude (deductively) that I will perform the indicated sequence of acts.

6.   Foreknowledge of One's Own Acts

I have shown that there are causally compossible worlds in which voluntary acts—i.e., acts which one *chooses* or *decides* to do—are scientifically predicted. Let us now see whether there are causally compossible worlds in which a person scientifically predicts one of his *own* acts. I think that there are such worlds and I shall illustrate by continuing the description of the world I was sketching earlier.

Having tested my book of life on a very large number of occasions during many months and failed to refute it, I become convinced that whatever it says is true. I have about as good inductive evidence for this proposition as I do for many another proposition I could be said to know. Finally, I get up enough courage to look at the very end of the book and, as expected, it tells when and how I shall die. Dated five years hence, it describes my committing suicide by jumping off the 86th floor observation deck of the Empire State Building. From a description of the thoughts which will flash through my mind before jumping, it is clear that the intervening five years will have been terrible. As the result of those experiences, I will have emotions, desires, and beliefs which will induce me to jump. Since I trust the book completely, I now conclude that I *will* commit suicide five years hence. Moreover, I can be said to *know* that I will commit suicide.

As described so far, we cannot consider my prediction of my suicide a "scientific" prediction. To be a scientific prediction the predicted event must be *deduced* from laws and antecedent conditions, while, as I have described the case, no deduction was involved. However, we might supplement the situation so as to include a deduction. The book may be imagined to list the relevant physical and psychological laws (in a footnote, say) and the relevant conditions which determine my committing suicide (my intention to commit suicide, my proximity to the fence surrounding the observation deck, the absence of guards or other interfering factors, etc.). From these laws and conditions I actually deduce my future action.[18]

This example shows, contrary to the view of some authors, that we can have inductive knowledge of our own future acts, knowledge which is not

---

[18] That these conditions will actually obtain is, of course, open to doubt. Moreover, I have not learned of *them* by scientific prediction. I have simply "taken the book's word"

based on having already made a decision or formed an intention to perform the future act. Stuart Hampshire, for example, has recently written, ". . . I cannot intelligibly justify a claim to certain knowledge of what I shall voluntarily do on a specific occasion by an inductive argument; if I do really know what I shall do, voluntarily, and entirely of my own free will, on a specific occasion, I must know this in virtue of a firm intention to act in a certain way."[19] The case outlined, I believe, shows that Hampshire is mistaken. In that case, there is a time at which I do have certain knowledge of what I shall do (at any rate, about as "certain" as one can be with inductive evidence) and yet I have formed no intention nor made any decision to perform that act. At the time I read the book's prediction, I do not intend to commit suicide. But although I do not intend to commit suicide, I fully believe and know that, five years later, I will intend to commit suicide. I firmly believe that, at that later time, I will feel certain emotions and have certain desires which will induce me to jump off the Empire State Building. At the time of my reading the book I do not feel these things, but I commiserate with my future self, much as I commiserate with and understand another person's desires, beliefs, feelings, intentions, etc. Still, my understanding of these states of mind and of the action in which they will issue is the understanding of a spectator; my knowledge of these states and of my future action is purely inductive. Moreover, this knowledge is of a particular voluntary act to be performed at a specified time. It will be a voluntary act in the sense that it will be performed as the result of a firm intention and choice, not because I am literally unable to act otherwise. The intention that it will result from, however, will not be formed until after I have had certain experiences, experiences which, at the time I am reading the book, I have not yet had.

We can imagine two alternative series of events to occur between my reading the book and my suicide. First, I might *forget* what I have learned from the book, and later decide to commit suicide. Secondly, while never forgetting the prediction, my attitude toward my future suicide may gradually change from mere inductive knowledge of the future suicide to *intention* accompanied by knowledge. In this second alternative, there is never any moment involving a radical change of stance *vis-à-vis* the future suicide. I never pass from a state of complete doubt about whether I will commit suicide to a sudden intention to commit suicide. Instead, there is a gradual

---

that these conditions will obtain; I have not deduced them from other, still earlier conditions. However, there are no restrictions on the manner in which a predictor comes to know antecedent conditions. One way predictors might learn about antecedent conditions is by using various measuring devices and instruments, the reliability of which is supported by inductive evidence. My book of life may be regarded as such a device, and my inductive evidence supporting its reliability may be as strong as that supporting the reliability of various other devices which scientists commonly use for obtaining knowledge of antecedent conditions.

[19] *Freedom of the Individual* (London: Chatto and Windus, 1965), p. 54.

change, over a five year period, from assent to the *declarative* proposition that I *will* commit suicide to assent to the *optative* proposition, "Let it be the case that I commit suicide." When I first read the book I am fully prepared to assent to the proposition that I *will* commit suicide. But I am saddened by the thought; my heart isn't in it. Later, as a result of various tragic experiences, my *will* acquiesces in the idea. I begin to welcome the thought of suicide, to entertain the thought of committing suicide with pleasure and relief. By the time the appointed time comes around, I am *bent* on suicide. This gradual change in attitude constitutes the difference between mere inductive knowledge of my future suicide and an intention to commit suicide. Hampshire claims that the first kind of knowledge of one's own action—i.e., knowledge unaccompanied by intention—is impossible. The present case, I believe, shows this claim to be mistaken.

Many philosophers seem to be very uncomfortable with the idea of a book of life. They believe that the existence of such books of life, or even the belief in determinism, would deprive us of all the essential characteristics of genuine action: choice, deliberation, etc. Richard Taylor has taken this position very clearly on the question of deliberation. For one thing, he maintains that if one knows that one is going to do a certain act, he cannot deliberate about whether or not to do it. "I want to argue that an agent cannot deliberate about what to do, even though this may be something that is up to him . . . , in case he already knows what he is going to do."[20] Now I think this point is correct. The agent who knows, as a result of reading his book of life, that he is going to commit suicide, cannot *deliberate* about whether or not to commit suicide. For deliberation implies the presence of some doubt as to whether the act will be done. Of course, the fact that one cannot *deliberate* here about whether to commit suicide does not imply that one cannot form an intention to commit suicide, or even that one cannot commit suicide voluntarily. It must be admitted, however, that *deliberation* would not be possible if we always knew inductively what we were going to do before we came to form an intention about it.

All this shows, however, is that deliberation is impossible if there is a book of life which the agent reads beforehand and which the agent believes to contain the truth. This hardly implies, however, that the mere *existence* of books of life is incompatible with deliberation. First of all, one might never read one's own book of life and therefore never learn (inductively) beforehand what one is going to do. Secondly, even if one reads one's own book of life, and reads a passage which says what one will do some time later, one might not (at least at first) believe it to be true. So one might disregard what one has read in the book, and set out to deliberate about what to do. Of course, if it really *is* a book of one's life, as opposed to a merely putative book of life, then the outcome of one's deliberation will accord with what

---

[20] Richard Taylor, *Action and Purpose*, p. 174.

the book predicted. This does not imply, however, that one's deliberation is irrelevant, illusory, or a mere sham. On the contrary, one's deliberation is probably a crucial causal condition of one's eventual action, and it is precisely this deliberation which the writer of the book of life had to take into account in ascertaining what one's eventual act would be.

Still less should we conclude that the mere truth of determinism, or the *belief* in determinism, is incompatible with deliberation. Now Taylor contends that the belief in determinism is incompatible with deliberation. He writes:

> What is inconsistent is for someone to affirm a theory of determinism and at the same time deliberate about some of his own future actions. . . . If a man believes, concerning some of the actions he is going to perform, that there already exist conditions causally sufficient for his performing them, and conditions which therefore render them inevitable, then he cannot deliberate whether or not to perform them.[21]

Taylor's reasons for this contention appear to be his belief that if it is determined that you will do A or determined that you will do $\bar{A}$, then it is not "up to you" whether or not to do A. It is not equally within your power to do A and to do $\bar{A}$. If your doing A is determined, then what you are going to do is inevitable, and hence out of your hands.

> . . . I maintain that even if one does not know what he is going to do, but nevertheless knows that conditions already exist which are causally sufficient for his doing whatever it is that he is going to do, then he cannot deliberate about what to do, even though he may not know what those conditions are. One can, in such a case, only guess or speculate about what he will do, or try to find out what it is that he will inevitably do. This is again a consequence of the fact that one can deliberate whether to do a certain act only if he believes it is up to him whether to do it or not, or that it is within his power equally to do it, *and* to forego it.[22]

But why should a person not believe that it is "up to him" whether or not to do A, even if he believes that either it is determined that he will do A or it is determined that he will do $\bar{A}$? I think that even if a person's action is determined, it may still be "up to him" what to do. Even if his action is determined, it may still be within his power to do A and equally within his power to do $\bar{A}$.

To clarify my position, it is essential that we distinguish two different kinds of ways in which an act may be determined. First, my performing the act of *not* taking a train to New York tonight may be determined by factors which causally necessitate that there will be no train going to New York

---

[21] *Ibid.*, p. 182.
[22] *Ibid.*, p. 177.

tonight. Here it is indeed not "up to me" whether or not I take the train to New York tonight; it is not within my power equally to take a train to New York and not to take a train to New York; it is inevitable that I *not* take a train to New York tonight. But this is because my action does not depend on my wants or on my choice. Even if I *want* to take a train to New York tonight, I will not succeed in doing so. It is not "up to me" whether or not to take a train to New York tonight because my choice in the matter is irrelevant. I will in fact *not* take a train to New York tonight, no matter what I want or what I choose.

A very different sort of case is where there *is* a train to New York tonight and I am in a position to catch the train. In this case, whether or not I take the train *is* "up to me," because my choice determines my action. If I want to take the train then I will do so, and if I want not to take the train, then I will not take it. Thus, it is within my power to take the train and within my power not to take the train. All this is quite compatible with the fact that I will in fact have just *one* desire in the matter, and it is also compatible with the fact that the desire which I shall in fact have is causally necessitated by prior events. Since it is *up to me*, therefore, whether or not to take the train to New York, it is perfectly proper for me to *deliberate* about whether or not to take it. Indeed, this process of deliberation may embody some of the events which causally necessitate my having the want which is among the factors that causally necessitate my action.

CHAPTER SEVEN

Ability, Excuses, and Constraint

1. Ability

At the end of the last chapter I indicated that the fact that an (actual) act *A* was determined does not entail that it was not in the agent's power to refrain from doing it. The fact that an act was causally necessitated does not entail that he was not able to do otherwise. In this section I shall present an analysis of the notion of "having it in one's power" to perform an act, or of "being able" to perform an act, which will, among other things, provide a defense for this position.

It must be admitted from the outset that there is at least one sense of "impossible" in which causal necessitation entails the impossibility of one's having acted otherwise. If *S*'s *not* doing *A* (at *t*) is causally necessitated, it follows that it was causally incompossible relative to actual events prior to *t* that *S* do *A* (at *t*). But I do not think that this sense of "impossible"—i.e., causal incompossibility relative to prior actual events—is the sense that is relevant to the question of whether *S* was *able* to do *A*, or whether it was in *S*'s *power* to do *A*. The failure to do *A* (at *t*) may have resulted from (at least) two quite distinct factors: either *S*'s *inability* to do *A* or *S*'s *disinclination* to do *A*. Prior events may have causally necessitated that *S* be *unable* to do *A* (at *t*) and thereby causally necessitated that *S* not do *A* (at *t*). Or prior events may have causally necessitated that *S* be *disinclined* to do *A* (at *t*) and thereby causally necessitated that *S* not do *A* (at *t*). In the latter case it would be incorrect to explain *S*'s failure to do *A* by saying that he was *unable* to do *A*.

Surely it is evident that we frequently fail to perform an act simply because we do not want to perform it, not because we are unable to perform it. If I do not watch television tonight because I know that there is nothing interesting on television tonight, and because I prefer to read a certain novel instead, it would be silly to conclude that I am *unable* to watch television tonight. Given that I have a television set in operating order, that the needed electricity is available, that my limbs can move in such a way as to transport me to the television set and turn it on, and that I am sufficiently rested to watch television without falling asleep, it follows that I am *able* to watch television tonight. The fact that I do not watch television because I would rather read a novel does not vitiate my ability to watch television. Moreover, even if my not wanting to watch television tonight is causally necessitated by prior events, I see no reason for saying that I am unable to watch television tonight.

It might be argued, however, that conditions of the sort indicated do not really entail that I am able to watch television tonight. In particular, it might be contended that a further requirement to be satisfied is that I am *able* to *want* to watch television tonight. If I am unable to want to watch television, and if my wanting to watch television is a causally necessary condition of my watching television, then, it might be argued, I am not able to watch television tonight. Unfortunately, it is far from clear what might be meant by saying that a person is "able" or "unable" to *want* to watch television; the notion of ability is not ordinarily applied to wants. True, we might wish to introduce a notion of "ability" that applies to wants. This might allow us to say that people with compulsions or phobias are "unable to want" to do certain things, and hence, in a sense, "unable" to perform these acts.[1] But even if we were to introduce such a notion, we would surely introduce it in order to *contrast* these cases with cases in which a person's not wanting to do something is caused in an "ordinary" way. Thus, we would not wish to say that if my not wanting to watch television tonight is causally necessitated by such events as my having been bored with television on many past occasions, my having enjoyed the first chapter of the novel I intend to read instead, etc., then I am "unable to want" to watch television tonight. In short, "inability to want" should not be regarded as co-extensive with "causally necessitated not to want."

Finally, even if we admit that there is a sense of "ability" in which a person is unable to perform an act if he has a phobia about performing such an act, or some other abnormal psychological state *vis-a-vis* this act, there seems to be *another* sense of "ability" to which phobias and other abnormal psychological states are irrelevant. Consider a Federal judge who is to rule on a certain desegregation case. Clearly there is a sense of "ability" in which he has the ability to order desegregation; it is "within his power," or "up to him," whether to order desegregation, in a sense in which the ordinary citizen does not have it within his power to order desegregation. Moreover, such a judge has this ability even if he happens to have a phobia against desegregation. There is still something very important that distinguishes him from ordinary citizens—an ability *he* has that they lack. Similarly, there is a sense

---

[1] Bernard Gert and Timothy Duggan attempt to work out such a notion, which they call the ability to "will," in their article "Voluntary Abilities," *American Philosophical Quarterly*, IV (1967), 127–35.

of "ability" in which a person who has a television set, who is sufficiently rested to stay up and watch it, etc., is "able" to watch television, even if he has an irrational aversion to it. This ability distinguishes him from a person who has no television set, or who is too tired to watch it, or who cannot turn it on because he is paralyzed. The sense of "ability" to which I am referring is the most basic, or fundamental, sense of "ability," which any stronger sense of "ability" must include or presuppose. This fundamental sense of "ability" is what I wish to analyze in this section.

When we say that a person has a certain ability, we often mean that he has a certain general capacity. We might say that Smith is able to play the piano, or able to run a mile in four minutes, or able to solve difficult mathematical problems. I am interested, however, in analyzing statements of the form "*S* is able to do *A* at (or by) time *t*," i.e., statements ascribing to an agent the ability to perform a specific act at a specific time. In this sense, a person is unable to play the piano at *t* if there is no piano in the offing at *t*, though he may still have the general capacity to play the piano.

Let me begin my analysis with the concept of a *basic act-type*, which was elucidated in Chapter Three. As the reader will recall, property *A* is said to be a basic act-type for agent *S* only if the following hypothetical statement is true: "If *S* were in standard conditions with respect to *A*, then if *S* wanted to do *A*, *S*'s exemplifying *A* would result from this want." Now if property *A* is a basic act-type for *S* at *t*, and if *S* is in standard conditions with respect to *A* at *t*, then I think that *S* is able to do *A* at *t*. For if *A* is a basic act-type for *S* at *t*, and if *S* is in standard conditions with respect to *A* at *t*, then the following causal conditional statement is true: "If *S* wanted to do *A* at *t*, then *S* would do *A* at *t*." This causal conditional statement, I believe, entails the statement that *S* is "able" to do *A* at *t*.[2]

_____

[2] Keith Lehrer has presented an argument purporting to show that no causal conditional statement of the form "*S* will do *A* if *C* obtains" can entail the statement "*S* can do *A*." Cf. "An Empirical Disproof of Determinism?" in Keith Lehrer, ed., *Freedom and Determinism* (New York: Random House, 1966). His argument consists in producing a pair of statements claimed to be jointly compatible with "*S* will do *A* if *C* obtains," but incompatible with "*S* can do *A*." These statements are: "*S* cannot do *A* if *C* does not obtain" and "*C* does not obtain." The conjunction of these statements, he contends, is compatible with "*S* will do *A* if *C* obtains;" but, since they entail "*S* cannot do *A*," they are incompatible with "*S* can do *A*."

To show in detail where Lehrer's argument goes wrong would require a discussion of temporal references (which Lehrer unfortunately omits) and/or counterfactual conditionals. I do not wish to pursue these matters here. Instead, I shall employ a *reductio* argument to show that something must be amiss with Lehrer's argument.

It is evident that there are some statements that can correctly be analyzed in terms of conditionals. A paradigm case of such a statement is

P: "*X* is soluble in water,"

which is analyzable as

Q: "*X* will dissolve if it is immersed in water,"

We have, then, a sufficient condition for saying that S is able to do A at t, a condition that is applicable when A is a basic act. But not all acts that one is able to do are basic acts, and therefore our analysis does not end here. I am able at present to turn on the light, but turning on the light is not a basic act-type. In order to take account of abilities to perform nonbasic acts, we must take account of the presence of relevant *generational* conditions. The fact that I am able to turn on the light is a function of the fact that I am already standing next to the light switch, that the switch is wired to the fixture, that there is a light bulb in the socket, etc. Because of these generational conditions, I am able to turn on the light by flipping the switch and I am able to flip the switch by moving my hand in a certain way. Moreover, I am able to move my hand in this way because this is a basic act-type for me at the present time.

There are, of course, a variety of different sorts of generational conditions that may be relevant to an agent's ability to perform a given act. In the case of turning on the light, only causal generational conditions are involved. These are the generational conditions that would allow my moving my hand in a certain way to generate my flipping the switch and the conditions that would allow my flipping the switch to generate my turning on the light. But in the case of the ability to checkmate one's opponent, say, *conventional* generational conditions are relevant. John is able to checkmate his opponent because the rules of chess and the configuration of the pieces on the chessboard allow his moving his hand in a certain way to generate his moving his queen to king-knight-seven and allow his moving his queen to king-knight-seven to generate his checkmating his opponent.

The notion of a basic act-type coupled with the notion of generational conditions provide the basis for a definition of ability. Before presenting such a definition (or definitions), however, we must give more careful attention to the temporal references occurring in statements of ability. In discussing

---

or, more accurately, as

    Q': "X would dissolve if it were immersed in water."

But if Lehrer's argument is sound, we can use an argument of the same form to "prove" that P cannot be correctly analyzed as Q (or as Q'). For consider statements

    R: "If X is not immersed in water it is not soluble"

and

    S: "X is not immersed in water."

R and S are jointly compatible with Q (and Q'). For let X be a piece of sugar, and imagine a magician such that if X is not immersed in water he changes its molecular structure so as to make it non-soluble, whereas if X is immersed in water it dissolves. Under these circumstances, it seems that R and S are jointly compatible with Q (or Q'). But R and S entail the negation of P. Hence, if all of this is correct, then Q (or Q') does not entail P.

We see, therefore, that Lehrer's form of argument leads to absurd conclusions, e.g., that P cannot be analyzed as Q (or as Q'). This shows, I believe, that there is something wrong with his form of argument, not that there is anything wrong with the claim that "If S wanted to do A at t, then S would do A at t" entails "S can do A at t."

someone's ability to do an act, we are interested in his ability to do it *at a certain time*, or *by* a certain time. Thus, we shall want an analysis of "*S* is able to do *A* at *t*." But just as a temporal reference is required in specifying the time of the act, a temporal reference is also required in specifying the ability.[3] I am not *now* able to turn on the light in the kitchen *now*; that is, I cannot turn on the kitchen light at this very moment, because I am not in the kitchen and hence not near the switch for the kitchen light. But I was able, a minute ago, to turn on the kitchen light at the present moment. If I had been asked a minute ago to turn on the kitchen light one minute later, I could have complied with the request. Thus, we must distinguish between the following two sentence-schemata, both in need of analysis: "*S* is able, at *t*, to do *A* at *t'*" and "*S* is able, at *t*, to do *A* at (or by) *t'*," where *t* is earlier than *t'*.

Let me begin by trying to analyze "*S* is able, at *t*, to do *A* at *t*." I propose the following definition.

> (I)   S *is able, at* t, *to do* A *at* t *if and only if:*
> *Either*   (1)   A *is a basic act-type for* S *at* t *and* S *is in standard conditions with respect to* A *at* t;
>
> or   (2)   *there is a basic act-type* A_1 *for* S *at* t *and a set of conditions* C* *such that* (a) S *is in standard conditions with respect to* A_1 *at* t, *and* (b) S's *doing* A_1 *at* t *would generate* S's *doing* A *at* t.[4]

Actually, the first disjunct in (I) may be regarded simply as a special case of the second disjunct, where A_1 is identical with *A* and where C* includes only standard conditions but no generational conditions. Bearing this in mind, we may simplify (I) as follows.

> (II)   S *is able, at* t, *to do* A *at* t *if and only if:*
> *There is a basic act* A_1 *for* S *at* t *and a set of conditions* C* *such that* (a) S *is in standard conditions with respect to* A_1 *at* t, *and* (b) *either* A = A_1 *or* S's *doing* A_1 *at* t *would generate* S's *doing* A *at* t.[5]

---

[3] This point is stressed by Keith Lehrer and Richard Taylor in "Time, Truth and Modalities," *Mind*, LXXIV (1965), 390–98, and by Roderick M. Chisholm in " 'He Could Have Done Otherwise,' " *The Journal of Philosophy*, LXIV (1967), 409–17.

[4] Conditions C* include both standard conditions for the basic act A_1 plus all relevant generational conditions. Notice that I do not say that conditions C* must all obtain "*at t.*" This is because some generational conditions may have taken place earlier than *t* (and perhaps some later than *t*). If *S* won his first chess game yesterday and hasn't won more since, then one of the generational conditions holds for *S*'s performing the act of winning his *second* chess game (today). Of course we might say that it is a fact *today* that *S* won his first chess game yesterday. But this raises metaphysical issues about facts that I would prefer to avoid.

If (II) is to be correct as an analysis of "*S* is able, at *t*, to do *A* at *t*," we must understand the notion of a basic act-type slightly more broadly than I have defined it until now. This is because there are some acts we are able to do which cannot be generated by a *single* basic act-token, such as moving one's right hand, but only by two or more *co-temporal* basic act-tokens, such as moving one's right hand while moving one's left hand. This introduces some complications.

Let me define the idea of a "compound basic act-type" as follows.

> *Property* A_n *is a compound basic act-type for* S *at* t *if and only if:*
>
> (1) A_n *is the conjunction of some properties* A_1, A_2, ..., A_m *each of which is a basic act-type for* S *at* t;
>
> (2) *it is physically possible for* S *to be in standard conditions at a single time with respect to each of* A_1, A_2, ..., A_m; *and*
>
> (3) *if* S *were in standard conditions at* t *with respect to each of* A_1, A_2, ..., A_m, *then if* S *wanted to do* A_1, A_2, ..., A_m *at* t, S*'s doing these acts at* t *would result from this want.*

Most pairs of basic act-types A_1 and A_2 are such that their conjunction, A_1 & A_2, is a compound basic act-type, according to this definition. This holds, for example, of the basic act-types *raising one's right hand* and *moving one's tongue*. But this is not true for all pairs of basic act-types. To take a trivial example first, both *raising one's right hand* and *lowering one's right hand* are individually basic act-types (for most people). But the conjunction, *raising one's right hand and lowering one's right hand*, is not a compound basic act-type for anyone. To take a less trivial example, *moving one's right hand up and down* is a basic act-type, as is *moving one's left hand in a rotating fashion*. But for many people, the conjunctive property *moving one's right hand up and down and* (*while*) *moving one's left hand in a rotating fashion* is not a compound basic act-type.

Having defined compound basic act-types, we can now simply say that any compound basic act-type is a basic act-type. Given this new, broader class of basic act-types, analysis (II) can stand as formulated.

Let us now ask how (II) is related to a hypothetical analysis of ability—e.g., to the analysans "If *S* wanted to do *A* at *t*, then *S* would do *A* at *t*." As we

---

[5] Definition (II), like (I), does not cover acts which are not basic acts but which would be on the *same level* as basic act-tokens. They could easily be taken care of with a slight addition, but they are such an insignificant class of acts that I have neglected them in order to avoid too much complication.

have seen, the fact that A is a basic act-type for S at t and the fact that S is in standard conditions with respect to A at t entail that if S wanted to do A at t then S would do A at t. Hence, where A is a basic act, my analysans and the hypothetical analysans are equivalent. But my analysans diverges from the hypothetical analysans when A is not a basic act. Suppose S is in a position, at t, to turn on the light at t and suppose that he has the needed basic act-type at t. Does it follow from this that S *will* turn on the light at t if he wants to turn on the light at t? No. Because although S may actually be in a position to turn on the light, he may not *know* that he is in a position to turn on the light. (Or even if he is told by a reliable authority that he is in a position to turn it on, he may not know just what to *do* to turn it on.) Though the light switch is in fact within his reach, he may not know where it is because it is disguised or hidden. In this case, definition (II) would have us say that S *is* able to turn on the light, whereas the hypothetical analysis would have us say that S is *not* able to turn on the light (because it is not true that if S wants to turn it on, then he *will* turn it on).

These considerations point out the necessity of distinguishing between an *epistemic* and a *non-epistemic* sense of "ability." In the case of the disguised light switch, we might be inclined to say that S is *able* to turn on the light but doesn't know it. Here we employ a non-epistemic sense of "ability," a sense in which saying someone is able to do A does not entail that he has the requisite knowledge or belief. But now consider Jones and his stalled car. Jones knows nothing about cars, and even though his engine needs but a small adjustment for which Jones has the necessary basic act repertoire, he does not know what to do. Here we would probably say that Jones is *not* able to repair his car, and in so saying we would be using an epistemic sense of "able," a sense which involves knowledge or belief. Clearly we use the term "able" in both senses, sometimes in the non-epistemic sense and sometimes in the epistemic sense. Definition (II) gives a non-epistemic sense of "able," which can be abbreviated as "able$_N$." With slight additions, we can define ability in the epistemic sense, to be abbreviated "able$_E$."

(II′) S *is able$_E$ to do* A *at* t *if and only if:*
(1) *There is a basic act-type* A_1 *for* S *at* t *which* S *knows (or truly believes) at* t *to be a basic act-type for him at* t;
(2) S *knows (or truly believes) that he is in standard conditions with respect to* A_1 *at* t; *and*
(3) *either*
   (a) S *knows (or truly believes) that* $A_1 = A$, *or*
   (b) S *knows (or truly believes) that there is a set of conditions* C* *such that his doing* A_1 *at* t *would generate his doing* A *at* t.

The hypothetical analysis of ability is much closer to (II') than it is to (II). For it is quite possible that the analysans of (II') holds true in precisely those cases in which the formula "If S wanted to do A at t, then he would do A at t" holds true.

Let me now turn to the more general question: is S able, at time t_1, to do A at (or by) t_n, where $t_1 \lesssim t_n$? (I shall use the symbol "$<$" to stand for "earlier than"; "$\sim$" will stand for "at the same time as"; and "$\lesssim$" will stand for "either earlier than or at the same time as.") Clearly, though someone may be unable, at t_n, to do A at t_n, there may have been an earlier time t_1 at which he was able to do A by (or at) t_n. At 8:00 I am not able to turn on the light at 8:00, because there is no bulb in the socket. But I was able, at 7:45, to turn on the light by (or at) 8:00, because at 7:45 there was still time for me to fetch a bulb, insert it into the socket, and flip the switch by (or at) 8:00. However, although I was able, at 7:45, to turn on the light by 8:00, I let my opportunity pass by not fetching the bulb. And this accounts for the fact that I am now, at 8:00, unable to turn on the light at 8:00.

In general, in order for S to perform A by t_n he must perform some acts prior to t_n which, together with the state of the rest of the world, cause him to be able, at some time t, $t \lesssim t_n$, to do A at t. For the most part, these "preparatory" acts are ones that would create generational conditions requisite for doing A. For example, if S wishes to turn on the light by 8:00, but there is no light bulb in the socket, then he must perform the act of fetching a light bulb and the act of screwing it into the socket. These acts, together with the antecedently present wiring system, etc., cause there to be a set of generational conditions C^* such that now, when S moves his hand in a certain manner, thereby flipping the switch, he will also turn on the light. There are some imaginable cases, however, in which the preparatory acts would be designed to affect standard conditions of certain basic acts, or even to affect the class of his basic act-types. To illustrate the last sort of case, consider a man who at one time has a paralyzed arm but who performs acts (e.g., going to the doctor) that cause him to regain the moving of this arm as a basic act. These preparatory acts result in his being able, at some later time, to perform acts that can be generated by his moving the arm.

With these points in mind, and using (II) as an analysis of "S is able, at A to do A at t," we can give the following definition of "S is able, at t, to do A_n, by t'," where $t \lesssim t'$.

(III) S *is able, at* t, *to do* A_n *by* t' *if and only if:*
    There is a set of acts $A_1, A_2, \ldots, A_i, \ldots, A_n$
    (n = 1, 2, . . .) *such that*
    (1) S *is able, at some time* t_1, $t \lesssim t_1 \lesssim t'$, *to do* A_1 *at* t_1, *and*
    (2)   *for each* A_i
        either   (a) $A_i = A_n$

or   (b)   *if* S *does* A_i *at* t_i, *this would,*
together with the state of the
world at t_i, *cause* S *to be able, at*
t_{i+1}, *to do* A_{i+1} *at* t_{i+1}, $t \lesssim t_i \lesssim t'$.[6]

A special case satisfying this definition is where $A_1 = A_n$. In that case S need not perform any "preparatory" acts in order to do A_n. He simply finds himself able, at some time between t and t' inclusive, to do the indicated act A_n. In the other cases, however, S must do one or more preparatory acts in order to do A_n by t'. Each of these preparatory acts, together with the rest of the world other than his own acts, would put him in a position (enable him) to perform the next preparatory act; and this series of preparatory acts would ultimately put him in a position, at or before t', to perform the indicated act A_n. These preparatory acts need not begin at time t itself, so I do not require $t_1 = t$. Moreover, these preparatory acts may be spread out in different ways over the interval from t to t'. Thus, t_{i+1} must be later than t_i, but it need not be merely an instant later.

According to this definition, S's being *able*, at t, to do A_n by t' does not depend on S's *actually performing* the sequence of acts from A_1 to A_{n-1}. S is able, at t, to do A_n by t' just in case he is *able* to do A_1 at t_1 and *if he were* to perform A_1 at t_1, this would, together with the state of the rest of the world, cause him to be able to perform A_2 at t_2, etc. Thus, even if S fails to perform A_1 at t_1 (or fails to perform any of the other acts A_i at t_i), it is still true that he is *able*, at t, to perform A_n by t'. By failing to perform A_1 at t_1, S may render himself *unable, at t_2*, to do A_n by t'. But this does not vitiate the fact that he was able, at t_1, to do A_n by t'.

The definition speaks of act A_i "together with the state of the rest of the world" at t_i, causing S to be able, at t_{i+1}, to do A_{i+1} at t_{i+1}. It should be noted, however, that in some cases the state of the rest of the world has the predominant causal role, and that the causal effect of A_i may be minimal. What is important is that the *conjunction* of A_i and the rest of the world would enable S, at t_{i+1}, to do A_{i+1} at t_{i+1}. This is satisfied even where the state of the rest of the world *by itself* ensures the ability *vis-à-vis* A_{i+1}. For example, in order to buy some bread at t', S must perform a sequence of acts including driving his car to the store. In order to drive his car he must perform the sequence of acts including (a) turning the ignition key and (b) releasing the emergency brake. Now although these two acts, turning the ignition key and releasing the emergency brake, must be performed in sequence, neither is really causally necessary for the performance of the other. Thus, although the act of turning the ignition key is, say, A_{10}, and the act of releasing the emergency brake is

[6] A very similar definition is given by Roderick M. Chisholm in a revised version of "He Could Have Done Otherwise," in Myles Brand, ed., *The Nature of Human Action* (Glenview, Illinois: Scott, Foresman and Co., 1970), p. 300.

A_{11}, it is false to say that the performance of A_{10} (at t_{10}) would *cause* S to be able, at t_{11}, to be able to do A_{11} at t_{11}. However, we can say that *the state of the rest of the world* at t_{10} (including the position of the emergency brake, etc.) together with the performance of A_{10} at t_{10} would cause S to be able, at t_{11}, to do A_{11} at t_{11}. Hence, the definition is satisfied.

Notice too that there may be more than one sequence of acts A_1, A_2, . . . , A_{n-1} which would result in S's being able, at some time t_n, $t_n \leqslant t'$, to do A_n at t_n. All the definition requires is that there be *at least one* such sequence. In our bread-buying case, for example, there may be one sequence in which turning the ignition key is A_{10} and releasing the emergency break is A_{11}, and another sequence in which A_{10} is releasing the emergency brake and A_{11} is turning the ignition key. This, of course, is irrelevant.

Definition (III) provides an analysis of the non-epistemic sense of "S is able, at t, to do A by t'." The epistemic sense of this notion could be defined by operating on (III) in the same sort of way that (II') was produced by operating on (II). But I shall not write out this definition. The main requisite here is that S know which acts A_i would enable him to do successive acts A_{i+1}.

Let us examine the relationship between ability and the passage of time. In general, the passage of time reduces the number of acts one is able to perform at some fixed time in the future. For example, consider the set of acts which S is able to perform at t_{10}. At a time substantially before t_{10}, say t_1, there is a large number of mutually exclusive acts that S is able to perform at t_{10}. He may be able, at t_1, to have dinner in San Francisco at t_{10}; and he may be able, at t_1, to have dinner in New York at t_{10}; and he may be able, at t_1, to have dinner in Paris at t_{10}; etc. But as time passes, some of the options S had at t_1 are foreclosed, because he does not perform the preparatory acts that that were necessary. In order for S to have dinner in Paris at t_{10}, he must board a plane for Paris at or before t_3, let us suppose. But if he fails to board a plane for Paris by t_4, then he is no longer able (at t_4) to have dinner in Paris at t_{10}. This may, of course, leave him the option of having dinner either in San Francisco or in New York. But perhaps, in order to have dinner in San Francisco by t_{10}, he must board a plane for San Francisco by t_7. If he passes this up by t_8, then it is no longer possible for him (he is no longer able) to have dinner in San Francisco at t_{10}.

The passage of time, however, does not work exclusively to *restrict* the range of alternatives. While the passage of time reduces the number of acts an agent is *actually* able to do, it may be accompanied by an increase in the number of acts which he *knows* he is able to do. In other words, while the passage of time may involve a loss in ability in the *non-epistemic* sense, it may be accompanied by a gain in ability in the *epistemic* sense. This is because a person normally *learns* of new opportunities as time passes. At t_1 S may be able$_N$ to perform any of 20 different acts at t_6, but he may only be able$_E$ to perform three of these acts. This is because at t_1 he is unaware of the requisite preparatory acts for doing the remaining 17 acts at t_6. As time passes he may lose the chance to do some of the original 20 acts. For example, at t_3 it may no longer be possible for him to do 10 of the original 20 acts, because there were preparatory acts that would have had to be done at t_1 or t_2, but which S failed to do. By the time t_3 rolls around, however, S may have learned how to perform some of the remaining 10 acts which he did not know how to perform at t_1. That is, he may learn, by t_3, what are the requisite preparatory acts for some of the 10 acts still open to him. If so, the number of acts he is able$_E$ to perform at t_6 may have *increased* between t_1 and t_3.

Notice that although an agent may be able (in either the epistemic or non-epistemic senses), at t_1, to do A by t_6, it may be *causally necessitated* that the agent *will not* do A by t_6. This is because it may be causally necessitated by events at t_1, or even earlier than t_1, that the agent will *not want* to do A by t_6. It may be causally necessitated that at each of the times $t_1, t_2, \ldots, t_6$ he does not want to do A by t_6. The fact that these desires are causally necessitated, however, does not preclude the fact that he was *able* to do A by t_6. Nor does the fact that his not doing A by t_6 was causally necessitated preclude the fact that he was *able* to do A by t_6. There may be events occurring now, at t_1, which causally necessitate that I will not want, or not choose, at t_4, to go to the concert at t_6. For example, suppose some person is now (at t_1) preparing to invite me to a gala party to be held at t_6. And this intention, together with a wide variety of other events at t_1, causally necessitates my being invited, at t_3, to go to the party, and causally necessitates my choosing, at t_4, to go to the party, and hence my choosing not to go to the concert. My choosing, at t_4, not to go to the concert in turn (in conjunction with other events) causally necessitates my not going to the concert at t_6. But none of this sequence of events and none of this causal necessitation need make it false that I was able, from t_1 through t_5 inclusive, to go to the concert at t_6. I was able all along to go to the concert inasmuch as I had the tickets, I had the necessary transportation, etc. My not going to the concert was not the result of *inability*, but simply the result of my choosing to go to the party instead.

2. Excuses

One of the main reasons philosophers have been interested in the concept of ability is its connection with responsibility or culpability. In this section I want to discuss briefly some of the ways in which a person may seek to exculpate himself, or more generally to defend himself, when he is blamed for performing an act or for failing to perform an act. I shall not try to present a general theory of responsibility, of blameworthiness, or of excuses. What I wish to do is merely to examine some of the important ways in which people can defend themselves against charges of culpability, and to see how they are related to determinism.

There are two important kinds of excuses I wish to discuss here: *inability* and *ignorance.*[7] Appeals to inability are perhaps the most common form of excuse, and many such appeals can be understood in terms of the sense(s) of "inability" that we have explicated in Section 1. If Johnny is excused for failing to shovel the snow because there are no shovels available, then his excuse is based on a sense of "inability" already discussed. But there are other excuses, or defenses, that must be construed as invoking senses of "inability" not discussed in Section 1. One of these, the "cost" sense of "inability", will be explored in a little detail. Appeals to ignorance also figure saliently among pleas for excuses. First, a plea of ignorance may be entered when one is blamed for failing to perform an act; the agent may say that he did not *know how* to perform the act. Secondly, a plea of ignorance may be entered when one is blamed for performing an act that should not have been performed; here the claim would be that one did not know that one was performing it, or that one was *going to* perform it.

Let me begin with a discussion of inability as an excuse or a defense. Traditionally this subject has been dealt with in terms of the apparently simple and straightforward maxim, "Ought implies can." But with the help of the distinctions made in the preceding section, we can see that the matter is not simple or straightforward at all. How, precisely, should we interpret the maxim, "Ought implies can"? Should we interpret it to mean: "S ought to do A at t implies that S is able, at t, to do A at t?" This principle seems to me very likely false. Consider its contrapositive, which is entailed by it: "S is not able, at t, to do A at t implies that it is not the case that S ought to do A at t." If this maxim is correct, then the fact that a student was in his dormitory room at the time of his final examination would imply that it is not the case that he ought to have been taking the examination in the classroom. Since he was, at t, in his dormitory, he was not able, at t, to take the examination at t. But of course this does not necessarily imply that he did not have the obligation to take the examination at t. It does not necessarily imply that he has a good excuse for not taking the examination at t. It all depends on *why* he was in his dormitory at t. If he was there simply because he didn't want to take the examination, then he does not have an excuse at all. On the other hand, if he was in his dormitory room because he was ill, then he does have an excuse, perhaps indeed a good excuse.

We see, then, that inability per se does not excuse. At least, the fact that S is unable, at t, to do A at t does not imply that S is absolved from responsibility for not doing A at t. Now perhaps a weaker interpretation of "Ought implies can" would make it unconditionally correct. If we interpret it to mean "S ought to do A at t implies that there was some time, at or before t, at which S was able to do A at t," then perhaps this maxim would be correct. This interpretation, however, is extremely weak, and would take

---

[7] If we employ the epistemic sense of "ability," appeals to inability and appeals to ignorance may overlap. But henceforth I shall employ only the non-epistemic sense of ability, unless I explicitly indicate otherwise.

the teeth out of almost any attempt to excuse oneself by appeal to inability. For almost any act for which one might plausibly be held responsible is such that there was *some* time at which the agent was able (in the non-epistemic sense) to perform the act at the requisite time.

We see, then, that the simple maxim "Ought implies can" does not readily explain to us precisely when inability provides an excuse. No doubt the fact that one was unable to perform an act often helps provide an excuse for having failed to perform it. But, except for a case in which one was *never* able to perform it, there are normally other considerations that are operative in deciding whether inability provides an excuse.

The maxim "Ought implies can" might be applied not only to cases where an agent fails to perform an act but also to cases where an agent performs an act he was not supposed to perform. If it is true that the agent was *unable not* to perform that act, then presumably he would be excused for having performed it. If he could not help but perform it, then he would not be regarded as responsible or culpable for having performed it. We should notice, however, that there are few if any cases in which ordinary *positive* acts, such as turning on the light, writing a letter, shooting a gun, etc., are such that the agent was literally *unable* to do otherwise, in the sense of "unable" given either by (II) or by (III). To be sure, there are cases in which physical forces external to the agent cause the movement of his limbs or body. In such a case, however, the agent's movement is not an *act* at all. Admittedly, if external forces push *S*'s hand and make it flip the light switch and thereby turn on the light, then *S* was unable to perform any act that was a contrary of turning on the light. And no doubt we would not hold *S* responsible for turning on the light. However, this is not a case in which *S* has performed an *act* which he could not help doing, for the turning on of the light was not an *act* of *S*'s at all.

Until now, my discussion of inability has presupposed the senses of "ability" presented in the preceding section. But, as noted earlier, there are other senses of this term that are equally important. Often when we proffer an excuse for failing to perform a certain act by saying that we *"could not"* do it we do not mean that we were literally unable, in one of the senses given in Section 1, to perform that act. Often we mean instead that it was too *difficult*, or too *costly*, or too *painful* to perform that act. Suppose, for example, that I have promised to meet you downtown to go shopping, but in the morning I cut my foot badly on some glass. I call you up and say: "Sorry, I can't go shopping with you today; I have cut my foot on some glass." In offering this excuse, I employ the word "can't," but obviously not in any of the senses of "can't" suggested in Section 1. Clearly, in the senses of "able" given in Section 1 (whether the non-epistemic senses or the epistemic senses) I *am* able to go shopping. The reason I say that I "can't" go shopping is that it would be too *painful* or too *difficult* for me to go shopping.

Excuses of this sort are not restricted to cases where the agent would undergo physical pain. Cases of a similar sort arise in which an act of the agent would involve some event to which he is *averse*, even though it would not involve physical pain. For example, *S* may say that he "cannot" attend a meeting he was supposed to attend because his wife is not home and he would have to leave their four-year-old home alone. Leaving the child home alone does not necessarily involve any physical pain, and surely no physical pain to *S* himself. Nevertheless, it is something to which S is *averse*. Using the term "cost" in connection with any aversive event, we may say that it would be too "costly" for *S* to attend the meeting; and because of this cost, he says that he "cannot" attend the meeting.

There are two sorts of cases in which an agent might say that he "could not" perform a certain act because of the "cost." In one sort of case he says that he "could not" perform act *A* because the performance of *A* would have required him to perform an act *on the same act-tree as A* to which he was averse. In the second sort of case he says that he "could not" perform act *A* because the performance of *A* would have required him to perform a *preparatory* act to which he was averse, or at least it would have required him to perform preparatory acts that would have *generated* (or been on the same act-tree as) some further act to which he was averse. The first kind of case is illustrated by our shopping example. I say that I "can't" go shopping because the performance of the act of going shopping would require me to perform the (basic) act of walking; and a performance of the act of walking would, in my present condition, generate an act of causing myself pain, to which I am averse. The second kind of case is illustrated by our meeting example. *S* says that he "cannot" attend the meeting because his attending the meeting would require him to perform the preparatory act of leaving the house, and the preparatory act of leaving the house would generate the act of leaving the child home alone, an act to which *S* is averse.

Sometimes we say that we "cannot" perform an act *A*, not because its performance would require us to perform some other act to which we are *averse*, but rather because its performance would require us to *forego* some other acts which we very much *want* to perform. As the economist's term "opportunity cost" suggests, there is a loss or a cost involved in passing up a good opportunity just as there is a loss or cost involved in performing an act to which one is averse. Thus, I might say that I "cannot" attend a meeting which has just been scheduled because I already have tickets to the Bolshoi Ballet that night, and it would be too "costly" for me to pass up such an opportunity.

Needless to say, not any or every aversion (nor any or every opportunity) will provide a legitimate excuse for an agent's failure to perform an act which he has a *prima facie* obligation to perform. The legitimacy of the excuse will depend on the nature of the aversion and the nature of the (*prima facie*) obligation. If a doctor is called at night to treat a sick and dying man, he cannot legitimately excuse himself for failing to go by pointing out that he would have to inconvenience himself, to which he is averse. A doctor is just expected to undergo this sort of inconvenience, despite his aversion to it.

It should be mentioned that an appeal to the "cost" of an act might be considered by some people to be a *justification* for its omission rather than an *excuse* for omitting it. Some philosophers might contend, for example, that the appeal to the prospect of leaving one's child home alone is a justification rather than an excuse for failing to attend the meeting. But I believe that in ordinary parlance this would be called an "excuse." If the agent were asked for his "excuse" for failing to attend the meeting, it would be perfectly appropriate for him to cite the fact that he would have had to leave the child home alone. In any case, whether we call it an "excuse" or a "justification," the agent may *defend* himself by an appeal of this sort; and he might formulate this defense by saying that he "cannot" or "could not" attend the meeting for this reason.

We see, then, that one thing we sometimes mean in saying that a person "cannot" or "could not" perform a certain act is that it would be, or it would have been, too *costly* to perform that act. Now there is a similar sense in which we might say that a person "cannot help" or "could not help" performing a certain act which he in fact performed. Suppose that S's child is kidnapped and the kidnappers threaten to kill the child unless S embezzles money from his company and gives it to them. Because S is extremely averse to letting his child be killed, and because he realizes that his *not* embezzling the money and giving it to the kidnappers would result in their killing the child, he proceeds to embezzle the money and give it to them. In this case it would be appropriate for S to say that he "could not help" embezzling the money, that he was "forced" to do it. Clearly S had at least a *prima facie* obligation to refrain from embezzling the money. But he might defend himself for having embezzled it by pointing to the prospective costs of not embezzling it. Notice that although S might say that he "could not help" embezzling the money, that he was "forced" to embezzle it, he does not mean that he was *unable* not to embezzle it, in any of the senses of "ability" presented in Section 1. Obviously, it was within S's power not to embezzle the money. But although it was within his power not to embezzle it, the prospective costs of not embezzling it were too great.

When a person says that he "could not help" doing act A, or that he was "forced" to do act A, he implies not only that it would have been too costly for him to *refrain* from doing A but also that he was *averse*, or at least *not attracted*, to doing A for its own sake (independent of the costs of not doing it). In saying that he was "forced" to embezzle the money, S implies that he did not want to embezzle the money, and even that there was no act he wanted to do which he believed would be generated by his embezzling the money.[8] If S had had a positive desire that (partly) motivated his embezzling the

---

[8] We might say, of course, that he wanted to cause the kidnappers *not* to kill his child, and that he believed this would be generated by his embezzling and giving them the money. But although we may speak of his "wanting" to cause the kidnappers not to kill the child, what is present is not really a *positive* want to cause them *not* to kill the child so much as an *aversion* to letting them kill the child.

money—e.g., if he had wanted to embarrass his boss and if he had believed that the embezzlement would cause embarrassment to his boss—then it would not be correct to say that S was "forced" to embezzle the money. To say that S was "forced" to embezzle the money is to imply that he embezzled it "against his will"—i.e., that he embezzled it despite the fact that he was *averse* to embezzling it. But if he had some other motivation for embezzling it, independent of the costs of not embezzling it, then he was not "forced" to embezzle it. (Of course, S might *claim* that he was forced to do it; but this would be a lie.)

Having discussed some species of excuses (or defenses) that appeal to *inability* in the "strict" sense and in the "cost" sense, let us now turn to excuses that appeal to some form of *ignorance* of the agent. Here again we shall be concerned with excuses *vis-à-vis* acts which an agent *failed* to perform, though he had a *prima facie* obligation to perform them, and with excuses *vis-à-vis* acts which an agent *performed*, though he had a *prima facie* obligation not to perform them. Let us begin with the former kind of cases.

If S is blamed for failing to perform act A at t, he might try to exonerate himself by indicating that he had been ignorant of the fact that he ought to do A at t. For example, a student may be unaware that he is supposed to take an examination on a certain day because the letter intended to inform him of the date of the examination does not reach him. The student's ignorance of the fact that this was the appointed examination day would excuse him for failing to show up and take the examination.

Another sort of excuse for failing to do A at t is that one was ignorant of the requisite way of doing A at t. One may have been ignorant of the preparatory acts necessary for doing A at t, or one may have been ignorant of the acts necessary to generate a performance of A at t. To illustrate ignorance of requisite preparatory acts, suppose S is supposed to meet a friend in midtown for lunch. While driving on the expressway, however, he finds that new construction makes it impossible to proceed along his usual route. Because he is unfamiliar with the streets he is forced to traverse he makes a bad turn which slows him down considerably and makes him miss the luncheon appointment. Although it may be true that there *were* acts he could have performed that would have enabled him to get to midtown on time, S did not *know* what these preparatory acts were: he did not *know how* to proceed in order to get to midtown on time. And this ignorance provides an excuse for his failing to make the luncheon appointment. An example in which ignorance of the requisite *lower-level* acts is the cause of failure to perform an act one is supposed to perform is where Shorty, whose job in a planned theft is to turn off the lights in the ballroom at an appointed time, fails to turn them off. At the appointed time Shorty finds himself standing in front of a very large set of switches, three of which control the lights in the ballroom. But although Shorty is right in front of the relevant switches, and although he is therefore able (in the non-epistemic sense) to turn off the ballroom lights, he does not know precisely what lower-level acts to perform—i.e., precisely which hand movements to make—in order to turn them off. Hence, he fails to turn off the ballroom lights.

It should be noted that ignorance of these sorts is not always an acceptable or valid form of excuse. Shorty's henchmen might protest that it was Shorty's job to *find out* which switches controlled the ballroom lights. They might not allow, therefore, that his ignorance was a legitimate excuse for failing to turn them off. We see, then, that whether or not ignorance is an adequate excuse depends on whether the agent had an opportunity to gain the relevant knowledge, on whether he could be expected to have obtained this knowledge, etc.

I turn now to cases in which an agent seeks to excuse himself for performing an act he should not (at least *prima facie*) have performed. A plea of ignorance may be entered here too. In particular, the agent may say that he was unaware of the fact that a certain act he intended to do would, if done, also generate an act which should not be done. *S* flips a certain switch with the intention of turning on the light. Instead, the switch starts up a certain machine which injures a workman. *S* has performed the act of causing an injury to the workman, but he can excuse himself, or at least mitigate the degree of his blameworthiness, by pointing out that he was ignorant of the fact that his flipping the switch would generate the act of starting up the machine, which would further generate the act of causing an injury to the workman. Here there is ignorance of a prospective case of causal generation, but ignorance can also arise for the other species of generation. Someone playing basketball for the very first time may be excused for goal-tending if he does not know of the existence of a rule prohibiting it. He is ignorant of the fact that blocking the ball on its way down would conventionally generate an act of breaking the rules and of giving the opposing team two points. To take another case, *S*'s driving at 55 m.p.h. may generate, by simple generation, the act of exceeding the speed limit. *S* may seek to be excused for this higher-level act on the grounds that he was ignorant of the speed limit—in other words, that he was ignorant of the fact that his driving at 55 m.p.h. would generate his exceeding the speed limit. This excuse would be plausible if the speed limit is poorly marked or obscured.

A man may be ignorant not only of the acts which would be *generated* by certain acts but also of what acts would be *on the same level* as certain acts. Oedipus, for example, was ignorant of the fact that his act of striking the man who forced him off the road would be on the same level as an act of striking his own father. That is, he was ignorant of the fact that this man was his father, and hence ignorant of the fact that he was about to perform an act of striking his father.

In all these cases, as before, ignorance is not necessarily an acceptable or valid excuse. Perhaps the agent who caused an injury to the workman, for example, should not have started pulling any switches before he knew for certain what the result would be. In a factory such precaution is mandatory. Similarly, the agent who exceeded the speed limit may be expected to look at the road signs more carefully even if they are not maximally visible. In these cases, the agent's ignorance does not completely absolve him from culpability, though perhaps the ignorance mitigates the degree of culpability or blameworthiness.

The reader will notice that none of the excuses (or defenses) I have considered are based on an appeal to causal necessitation *per se*. This is because I do not believe that the causal necessitation of an act (or the omission of an act) *by itself* is an excuse or a defense. Johnny cannot be excused for not shoveling the sidewalk simply because his not shoveling it was causally necessitated. Perhaps the factors which causally necessitated his not shoveling the sidewalk consisted (in part) in his preferring to stay in bed and sleep rather than to go outside and shovel the sidewalk. In such a case, Johnny does not have a good excuse, or an excuse at all, for failing to shovel the walk. Admittedly, *certain* kinds of causal necessitation do provide excuses—e.g., causal necessitation involving inability, or ignorance, or costs of a relevant sort. If Johnny's not shoveling the walk was causally necessitated (in part) by there being no shovel available, then he has an excuse. Or if his not shoveling the walk was causally necessitated (in part) by his not knowing (through no fault of his own) where the shovel was, then he has an excuse. And if his not shoveling the walk was causally necessitated (in part) by his having a high fever, then he has an excuse (or a defense). But the simple fact that his not shoveling the sidewalk was causally necessitated does not imply that he has an excuse or a defense.

Now one might contend that if an agent's act is causally necessitated by a desire or aversion and if, moreover, this desire or aversion is causally necessitated by still earlier events, then one cannot be blamed for one's act. If prior factors determine what desires one will have or choices one will make, how can one be held responsible? Surely if one's desire is caused by a hypnotist or if it is caused by a scheming scientist performing an operation on one's brain, then one would not be held responsible for the acts which flow from this desire. Similarly, if one's desires are causally necessitated in any other way, one should not be held responsible for the resulting acts.

We can admit that when an agent's desires or aversions are caused in *certain* ways—e.g., by brain surgery or perhaps by hypnosis— then the agent may not be held responsible for acts which flow from these desires or aversions. It does not follow, though, that the existence of *any* causes of an agent's desires or aversions should absolve the agent from responsibility for acts which flow from them. I am inclined to think that only *special* kinds of causal necessitation, such as brain surgery or perhaps hypnosis, tend to void an agent's responsibility, but that the "normal" ways in which desires are caused do not justify absolving the agent from responsibility. The difficult problem, of course, is to specify in detail which kinds of causes do and which kinds of causes do not void responsibility and to give a rationale for the distinction. I do not have a general answer to this complex but important problem.

3. Constraint

The issue of brain surgery and hypnosis raises the question of when the action of one agent can be viewed as somehow constraining another agent. The importance of this issue is related to the importance of distinguishing between constraint and mere causation (or causal necessitation). In the history of the controversy concerning free will and determinism it has often been pointed out that causal necessitation is not equivalent to compulsion, constraint or coercion; that the fact that an agent's act is causally necessitated does not entail that he is compelled or constrained to do it.[9] Now I wish to elaborate this theme with special attention to the causal effects that one agent has on the action of another. It would be a mistake to think that whenever the action of one agent has a causal effect on the action of a second agent, or even when the action of one agent is among the factors that causally necessitate the action of a second agent, then the second agent has been "constrained" by the first agent. Only a proper subset of the ways of causally affecting the behavior of another agent should be regarded as constraint. My purpose is, first, to mention some of the ways of causally affecting the behavior of another that do *not* constitute constraint, and, secondly, to try to elucidate a few of the ways of causally affecting the behavior of another that *do* constitute constraint.

Let us begin, then, by looking briefly at ways of affecting someone else's action that do not constitute constraint. We can divide the factors that are causally relevant to a man's action into three: (a) his wants or aversions, (b) his beliefs, and (c) his abilities, including both his basic act repertoire and generational conditions. There are ways of affecting each of these factors, and thereby affecting his behavior, that do not constitute constraint.

It should not be thought that the only way of affecting an agent's wants or aversions is by devious methods such as hypnosis, brain surgery, or perhaps subliminal advertising. There are thoroughly innocent ways of affecting the wants or aversions of another agent—e.g., by making suggestions, offers, and the like. S^* may suggest to S that they go to a movie together, and this suggestion may arouse in S a desire to go to the movie. If, as a result, they do go to the movie, we can say that S^* caused, or partially caused, S's act. Indeed, the action of S^* may even be among some factors which causally necessitated S's going to the movie. Nonetheless, it would clearly be incorrect to say that S^* *constrained* S in any way, or that he *coerced* S into going to

---

[9] Cf. Moritz Schlick, *Problems of Ethics*, trans. David Rynin (Magnolia, Mass.: Peter Smith, Publisher 1962), Chap. VII, and John Stuart Mill, *An Examination of Sir William Hamilton's Philosophy* (London, 1867), Chap. XXVI.

the movie. The same is true if S^* indicates to S that it is a bad movie, thereby creating in S a disinclination to go to the movie. If S had previously been planning to go to the movie, and if this newly acquired disinclination results in his not going to the movie, then we can say that S^* caused, or partially caused, S's refraining from going to the movie. But again it would be incorrect to say that S^* *constrained* S at all.

In the previous paragraph we examined ways of affecting his action via his wants and aversions. Similarly, one agent often affects the action of another via his beliefs. S may want to perform a certain act A but not know *how* to do it—he may not know what acts would generate act A or he may not know what preparatory acts to perform to put himself in a position to do A. If S^* tells S how to perform act A this may result in his actually performing A, though without this information S would not have performed A. Hence, the act of S^* of giving this information to S is a partial cause of S's doing A. Nevertheless, S^* obviously has not constrained S.

The third factor that is causally relevant for action—viz., ability—can also be affected by another agent. S^* may affect the action of S by affecting generational conditions relevant to the performance of certain acts by S, or by affecting whether or not S is in standard conditions *vis-à-vis* certain basic acts, or by affecting whether or not certain properties are basic acts for S at a certain time. Now some of the ways in which S^* can affect the ability of S, and thereby the action of S, would certainly count as constraining S, as we shall see shortly. But there are other ways of affecting S's action via his ability that do not involve constraint.

First, S^* may bring about certain generational conditions that allow S to do a certain act. For example, S^* may give S a pomegranate and thereby put S in a position to perform an act of eating a pomegranate. Secondly, S^* may cause S to be in standard conditions with respect to a basic act-type, which would not have been the case without S^*. For example, S^* may cut the ropes which bind S's hands to the bed, thereby causing S to be in standard conditions with respect to the basic act-type of moving his hands. Thirdly, S^* may cause S to acquire a new basic act-type, or cause S to regain a basic act-type that he had lost. For example, S^* may cure S of paralysis in his legs, thereby causing S to regain the property of moving his legs as a basic act-type. In any of these cases, once S is enabled by S^* to perform the given act, he may actually choose to perform it. He may choose to eat the pomegranate, move his hands, and move his legs (respectively). In each of these cases, then, S^* will have played a role in bringing about S's doing this act. Indeed, the action of S^* may be among a set of factors that causally necessitated S's doing this act. Clearly, however, in none of these cases has S^* constrained, compelled, or coerced S in any way.

I turn now to a discussion of some of the ways in which S^* can affect the action of S that *would* count as forms of constraint. I shall not attempt to give an exhaustive list of the forms of constraint, but merely to cite and examine a few of the most obvious species of constraint.

As I shall employ the term "constraint," it will function as a term of success. That is, S^* will be said to have constrained S only if S^* succeeds in causing S to perform an act which S would not otherwise have performed or in causing S not to perform an act which he otherwise would have performed. Thus, if S^* tries but fails to affect S's behavior, then he will not be said to have constrained S.

The most straightforward way of constraining S is to render him unable, in the sense of Section 1, to perform an act that he wants to perform. This can be achieved in three different ways, corresponding to the three ways of *enabling* someone to perform an act. First, one can eliminate a property from the basic act 'repertoire of S, e.g., by causing him to be paralyzed. Secondly, one can cause S not to be in standard conditions with respect to a basic act-type, e.g., by placing handcuffs on him. Thirdly, one can eliminate generational conditions necessary for S's performance of an act. For example, if S^* steals S's violin, he may cause S to be unable to practice the violin. If S was intending to practice the violin, then S^* causes him not to perform an act he otherwise would have performed, and hence constrains him.

It might be suggested that the term "constraint" is appropriate only when S^* *intentionally*, or at least *knowingly*, causes S to be unable to perform an act. It is arguable that if S^* (falsely) believes that S has *two* violins, and hence believes that his theft would not render S unable to practice, then S^* does not "constrain" S. I am uncertain on this point. In the case of "coercion," I think it is clear that intention or knowledge is required; but this is less clear in the case of "constraint."

Causing S to be unable to perform an act, in the sense of Section 1, is not the only way of constraining him. Constraint is also exemplified when S^* makes it *costly* or *difficult* for S to perform an act, and thereby deters S from doing it. Deterrence can be accomplished in two ways. First, by eliminating certain generational conditions relevant to the performance of act A, S^* may make it impossible for S to perform A in the easiest, or most convenient, manner. Although S may still be *able* to perform A, in the sense of Section 1, the remaining way or ways of performing it may be too costly or unattractive. Similarly, by eliminating conditions relevant to the performance of acts *preparatory* to the performance of A, S^* might leave S with only costly or unattractive sequences of acts that would have to be performed in order to enable him to perform act A. Secondly, S^* may deter S from performing A by arranging, or threatening to arrange, that certain aversive consequences will ensue if S does A. In our terminology, we can say that S^* arranges, or threatens to arrange, that S's performing A would causally generate S's bringing about E, where E is some event to which S is averse.

Let us consider some illustrations of these two ways of deterring S from the performance of an act. Suppose S^* wants to keep S from eating dinner in his apartment tonight, so he cuts the cables of the apartment building's elevator. S arrives at his apartment building after a hard day's work, intending to eat dinner in his 14th floor apartment. Although he is not literally unable to eat dinner there, since he is able, in the sense of Section 1, to walk the stairs to the apartment, he is understandably averse to the performance of this preparatory act, and decides to eat dinner at a restaurant instead. It is evident that S^* has constrained him. The second sort of case can be illustrated by any example of a (successful) threat. Suppose S's boss threatens to fire him if he performs act A. This makes act A considerably more costly for S than it otherwise would be, for it means that his performing A would causally generate the act of bringing it about that he loses his job, an act to which he is very averse. If, as a result, S decides not to do A, but otherwise would have done A, then S^* has constrained S.

In cases of threats, S^* may not actually affect any generational conditions relevant to S's doing act A. If, in making the threat, S^* has no intention of carrying it out, or lacks the ability to carry it out, then he does not really arrange that S's doing A would generate S's bringing about event E. If the boss doesn't really intend to fire S, then it is false that S's doing A would generate his causing himself to lose his job. S is deterred from doing A, however, because of his *belief* that his doing A would generate his causing himself to lose his job. Thus, by making the threat, the boss considerably reduces the *expected value* for S of doing act A.

One should not conclude that anyone constrains S who causes S to believe that his doing A will have aversive consequences, and thereby deters S from doing A. If a friend *warns* S that his doing A will cause his boss to fire him, the friend does not constrain S. If S is deterred from doing A by this warning, then the "source" of the constraint is the boss, not the friend. More precisely, if the boss does intend to fire him if he does A, and if this fact is conveyed by the friend to S, then the source of the constraint is the boss rather than the friend. For it is the boss who brings it about that S's doing A would cause him to lose his job. But if the boss has no intention to fire S, and does nothing to imply that he has such an intention, then he cannot be considered a constrainer of S. Two possibilities remain. Either the friend is lying to S, or the friend is simply honestly misinformed about the boss's intention. In the first case, I think we would say that the friend constrains S. In the second case, where there is just an honest misunderstanding, we might deny that S is constrained by anyone.

The examples of constraint considered thus far have been ones in which S^* causes S *not* to do an act he would otherwise do. Let us look next at cases of constraint in which S^* causes S to *perform* an act he would otherwise not perform.

The commonest cases in this category again involve threats. For example, S^*, who has kidnapped S's child, threatens to kill the child unless S gives him $500,000. Here S^* affects the cost to S, or rather, the expected cost, of various courses of action. Specifically, he makes it very costly for S not to give him $500,000; for S's act of not giving S^* $500,000 will now generate, or can be expected to generate, the further act of causing S^* to kill the child, an act (or consequence) to which S is very averse. Although cases of threats are the commonest cases in which one is constrained, or coerced, into performing an act one would not otherwise do, other kinds of cases are conceivable. Without threatening S overtly, S^* may arrange conditions so that a certain aversive event will occur unless S performs act A. For example, S^* may arrange that a bomb will go off unless S does act A, an act that S finds very unattractive. If S learns of these conditions, and feels forced to do A despite his aversion to it, we might say that he has been constrained or coerced by S^*. At any rate, it would be correct to say this as long as S^* made these arrangements *in order* to get S to do A, or with the *knowledge* that it would motivate S to do A.

Having discussed various species of constraint, let us discuss briefly some of the factors that might be considered in assessing the degree, or severity, of constraint exercised by S^* with respect to S. First, where S is constrained to perform an act to which he is (antecedently) averse, the extent of the constraint might be measured by the extent of this aversion. Thus, someone is more seriously constrained when he is forced to give up \$500,000 than when he is forced to pay \$100,000 (other things being equal). Similarly, when someone is prevented from performing an act he very much wants to do, the degree of constraint might be measured by the value of the foreclosed activity. A second, and more plausible, way of assessing the degree of constraint is in terms of the *difference* in utility, or value, that is brought about by the action of S^*. If S^* prevents S from doing A, or deters S by threat from doing A, then the degree of constraint is not the value of act A itself, but the *difference* in value between A and the next best alternative available to S. If S only slightly prefers going for a drive to going for a walk, and if S^* prevents him from going for a drive by letting the air out of his tires, then the extent of constraint is not proportional to the value of going for a drive but proportional to the difference in value between going for a drive and going for a walk. (In this case, though, one must also take account of the cost to S of re-inflating the tires.) A third possible measure of constraint is the value of the sanction S^* threatens to impose on S unless he acts in accordance with S^*'s wishes. For example, if S^* threatens to bring about E unless S does act A, then this proposal would have us measure the extent to which S^* constrains S by the degree to which S is averse to E. This suggestion, however, is counterintuitive. If S's wife threatens to leave him unless he washes the dishes, and if this succeeds in inducing him to wash them, then the extent of the constraint is not a function of the disutility he assigns to her leaving him. Rather, it is a function of the disutility he assigns to washing the dishes, or the difference in utility between washing the dishes and doing whatever he would have done instead of washing them.

Our discussion has shown that the fact that S's act A was causally necessitated does not entail that S was constrained to perform A. Specifically, we have seen that the mere fact that acts of agent S^* were among a set of events that causally necessitated S's doing A does not entail that S^* constrained S. We can construct *some* cases in which act A is causally necessitated, in part, by the action of S^* and in which S^* *does* constrain S. But equally, we can construct *other* cases in which act A is causally necessitated, in part, by the action of S^* and in which S^* does *not* constrain S.[10]

We might note in this context that the writer (or writers) of the book of life discussed in Chapter Six does not constrain the agent whose book it is, despite the fact that the writer of the book performs acts which are included among events that causally necessitate some of the agent's acts. The writer of the book of life writes certain sentences in the book which, when read by the agent, result in his performing certain acts. For example, when the agent reads the sentence indicating that he will leave the library and go to the President's office, he is reminded that he has an appointment with the President of the University, and this results in his leaving the library and going to the President's office. But although the writer's act of writing this sentence may have been a factor in the causal necessitation of the agent's leaving the library and going to the President's office, this is not a case of constraint. The writer of the book of life has, in effect, simply reminded the agent of something he had intended to do in the first place.

I have made no attempt in this section to give an exhaustive list of the ways in which one agent can constrain another, just as I made no attempt in the preceding section to give an exhaustive list of the sorts of excuses a person can offer for his action or inaction. What I have tried to do is simply to illustrate a few of the different ways in which one agent can affect the behavior of another agent and to indicate which of these would be classified as constraint and which would not be so classified. One of my purposes has been to show that causal necessitation *per se* does not tell us much about constraint. This negative point, of course, is not a substitute for a detailed analysis of the concept of constraint. A positive analysis of this notion, and of the related notion of coercion, is obviously an important task for ethics.[11] Any adequate account of freedom will surely presuppose or involve a careful analysis of constraint or coercion. Although I have not tried to present a full analysis of constraint, I believe that I have shown how the theory of action developed in this book can be of use in such an analysis. Ultimately, the success of the theory I have proposed depends on its usefulness in dealing with topics such as constraint, responsibility, and ability. The present chapter

---

[10] I do not believe that causal necessitation is *necessary* for constraint any more than it is *sufficient* for constraint. In my discussion of constraint I have said that the action of S^* must partially *cause* S to perform a certain act or to refrain from performing a certain act. But I have not said that the action of S^* must be among a set of factors which *causally necessitate* S to perform a certain act or to refrain from performing a certain act.

[11] For a detailed analysis of the concept of coercion, see Robert Nozick's recent paper, "Coercion," in S. Morgenbesser, P. Suppes, and M. White, eds., *Philosophy, Science, and Method*, (New York: St. Martin's Press, 1969).

shows how the central concepts of my theory, e.g., the concept of generation and the concept of a basic act, can be of great value in these contexts.

Epilogue:
A Look Back
and A Look Ahead

This book has had two major objectives: first, to develop a set of conceptual tools for dealing with human action, and second, to use these tools in defending a causal model of human behavior in which wants and beliefs play a crucial role. Let me briefly review the main results.

In the first two chapters (and part of the third) I analyzed the concept of an act and formulated procedures for dealing with acts in a precise, yet general, way. I argued for a "property" criterion of individuating act-tokens, according to which particular instances of different properties, such as John's turning the key and John's unlocking the door, are different act-tokens. Having denied the identity of such pairs of act-tokens, I then explicated their relationship in terms of the concept of "level-generation." Other act-relationships, such as co-temporality, subsequence, etc., were also explored. Techniques for diagraming the various acts of a given agent were introduced. With the help of these diagrams, especially "act-tree" diagrams, it is easy to see how all of an agent's acts are generated by, or in some other way stem from, an agent's basic acts. Ultimately, in fact, the idea of an act-token was so defined that every act-token is either a basic act-token, is level-generated by a basic act-token, is on the same level as a basic act-token, is a sequence of basic act-tokens (or a sequence of act-tokens level-related to basic act-tokens), or is a temporal part of a basic act-token (or a part of an act-token level-related to a basic act-token).

The idea of a basic act-token is dependent on the notion of a basic act-type, which was in turn explicated in terms of the causal propensities of certain wants. A property was said to be a basic act-type if one's desire to exemplify it would result in one's exemplifying it, with no dependence on level-generational knowledge or cause-and-effect knowledge. A basic act-token was said to be an instance of a basic act-type, an instance that is caused by an appropriate set of wants and beliefs, but which is not generated (except perhaps by augmentation generation) by any other property-instance that fulfills these conditions.

222

On my view, then, the idea of a basic act-token, and *ipso facto* the idea of an act, presupposes that behavior is caused by wants and beliefs of the agent. Many recent philosophers have contested the view that wants are causes of action, but I defended this view in Chapters Three and Four. The concept of a want, at least an "occurrent" want, I contended, is the concept of a mental event that has a tendency, together with beliefs, to result in action. There is, therefore, a logical connection between the concept of a want and the concept of action as well as a causal connection between particular wants and particular act-tokens.

The heart of my theory of action, we see, contains the following elements: (1) the analysis of an act-token as the exemplifying of a property by a person (at a time); (2) the relation of level-generation, plus various other act-relations such as co-temporality, subsequence, etc.; (3) the notions of a basic act-type and a basic act-token; and (4) the idea of want-and-belief causation. With these fundamental ideas at hand, I tried to give a coherent picture of human action and attempted to deal with a few of the specific problems concerning action that have been raised in the literature.

The concept of *intentional* action was analyzed in terms of causation by a desire to do a certain act together with level-relational beliefs *vis-à-vis* that act. For example, S's act A is intentional if (i) S wanted to do act A'; (ii) S believed that A' would be level-generated by A which would be level-generated by basic act A_1; (iii) this want and these beliefs caused his doing A_1; and (iv) act A was level-generated (in the anticipated way) by basic act A_1. The notion of a *reason* for action was explicated in a similar way. We can say that A' was the *reason* for S's doing A if S wanted to do A', believed that A would level-generate A', and, as a result of this want and belief, did A (in the anticipated way). The concept of *agency* was also said to be compatible with, indeed perhaps explicable in terms of, want-and-belief causation. That an agent's acts are caused by his wants and beliefs, I argued, does not imply that he is not the *source* of his acts. On the contrary, to say that they are *his* acts implies that they are dependent on *his* desires. Want-and-belief causation was again a central ingredient in my discussion of *practical inference*, including *deciding* and *deliberating*. Practical inference was viewed as a causal chain in which initial wants and beliefs lead to new wants.

In Chapter Five I sought to illustrate how pervasive are such factors as wants and beliefs even in the literature of the behavioral sciences. Furthermore, I argued that even those theories of behavior that make no reference to wants and beliefs need not be incompatible with the want-and-belief scheme of action. Many factors of concern to empirical scientists are either *causes* of wants or beliefs or somehow *correlated* with wants or beliefs. It seems to me important that we attempt to reconcile the want-and-belief model with other, apparently incompatible, accounts of behavior. A host of our commonsense notions in law, in morals, and in practical affairs presuppose the notion of want-and-belief causation. Since we are unlikely to give up these deeply imbedded commonsense notions—to do so would wreak havoc to our entire conceptual scheme—we must try to reconcile these notions with theories propounded in the behavioral sciences.

In the final two chapters I addressed myself to certain longstanding issues in the free-will controversy. I contended that the matter of predictability in human behavior does not provide grounds for the denial of determinism. In a relevant sense of "predictable," human behavior may well be predictable, but this does not mean that there can be no deliberation, decision, or choice. Moreover, as I tried to show in Chapter Seven, even if it is determined that *S* will do *A* at time *t*, he may also be *able not* to do *A* at *t*. The fact that *S*'s doing *A* at *t* was determined does not imply that he was *unable not* to do *A*, nor that he should be excused or absolved from responsibility for doing *A*.

The analysis of ability in Chapter Seven, and the ensuing remarks on excuses and constraint, made use of many, if not all, of the fundamental ideas developed in the book. The analysis of ability shows how an agent's ability to perform an act depends on (a) his basic act repertoire, (b) generational conditions, and (c) his beliefs. The ease encountered in analyzing ability suggests that the conceptual tools and techniques presented in earlier chapters may have wide potential applicability. Where, then, might one go from here?

First, it is important to explore the generalizability of the property criterion of act-individuation. My analysis of acts involves an ontology in which substances are primary, and acts are construed as the exemplifications of properties by certain substances—i.e., persons. Can this ontology be extended to events in general? I have suggested in two or three places that a similar treatment might be given of physical events, but new problems would arise in trying to make this extension. Where acts are concerned, it is clear what the substance is that exemplifies the properties; it is the human agent. (To be sure, there are problems in analyzing the notion of an agent or person, but there are no practical problems, for the most part, in identifying individual agents.) In the case of many physical events, however, it is difficult to decide what substance or substances are the "subjects" of the event. There is an additional problem of deciding when, if at all, the exemplifying of a property P by an object O is identical with the exemplifying of a property P' by the physical parts of O, where $P \neq P'$. Despite these problems, however, it is important to see whether, and to what extent, our account of act-tokens can be carried over to physical events.

The usefulness of the property criterion as a criterion of *acts* should also be explored in various domains. How would this conception of an act work out, for example, in the law? Here is a fertile area for investigation. It is often crucial in the law to be quite specific concerning the act or acts for which an agent is punishable. Of special interest are cases in which a person is punishable for more than one act on the same act-tree, where there are different penalties for these different acts. My "fine-grained" method for individuating acts should be helpful in analyzing these cases. My account of intentional action may also be of relevance to the philosophy of law, as well as my discussion of inability, ignorance, etc. I have not attempted to relate my discussion of these problems to the law, but it should be evident that these topics are important for jurisprudence.

My theory of action might also be applicable to the theory of decision-making. We may conceive of an agent, at any given time, as choosing between various sets of incompatible basic acts. His choice between them should be a function not only of the value of those basic acts themselves, but also of the value (or utility) of the acts which would be *generated* by them. The usual versions of decision-theory are formulated in terms of the *outcomes* of the acts of the agent. In our framework this might be re-expressed in terms of the *further acts* that would be generated (especially *causally* generated) by a given basic act or set of basic acts. Instead of speaking of the probability of the *outcomes*, given the acts, we can speak of the probability of the further *acts* being generated, given the performance of the basic acts. Thus, we can think of an agent as choosing between various possible *act-trees* that would result from various possible choices of basic acts. Other agents could affect the choice possibilities of a given agent by bringing about changes in generational conditions, thereby affecting the set of acts that would be generated by his performance of specified basic acts. This would provide us with an alternative way of formulating the role of an opposing player in a game situation.

Most of the discussion in this book has focused on the acts of single agents, rather than the relationship between acts of several agents. It is obvious from the final section, on constraint, that the theory can also be used to study the *interactions* of two or more agents. I regard this area as potentially the most fertile for the extension of my model of action. Take, for example, the concept of power. What does it mean to say that an agent, S_1, has power over a group of other agents? What does it mean to say that agent S_1 has *more* power over that group than S_2 has over the same group? An approach to this problem can be made with the help of an analysis of ability. The power of an agent over others depends on his ability to perform acts that affect the welfare, or utility, of the other agents. It depends, indeed, on the *sequences* of such acts that he has the ability to perform. The ways in which he can affect their welfare can be broken down into several categories. On the one hand, he can affect their welfare by physically harming them. But also, he can affect their welfare by affecting the generational conditions which enable them to perform acts they desire, or by affecting their fund of information which bears on their success in executing acts they want to perform. At the same time, the power that S_1 has over a group of people also depends on *their* abilities to affect *his* welfare. If the group is in a position to respond to the acts of S_1 by some form of punishment or reprisal, then it may be *costly* to S_1 to affect their welfare. Thus, although he may be able to affect their welfare, he will be less likely to do so, and his power over them will correspondingly be diminished.

The picture I have drawn here of a human agent is that of someone whose action flows from his desires, beliefs, and primitive abilities (basic act-types). The scope of his action is also affected by the environment, which provides generational conditions for the performance of further acts. Can a similar picture be drawn of a *group* of human agents, such as a family or a nation? We often speak of a nation as *performing* acts—e.g., making war, sending men to the moon, etc. Is this just a metaphor, or is there a precise parallel to the notion of an act in the case of nations? There certainly are desires and beliefs of the citizens that compose a nation, but can these desires and beliefs be "added" or "combined" in any significant way? And do they really result in the actions of a nation in the way that the desires and beliefs of a single human being result in his action? It would seem that certain citizens of a nation—e.g., the President—are able to act "in behalf" of the nation in ways that do not correspond to the desires and beliefs of the nation, and this seems to suggest an important disanalogy.

These sorts of questions, needless to say, are very old questions in the history of social and political theory. Nevertheless, the model that has been presented here may provide a framework for dealing with these questions in new ways. Any theory should be measured in terms of its fruits, and if the theory of action proposed here has interesting applications in any of the areas I have mentioned, that is the best support that can be given for it.

Index